Hearing and Knowing Music

Hearing and Knowing Music

THE UNPUBLISHED ESSAYS
OF EDWARD T. CONE

Edited and with an Introduction
by Robert P. Morgan

PRINCETON UNIVERSITY PRESS
PRINCETON AND OXFORD

Published by Princeton University Press,
41 William Street, Princeton, New Jersey 08540
In the United Kingdom: Princeton University Press,
6 Oxford Street, Woodstock, Oxfordshire OX20 1TW

Library of Congress Cataloging-in-Publication Data

Cone, Edward T.
    Hearing and knowing music : the unpublished essays of Edward T. Cone / edited and
with an introduction by Robert P. Morgan.
        p. cm.
    Includes bibliographical references and index.
    "Published Works of Edward T. Cone": p.
    ISBN 978-0-691-14011-7 (hardcover : alk. paper)   1. Music—History and criticism.
I. Morgan, Robert P.   II. Title.
    ML60.C773H43 2009
    780—dc22

                                                                        2008049313
British Library Cataloging-in-Publication Data is available

This book has been published with the generous support of the Princeton University
Department of Music

This book has been composed in Sabon
Printed on acid-free paper. ∞
press.princeton.edu
Printed in the United States of America
10 9 8 7 6 5 4 3 2 1

To George Pitcher

Contents

Musical Examples

Tables

Acknowledgments

OF THOSE WHO HELPED BRING THIS BOOK TO LIFE, Scott Burnham, Professor of Music and Chair of the Music Department at Princeton University, played a particularly critical part. When he first heard that Edward Cone had left a collection of unpublished essays after his death, Scott not only expressed enthusiasm that they be made public but conveyed his belief, Cone having taught exclusively at Princeton, that they should be published by Princeton University Press. He personally delivered the manuscript to the Press to argue for its consideration, which no doubt eased that process considerably; and he was instrumental in securing a subvention from the Princeton Music Department to help defray publishing costs.

My first two contacts at Princeton University Press, Fred Appel and Claire Tillman-McTigue, offered much help and unfailing support throughout the publishing process, as did all the other staff with whom I worked. Special thanks go to Kathleen Cioffi, the production editor, for her tireless efforts in putting the book into final shape for the printer. Jodi Beder, an accomplished professional musician herself, copyedited the entire manuscript with understanding and a light yet firm hand, saving me from countless errors. I also thank the two anonymous readers who wrote unusually helpful responses after seeing the first draft of the manuscript. I adopted many of their suggestions, especially those regarding the introduction. Equally essential were my wife Carole Morgan, who undertook the task of converting the essays into digital form, and my friend and Yale colleague Ellen Rosand, who checked and corrected the Italian translations. Donna Anstey of Yale University Press and Keith Towndrow of Ashgate Publications graciously allowed me to use material that had appeared in different form in two earlier articles.

My greatest debt goes to Ed Cone's partner George Pitcher, who discovered the essays following Ed's death and, suspecting they were of uncommon interest, asked me to look them over. George participated actively in all aspects of the project, reading the edited version of all the essays and offering much useful advice. I am especially grateful for his sensitive and sympathetic reading of two earlier versions of my introduction. It is with particular pleasure that I dedicate this volume to him.

Hearing and Knowing Music

Introduction

EDWARD T. CONE WAS one of the most important writers on music of the past century. But he was also unusual in several other respects. In addition to being a writer, he was active as a composer, and always considered himself first and foremost in that light;[1] and he performed frequently as a concert pianist, though usually remaining close to home. He held a prominent position as a member of the Music Department at Princeton University, where following military service during World War II he taught without interruption from 1946 until his retirement in 1985 and remained in close contact until his death in 2004.[2]

Nevertheless, for many Cone is best known for his critical work, though not least for its reflection of his interests as a composer and performer. Princeton was ideally suited to foster his gifts as a writer, for it encouraged its composers to be thinkers as well as active professionals. Two of Cone's Princeton colleagues, Roger Sessions, his former teacher, and Milton Babbitt, his friend and contemporary, are almost as famed for their critical work as for their music. Yet even in this company Cone's writings set him apart. As the author of two influential books, editor of seven others, and creator of over sixty published articles, plus numerous reviews and occasional poems, he enjoyed a uniquely prominent position in the world of musical scholarship.

Although Cone's sizable and varied output helps explain his importance as a writer, his distinctiveness stems especially from the quality of his written output. There simply is no bad or uninteresting work. And Cone occupied a special niche, as he always wrote from the perspective of a practicing musician. He did not participate actively in professional scholarly groups, although he occasionally joined and supported them; and I doubt if he ever submitted a paper for inclusion at a professional meeting. Yet he was often invited to present talks or participate on panels

---

[1] A catalogue of Cone's compositions, including dates of composition and performance information, as well as reproductions of (at least) the first page of score for each work and movement, has been compiled by Jeffrey Farrington and is available on CD in Adobe Acrobat 7.0 format. For additional information, interested readers should contact http://music.princeton.edu/The_Music_of_Edward_T_Cone.pdf.

[2] Cone himself attended Princeton, receiving his undergraduate and MFA degrees there in 1939 and 1942. Not surprisingly, his name was included in a list of 250 distinguished Princeton graduates recently submitted by the *Princeton Alumni Weekly* to a committee charged with identifying the 25 most influential alumni ever to attend the university.

at such gatherings. For example, he was invited to deliver the keynote address at the 1987 meeting of the Society for Music Theory; and his book *The Composer's Voice* was chosen as the topic of a paper session at the 1988 annual meeting of the American Musicological Society, for which he responded to all the contributors.[3]

Cone's independence also stems from the variety of his output. There are carefully argued theoretical and analytical studies (both of his books); considerations of style in individual eighteenth-, nineteenth-, and twentieth-century composers ("Bach's Unfinished Fugue in C minor," "Inside the Saint's Head: The Music of Berlioz," "The Uses of Convention: Stravinsky and His Models"); ruminations on opera and operatic characters ("The World of Opera and Its Inhabitants"); less technical commentaries on musical meaning and criticism ("Musical Theory as a Humanistic Discipline"); contributions to concert programs ("Roger Sessions: Symphony No. 6"); consideration of the musical writings of a literary critic ("Dashes of Insight: Blackmur as Music Critic"); and a personal appreciation of his two famous art-collecting aunts ("The Miss Etta Cones, the Steins, and M'sieu Matisse"). One would be hard pressed to find another musician able to challenge this range.

This variety was consistent with one of Cone's most fundamental tenets: that music should be viewed as part of a larger cultural matrix, not as a specialized topic isolated from other intellectual concerns. This is evident even in the forums in which he published his work, which were often directed toward readers of general, as opposed to specifically musical, interests: books such as *Sound and Poetry*, edited by Northrop Frye, and *The Legacy of R. P. Blackmur*, compiled by Joseph Frank, Edmund Keeley, and Cone himself; and journals such as *Art News*, *Critical Inquiry*, the *Georgia Review*, *Perspectives USA*, *Proceedings of the American Philosophical Society*, and the *American Scholar* (where no less than five of his articles appeared).

Though Cone's work is well known to music scholars, its breadth undoubtedly contributed to his position as an outsider. Indeed, he did not think of himself as a professional musical theorist or musicologist at all, but rather as someone he would probably have called a "music critic" (though obviously one of a special sort). Nor did he collect disciples or actively pursue fame, activities that would have conflicted with his deeply engrained professional reserve. Cone no doubt welcomed his status as outsider. It allowed him the freedom to write about whatever he wished, and it encouraged him to develop the unruffled, nonpolemical, yet highly

---

[3] These papers and Cone's responses were published in the *College Music Symposium* 29 (1989): 1–80. Cone's responses are on pp. 75–80.

independent style that characterized all his work.[4] At the same time, the variety of Cone's work may help explain his prominence outside the field of music, as well as the importance of nonmusical ideas for his thought—even though he scrupulously avoided professional jargon of any kind, whether musical or otherwise.

I was fortunate to have studied with Cone at Princeton both as an undergraduate and graduate student; and I became his friend and remained in touch with him until his death. Along with that of many others, my life and work were profoundly influenced by his example. In consideration of his importance as a writer, plus the fact that so much of his critical work appeared in journals rarely seen by musicians, I brought out a collection of his essays in 1989 to make them more readily available.[5] Thus it was a particular pleasure to learn from Cone's lifetime partner, the philosopher George Pitcher, that he had left behind a sizable body of unpublished material consisting of papers read on various occasions. After looking these over, I became convinced, along with Pitcher, that their quality warranted publication as a book.

Neither Pitcher nor I know when most of these papers were written, or where they were first presented. Only one, "The Irrelevance of Tonality?," refers in its two versions to specific locations: Cornell University and the Lawrenceville School, near Princeton. (This is also the only essay I knew beforehand, having heard Cone read a version of it at Swarthmore College in the late 1970s or early 1980s.) Three of the essays, "The Silent Partner," "Mozart's Deceptions," and "Siegfried at the Dragon's Cave," were essentially in final form, cleanly typed and with detailed footnotes and prepared musical examples. Only one other essay, however, "Schubert's Heine Songs," contained a prepared example, and only a single one previously published in a related article. Though all the remaining essays were also typed, they often had multiple versions; and they contained numerous penciled corrections and occasional suggestions for additional ideas and compositions.

Nevertheless, of the fifteen essays received, only one, evidently written to introduce a performance of the Beethoven Fourth Piano Concerto (presumably played by Cone himself), seemed too occasional for inclusion. Even those in rough form were of remarkably high quality and, with minor exceptions, could be easily prepared for publication. As Cone's readers know, he was a consummate prose stylist, which eased

[4] Cf. Fred Maus's remarks on Cone's writing in his excellent introduction to the Cone panel mentioned in note 3 (*College Music Symposium* 29: 2).

[5] *Music: A View from Delft*, ed. Robert P. Morgan (Chicago: University of Chicago Press, 1989).

their preparation considerably. For the most part my contribution was limited to minor adjustments: selecting from multiple versions, inserting missing words and phrases, reordering sections, providing translations, and occasionally adding brief statements for clarification. For some articles I introduced subdivisions through spacing, Roman numerals, or verbal headings (as Cone himself often did); while in others, especially "Stravinsky's Sense of Form," I fleshed out graphic formal analyses that were probably intended originally as self-reminders. But in all cases I tried to follow Cone as closely as possible, retaining the content and character of his original text so that he could speak in his own voice.

A few particulars might be mentioned. I have not altered the essays' consistent use of the pronoun "he" to designate persons of either sex, since for Cone and his generation this was the standard and accepted manner of expression. Nor have I attempted to assign dates to the essays. This probably would have proved impossible; but in any event, the essays give little suggestion of chronological progression or development: they are all the fruit of a mature writer and thinker. No doubt those expert in particular areas will find some of the essays dated; but in my view, this does not detract from their quality, and I have made no effort to bring them up to date (for example, by introducing additional citations). The essays stand as they are: authentic representations of Cone's wonderfully individual and effective critical manner.

For the most part, footnotes were supplied without difficulty. When Cone quoted others, he often included citations in parentheses or in margins; and when he did not, a check of standard references was normally all that was needed. Cone also occasionally indicated that a passage from the text should be placed in a footnote, and in a few instances I relocated other material there as well. Finally, in the very few cases where additional explanation seemed necessary, I added footnotes of my own, distinguished from Cone's by being placed in brackets.

The musical examples posed a more difficult problem. Aside from the three "finished" ones, almost all of the essays deal, often in considerable detail, with musical passages identified by name but not measure number. Though there were frequently copies of score accompanying the essays, these consisted of multiple pages without any additional indications. With the exceptions noted, then, the essays had no prepared examples. (Cone himself no doubt played all of the examples, or portions of them, verbally indicating measure numbers where necessary.) This meant that the precise location of most passages had to be surmised from the text. In the great majority of cases in which Cone did not specify measure numbers, I have inserted them myself, placing them in brackets. (Although I feel reasonably confident that the passages have been correctly identified, I confess that in a few instances they were by no means obvious.) If these numerous indications seem obtrusive, their presence reflects a wish to make the book as user-friendly as possible, especially for those less familiar with particular compositions. But I have reluctantly decided to include only those musical examples Cone prepared himself. This seemed the best solution, given that so many pieces were discussed. To have included all would have created an impractically long book; and deciding which ones to incorporate and where they should begin and end would have required arbitrary decisions. In any event, the works are almost without exception well known and readily available.

There is no doubt that Cone would have made significant alterations if he had published these essays himself—fleshing out some passages, compressing others, reworking formulations, and probably adding or deleting entire segments. But not wanting to make these decisions for him, I have kept the essays as much as possible as he left them. And most of the changes I made were sufficiently minimal not to require identification as such.

Taken together, these essays offer an eminently readable collection and provide an impressive sample of Cone's critical work. One will find some surprises, such as the essay on Debussy, a composer Cone addressed only sporadically in his published work. There are also two essays that develop a theory of "composition as criticism," an idea close to Cone but one not previously investigated in depth. The essays are equally valuable, however, for the way they enrich—often in unexpected ways—topics addressed at length in Cone's published work, including musical meaning and understanding, the role of memory, operatic versus normal reality, the relationship between temporal and atemporal conceptions of form, and the music of Schubert and Stravinsky. Consistent with all of Cone's work, the essays are elegant yet simple in style; and each is carefully framed to highlight a central point.

As an individual, Cone was engaging and attractive; yet he maintained a somewhat reserved public persona. He was in many respects shy with strangers, and it often took some effort to get to know him well. Yet the payoff was rich. One gained a devoted friend and staunch ally—someone who could be critical yet remain gracious and understanding. He was a natural teacher, possessing passionate beliefs yet always respectful of conflicting ideas. There was never any "show" in his manner. It did not seem to occur to him to try to impress those around him—even if he invariably did. He imparted his wisdom enthusiastically, yet with grace and humility.

These personal traits are reflected in Cone's writing style. Although he expressed himself beautifully, he did so without pose or any attempt to harangue or cajole. And despite his consummate musicianship, Cone's technical acumen was offered with a light hand, so that his articles, though theoretically informed, do not seem "theoretical." Technical details, even when present, are emphasized not for their own sake but for their critical role in engendering a uniquely musical response—something that for Cone was ultimately the only meaningful kind. What was essential in listening to music, then, was the listener's musical experience. One of the essays in this volume, "Hearing and Knowing Music," which gives it its title, sums up Cone's position perfectly: neither hearing nor knowing is sufficient in isolation, for the two must work in tandem, enriching and strengthening one another. This probably accounts for music's special importance for Cone: it is directly linked to our innermost natures, to the way we hear and the way we think.

Though the present fourteen essays were intended for informal presentation, they are entirely comparable in quality to Cone's published essays (which themselves seem to suggest that they be read out loud). Cone was a gifted lecturer: a master of his materials and deeply committed to communication. By performing his own musical examples, he enlivened his talks, adding greatly to their individuality and their intimacy. These qualities come through clearly in this new collection; and readers who knew Cone should be able to recognize his voice, and perhaps even hear him playing the examples.

I have grouped the articles into four sections—on aesthetics, opera and song, composer as critic, and the analysis of individual composers—and supplied brief introductions for each. Inevitably, the divisions are partly arbitrary. As always with Cone, the range of topics is great, including such matters as the role of music in culture, the nature of musical hearing, the history of tonality, the relationships between music theater and the real world, connections between composition and criticism, and the character and design of works by individual composers.

Though those familiar with Cone's critical work may recognize occasional overlaps with his published writings, the relationship is in most instances sufficiently minor to require no comment. In two cases, however, I do mention connections in the introductions. Since I also comment there briefly on each of the essays, I can close here simply by asserting that this collection provides an important addition to Cone's published work. It develops his views regarding the different possibilities of musical meaning (symbolic, programmatic, emotional, literal); explores the kinds of compositional insights informed musical commentary can contribute to musical discourse; and, by example, provides an invaluable lesson in the varied uses of music analysis.

PART I

Aesthetics

THE FIRST GROUP OF ESSAYS addresses aesthetic issues: the musical composition in general culture, the listener's role in comprehending music, the historical nature of tonality, and the role of intellect in musical understanding. The first, "The Missing Composer," part of which was evidently read as an introduction to a conference at Princeton University, takes as foil E. D. Hirsch's widely discussed 1987 book, *Cultural Literacy*, whose shortcomings offer Cone an occasion to plea for music's rightful position in intellectual life. For Cone, musical literacy cannot be measured simply by what one knows, but only by what one ought to know; and it depends not just upon shared knowledge but upon shared experience as well.

"The Silent Partner" relates to Cone's influential idea of musical "voice," arguing that music should not be understood simply as a score or performance but as a "heard performance of a score." Listeners, armed with "techniques of recall," "take part in the musical action— [they do] not merely . . . contemplate it." This symbiotic relationship is often exploited by composers, who write passages that require the active contribution of the listener to achieve their full effect.

The decision to include the third essay, "The Irrelevance of Tonality?," in this section may seem surprising, as it focuses on a more technical matter: the nature of tonality in nineteenth- and twentieth-century music. But Cone's response to this question, one that engaged him throughout his career, played a central role in shaping his view that music is first and foremost an historical phenomenon, and must be analyzed as such. The essay is also valuable in further developing distinctions regarding tonality in the twentieth century first introduced in Cone's influential 1974 essay "Sound and Syntax: An Introduction to Schoenberg's Harmony."[1] (This portion, encompassing the second and third parts of the essay, was in particularly sketchy form and required unusually extensive editing.) The topic's importance is also reflected in the sizable body of writing Cone devoted to the subject, including the two versions from which the current essay was compiled, as well as lengthy notes for a semester-long seminar.

The last essay, "Hearing and Knowing Music," from which this book takes its title, was no doubt intended to recall the first chapter of Roger Sessions's *Questions about Music*, "Hearing, Knowing, and Understanding Music" (quoted by Cone in "The Silent Partner"). It is a wide-ranging consideration of the need for listeners to grasp music's "symbolism"— that is, its ability to refer to things that transcend the particular musical

---

[1]Edward T. Cone, "Sound and Syntax: An Introduction to Schoenberg's Harmony," *Perspectives of New Music* 13, no. 1 (1974): 21–40; reprinted in *Music: A View from Delft* (Chicago: University of Chicago Press, 1989), p. 250.

moment—if they are to have complete musical experiences. Such symbolic references may be specifically musical, even internal to the same composition; but they can also relate to programmatic and textual matters, stated or not. This leads Cone to state that the appreciation of "music of any profundity at all is a highly intellectual activity," bringing us back full circle to the premise behind the opening essay. This final essay, underlining one of the most important components of Cone's aesthetic, not only complements the others in this first group but provides an effective introduction for the three essays on opera and song in the following section. One brief segment—on Wagner's setting of the words "Ruhe, du Gott"—appeared previously in somewhat different form in Cone's article "On Derivation: Syntax and Rhetoric,"[2] but is retained here to preserve its central role in the present argument. In addition, the essay's account of Beethoven's Piano Sonata Op. 109 offers a variation of an analysis that appeared some years ago in the last chapter of *The Composer's Voice*.

[2] Edward T. Cone, "On Derivation: Syntax and Rhetoric," *Music Analysis* 6, no. 3 (1987): 237–56.

The Missing Composer

A FEW YEARS AGO a little book by E. D. Hirsch, Jr., *Cultural Literacy*, promised to reveal, according to its subtitle, *What Every American Needs to Know*.[1] Its eloquent plea for a more rational system of education based on a modicum of shared knowledge was supplemented by a list of "What Literate Americans Know." So far as music is concerned, at least, that list made melancholy reading; and it still does in the updated and expanded edition that appeared a year later, whether we take it as detailing what literate Americans actually do know, or what they ought to know.[2]

The list is, as one would expect, limited to Western music since 1700; even within those limits it reveals many biases and blind (or deaf) spots. No English composer is mentioned, and only one French. (No, it's not Debussy; it's Bizet.) Of the four operas that make the list, none is German. Schubert is there, but not Schumann; Stravinsky and Prokofiev, but not Schoenberg and Shostakovich; Berlin and Gershwin but not Kern; and certainly not Copland or Carter. The only instrumental title specified, beyond Sousa marches and Strauss waltzes, is Handel's *Water Music*! The most numerous category of composition is that of popular song: nursery songs, hymns, the standard Stephen Foster repertoire in detail, modern "folk" songs, "White Christmas," and so on.

One can of course deplore certain inclusions and exclusions. More important, however, is the attitude suggested by the "classical" choices that do make the grade. By mentioning Beethoven but none of his symphonies, Schubert but none of his songs, Wagner but none of his music dramas, the list seems to be saying: what is important is not familiarity with works of art, but knowledge of facts about them. The book actually makes this point of view explicit in its recommendation of what it calls *schemata*. A schema is a rough model that supplies just enough relevant information about a given subject to enable one to read or converse on a

---

[1] [E. D. Hirsch, Jr., *Cultural Literacy: What Every American Needs to Know*, with an appendix "What Literate Americans Know," by E. D. Hirsch, Joseph Kett, and James Trefil (Boston: Houghton Mifflin Company, 1987).]

[2] [Cone is apparently referring to E. D. Hirsch, Joseph Kett, and James Trefil, *The Dictionary of Cultural Literacy* (Boston: Houghton Mifflin, 1988), which consists of an expanded and annotated version of the list published in the original book. The remainder of his essay, however, refers only to the first book.]

superficial level. Such a schema for Beethoven might be: "Austrian composer, Napoleonic period, nine symphonies, deaf." Obviously one need not know any of Beethoven's music to construct such a schema: one may never have heard a note. But one can carry on what might be called cocktail conversation: "To think that he wrote his best music when he was stone deaf!"

Is that what we mean by literacy in the arts? Isn't the view of culture presented here the one illustrated by the cartoon, "Quick, Mac, where's the Mona Lisa? We're double-parked!"? And isn't the type of music education that such a view encourages the one that Virgil Thomson excoriated years ago as the "Appreciation racket"?

The only kind of schema that makes sense for dealing with composers—or with artists of any kind—is that of style. When we hear the word "Beethoven" we must respond, not with a bunch of facts about the man, but with an aural concept of the style of his music—of the way it sounds. And the only relevant schema for the individual composition is the work itself: not words *about* it but the memory *of* it. And that means we must know a sufficient number of his compositions—and know in the sense of being able to remember, not just to have heard them. For the schema of the individual artwork can only be based on an aural image. When we read the words "Beethoven's Fifth," they must convey an image of sound, and I don't mean simply the opening motto. Interestingly, this is what the list itself implies when it labels the Parthenon as a visual image. And I think it is also implied by the presence of so many old favorite songs: these are present to all of us as audible images—music as well as words. Such knowledge is essential. And as for those songs, I'm not objecting to their presence on the list; I am only suggesting that a musical literacy that is restricted to that source of musical imagery is neither wide nor deep.

The way to understand music is thus through first-hand experience. Only on that basis can one then begin to appreciate the role of music in our cultural history; only then can one realize that Western music is one of our proudest intellectual achievements. In other words, only experience of music as a fine art can lead to understanding of music as a liberal art.

There is another point. In arts the list is restricted to what literate people do know. But in science, as I mentioned, it is broadened to include what they ought to know. In "A Note on the Scientific Terms," an appendix supplied by the physicist James Trefil, one reads:

Because there is little broad knowledge of science even among educated people, the kind of criteria used to compile our lists for the humanities and social sciences—for example, would a literate person be familiar with this term?—

simply can't be used for the natural sciences. The gap between the essential basic knowledge of science and what the general reader can be expected to know has become too large.[3]

This is typical of our reverence for science and I am not against it. But it is true for the arts as well. And indeed the list makes a small move in this direction by including stylistic and technical terms in visual art: for example, the architectural orders, abstract expressionism, impressionism, art nouveau, art deco, etc. But this doesn't call for much real knowledge. And in music the intellectual level is even lower: musical instruments, directions like *crescendo* (but no *diminuendo*), *pianissimo* (but no *piano*), and a few forms like concerto, sonata, symphony (so that you can read a concert program). There is no sense that music is an intellectual activity, and that Western music especially is one of the supreme intellectual achievements of mankind. Melody is there, and rhythm, but not harmony and counterpoint, which make Western music what it is and differentiate it from other music. Nor, certainly, is tonality: the sense of key and the structure of music necessary to convey and exploit that sense of key. A proper schema for tonality would cover the history of music from the use of modal scales in Greek antiquity, through the early Christian adaptation of those modes, the rise of polyphony in the Middle Ages, the discovery of the implications of harmony in the Renaissance, the gradual development of the modern tonal system in the sixteenth and seventeenth centuries, its flowering in the eighteenth and nineteenth centuries, its overelaboration in the late nineteenth and the crisis of the twentieth century, with the possibility of atonality and substitute systems such as the twelve-tone system. Is all that too much to expect of a normally literate person?

That reminds me of another crucial omission in the list: Arnold Schoenberg. By anybody's count, he was one of the two most important composers of the twentieth century, and actually one of the easiest for whom to give a schema (in the bad sense): Austrian composer associated with the rise of atonality and the development of the twelve-tone method. And it is much easier to give a quick explanation of the twelve-tone method than of tonality (which you really have to experience to understand).

All this is by way of showing what real literacy in music involves, and I'm sure that proponents of the other arts could show corresponding concepts. But of all this, there is nothing in the book. The arts—even literature—are reduced to names, titles, isolated words. This reflects a common view: that the arts are not intellectual pursuits.

[3] [*Cultural Literacy*, p. 148.]

What then do the arts really have to do with culture? Hirsch's book treats culture as shared knowledge. But I believe that there is another equally important aspect of culture: shared experience. It is not sufficient, for example, for a people to have a common history: they have to share that history. One way is to keep the history alive—as, for example, Jewish tradition and ritual does at the Passover, Christian ritual during Holy Week; or, for another, as the Old South did in keeping its memories of the Civil War alive. But for most of us, our history is not alive. What keeps it alive for us is Art and Literature. *Gone with the Wind* may not be a great novel, but it has made the Civil War a national experience for a generation. *Washington Crossing the Delaware* may not be a great painting, but it again has given us all a shared experience.

But shared artistic experience is not to be limited to historical re-creation. Shared *aesthetic* experience is a powerful force for community, even when—maybe especially when—it is not overtly realized as such. Probably architecture is the most obvious example. Hasn't the culture of Italy, for better or for worse, been largely shaped by the constant architectural presence of Imperial Rome? And didn't the cultural synthesis of the High Middle Ages depend on the fact that the philosophy and religious ideals of the period were not just taught and talked about but were actually *experienced* in the gothic edifice of the cathedral itself—as Erwin Panofsky and other art scholars have convincingly shown?

What I am primarily interested in, of course, is shared musical experience. I am afraid that in our own country today the musical experiences most widely shared are country music and rock—alas, not even good jazz anymore. But contrast certain European countries. In Vienna you can still choose the musical Mass you want to hear on Sunday in any one of several beautiful baroque churches: a shared experience of ritual, music, and architecture.

Or consider the example of Berlioz, who was acutely aware of the role of his art as a source of shared experience. And he wanted the experiences to be widely shared—no chamber music for him! His *Memoirs* include a telling story:

> In 1840, as the month of July drew near, the government proposed to celebrate the 10th anniversary of the 1830 Revolution with public ceremonies on an imposing scale. The relics of the glorious victims of the Three Days were to be translated to the monument lately erected to them in the Place de la Bastille. The Minister of the Interior decided to commission me to write a symphony for the occasion. I wished, to begin with, to recall the conflicts of the famous Three Days amidst the mourning strains of a bleak but awe-inspiring march; to follow this with a kind of funeral oration or farewell address to the illustrious dead, while the bodies were lowered into the cenotaph; and to conclude

with a hymn of praise at the moment when, the tomb being sealed, all eyes were fixed on the high column on which Liberty with wings outspread seemed soaring towards heaven like the souls of those who had given their lives for her.[4]

Can you imagine the National Endowment for the Arts commissioning such a work from the leading radical composer of today—one who was constantly at war with the accepted musical values and academy of his day—and his accepting the commission in that spirit? But that is what it means to have a true national culture, and for the arts to take their place in it.

In conclusion, let me read another passage by James Trefil, defending his inclusion of scientific terms that *ought* to be known by the public:

In the end, the purely instrumental utility of scientific knowledge may be less important than the wider value to be gained from being acquainted with science as one of the great expressions of the human spirit. Science has been and continues to be one of the noblest achievements of mankind. From a humanistic point of view, its attainments are on a par with great achievements in art, literature, and political institutions, and in this perspective, science should come to be known for the same reasons as these other subjects.[5]

Now read it again, substituting music.

[4] [Hector Berlioz, *Memoirs*, trans. and ed. David Cairns (New York: Alfred A. Knopf, 1969), p. 253.]
[5] [*Cultural Literacy*, p. 151.]

The Silent Partner

IN ORDER TO EXPLAIN my title, I start with a well-known example, the opening Adagio of Beethoven's *Sonata quasi una fantasia*, Op. 27 No. 2. We are so familiar with this famous movement that we do not realize how strangely it begins. After an introduction, the first theme enters—but its opening phrase immediately modulates from the tonic C-sharp minor to the relative major, E. And the next phrase, separated by an extra measure and a shift to E minor, is already a transition to the second subject. What has happened to the original key, and to the first theme? Certainly it is possible to begin a lyrical melody with a modulation—but normally that is followed by a return to the original key, before further excursions are made. That in fact is what does happen in the recapitulation: from tonic to relative major, then relative major back to tonic. But how should we understand the beginning? The trouble arises because we accept the opening phrase as pure introduction. A much more satisfactory form results if we hear that phrase not as introduction but as proto-thematic, adumbrating the melody that is openly stated by an answering phrase. Then we have a normal modulating period whose first phrase establishes the tonic and whose second moves to the relative major.

How can that interpretation be established in performance? If the pianist tries to emphasize a concealed melody—perhaps the right thumb line, or perhaps the top notes of the arpeggios—he destroys the mysterious atmosphere and ruins Beethoven's carefully composed effect of a gradually emerging melody. So the pianist must give only the merest hint—probably rhythmic rather than melodic, letting the increasingly rapid chord changes above the slowly moving bass suggest that the phrase may be at least partially thematic and not purely introductory. But the pianist can be successful only if the listener assumes the role of active collaborator. He or she must follow those progressions and try to understand their significance. One might say that both the listener and the pianist must practice, that only through repeated hearings or playings can one comprehend the formal role, and therefore the expressive significance, of the passage. Certainly in my case, only after having heard the sonata many times—indeed, after having learned to play it—did the advantage of such a reading occur to me.

Roger Sessions entitled a well-known book *The Musical Experience of Composer, Performer, Listener*.[1] And by now the identity of the silent partner of my own title has, I hope, become clear. It is, of course, the listener.

I

A novel, according to Wolfgang Iser, implies an appropriate reader toward whom it is directed.[2] In the same way, a composition implies its ideal listener. That is why in an earlier article, I have expressed my dissatisfaction with pure syntactic analysis, whose "aim is to arrive at a spatially oriented view of the composition as a whole, and [whose] method is atemporal study."[3] For such analysis, I insisted, "does scant justice to our experience of hearing a composition in real time."[4] It should therefore, as I recommended, be complemented by a diachronic analysis—one based on an examination of the composer's strategies as they reveal themselves during the actual temporal course of a composition. Such an exercise would share some of the aims and methods of analysis based on phenomenological principles.[5] My own approach makes an assumption which those influenced by certain literary theories would no doubt consider untenable: that it is not only possible but desirable to determine how a composer meant for a work to be heard. That is why in a later essay I referred to "intentional analysis."[6] For diachronic analysis, the analysis of how music moves through time, although by no means limited to a definition of the composer's intention, should take it into account.[7]

---

[1] [Roger Sessions, *The Musical Experience of Composer, Performer, Listener* (Princeton, NJ: Princeton University Press, 1950).]

[2] [Wolfgang Iser, *The Implied Reader* (Baltimore: Johns Hopkins Press, 1974).]

[3] ["Three Ways of Reading a Detective Story—Or a Brahms Intermezzo," *Georgia Review* 31, no. 3 (1977): 554–74; reprinted in Edward T. Cone, *Music: A View from Delft* (Chicago: University of Chicago Press), p. 85.]

[4] [Ibid., p. 86.]

[5] See, for example, Thomas Clifton, *Music as Heard* (New Haven, CT: Yale University Press, 1983); and Lawrence Ferrara, *Philosophy and the Analysis of Music* (New York: Greenwood Press, 1991).

[6] [Edward T. Cone, "Ambiguity and Reinterpretation in Chopin," in *Chopin Studies 2*, ed. John Rink and Jim Samson (Cambridge: Cambridge University Press, 1994), p. 141.]

[7] Lawrence Ferrara's view, based on a consideration of contemporary works, seems to me to be even more generally applicable in this regard: "Musical significance cannot be limited to the composer's intentions . . . [T]he composer's sense of his own work should not be dismissed but also it should not be the limit to what a work can mean. I cannot provide general rules for the balance between a composer's intentions and a listener's inventiveness. Such a balance must be achieved at the level of criticism, not theory." [*Philosophy and the Analysis of Music*, p. 35.]

To establish how a work is to be heard is to establish how it is to be listened to. In clarifying the composer's aims, intentional analysis at the same time defines the listener's role—more strictly, the listener's job—as my little discussion of the Beethoven sonata tried to demonstrate. Music is not simply a score, nor even a performance of a score, but rather a heard performance of a score. To be sure, the listener may be the performer, or the composer may be both; the composition may be mentally performed and therefore silently heard; but the principle remains.

No composition lacks an implied audience of some sort, but it is my further contention that the listener's investment in the musical enterprise considerably increased during the nineteenth century. In earlier periods, as we know, performers, particularly solo performers, overtly collaborated with composers. In the later eighteenth century, and on into the nineteenth, however, their activities were increasingly restricted, for music was being notated in ever more exact rhythmic and dynamic detail. Even the solo concerto, in the hands of Beethoven and others, turned away from individualized embellishment and even from improvised cadenzas. Although still a partner, the performer was becoming less a co-composer than an interpreter, a guide to assist the listener in his newly exacting task.[8] For, more than ever before, the listener must now take an active part. The complexity, unpredictability, and ambiguity that characterized much Romantic music required an audience willing to join the performer in a collaborative effort to comprehend its messages—musical and sometimes extramusical. Musical form itself became more demanding of the audience: the monothematic fugues and concertos, with their periodically recurring subjects, gave way to an ever more complex sonata form with its multiplicity of themes and textures. All music, of course, demands of its audience what Roberto Gerhard called "a willing ear";[9] and Roger Sessions's elaboration of that notion applies neatly to the requirements of the nineteenth century: "not only an ear that is free of prejudice, but an ear that is attentive, curious, and persevering as well."[10]

Sessions's insistence on freedom from prejudice is valid only if "prejudice" is understood in its pejorative sense; for certain predispositions are expected—even demanded—of every listener. Composers have often had occasion to decry the refusal of audiences to tolerate unfamiliar dissonance. But as the system of tonality was developed, composers came to

---

[8] Italian opera was, of course, *retardataire* in this regard. See the contrast of Rossini with Beethoven in Carl Dahlhaus, *Nineteenth-Century Music*, trans. J. Bradford Robinson (Berkeley and Los Angeles: University of California Press, 1989) [pp. 9–10].

[9] [Roberto Gerhard, "The Contemporary Musical Situation," *The Score* 16 (June 1956): 7.]

[10] [Roger Sessions, Questions about Music (Cambridge, MA: Harvard University Press, 1970), p. 13.]

depend on bias of a more friendly kind—on the predictability of response to functionality. The establishment of a harmony as functional—say, as a dominant—meant that it was activating a certain disposition in the listener, the expectation of a familiar course of action, which, whether or not actually forthcoming, was implied by the harmony and hence was part of its meaning.

The so-called deceptive cadence, for example, worked because it *was* deceptive: it led the listener to expect one outcome and then produced another. The composer could depend on that expectation, which was grounded in the syntax of the tonal system. But matters were not always so simple, even with composers like Mozart and Haydn. An apparently unambiguous dominant seventh might turn out to be an augmented sixth; a diminished seventh might be reinterpreted; a resolution might be postponed. Complications of this kind increased as music moved into the nineteenth century, and each of them made further demands on the listener. No longer could he rely on a conventional response to a well-known harmonic situation. The harmony itself might be strange, or if familiar it might acquire new significance as the result of its context. Thus the listener had to work harder than before in order to comprehend the harmonic structure. The ambiguity characteristic of so much nineteenth-century harmony could operate only as a result of the interpretations adduced by the sensitive listener. Those often depended on what might be called implicit or connotative functionality: harmonic meaning that is suggested rather than explicitly denoted in terms of an actual progression.

Implication can often be misleading, although with positive aesthetic results. That is because the expressive effect can depend on the listener's uncertainty, if not his downright misconception. Naturally, it is difficult today to listen to familiar works with fresh ears; yet that is what we must often do if we are to receive their full message. Hearing them, we must sometimes do our best to ignore our knowledge of the course of musical events. Only then can we fully assume the listener's role.

Thus, when I describe the listener's task as one that relies to a large extent on memory, I mean to include its suppression as well as its exercise. As we hear a composition, we must constantly keep in mind its themes and developments as they have been presented to us, and we must also apply our knowledge of the style and of the type of musical structure embodied by the composition; but at the same time we must try not to let our recollection of previous hearings unduly influence our expectations at each moment. (That ambiguity is one that is familiar to us as readers of fiction. For example, in order to enjoy a mystery story or a tale of suspense when we reread it, we must try to suppress our memory of its outcome.[11])

---

[11] I discuss this point further in "Three Ways of Reading a Detective Story" (see note 3).

II

As an example of the rewards accruing from both the exercise and the suppression of memory, consider the opening of the second movement of another famous Beethoven piano sonata: the "Waldstein," Op. 53.[12] It is difficult to recall one's own first hearing of a work as often played as this one, or to imagine how it must have sounded to its contemporaneous audience; but let us try. What harmonic associations are suggested by the opening measure? The listener, whether of our own or Beethoven's day, who encounters this movement for the first time can have no way of knowing, without reference to a score, the spelling of the chord arpeggiated there. The tempo gives him ample time to savor the chord, to come to terms with it, to adopt a specific attitude of expectation. What is that to be?

For an answer I refer to a formula that had previously been adopted by numerous openings, from Bach (e.g., the Prelude No. 7 in E-flat major in the *Well-Tempered Clavier* I), through Mozart (the Piano Quartet in E-flat K. 493) to Beethoven himself (the Piano Trio Op. 1 No. 1). In each case an apparent dominant seventh turns out to be V7/IV in a IV–V–I cadential progression—often over a tonic pedal. The educated listener, recalling such passages, would have every reason to expect a similar progression here (see ex. 2.1a). That, as we now well know, is not what he gets. The apparent dominant seventh turns out to be an Italian sixth (ex. 2.1b). What can that mean? The sophisticated listener, given an entire measure to take in the resolution to E, will probably locate that as the dominant of a hypothetical A. And if he is really acute, he will recognize that the composer is subtly recalling the same progression in the first movement. There it was indeed utilized to effect a modulation to A (mm. 181–91). Can that be the case now? Again expectation is defeated: m. 3, far from confirming A, makes a minor triad of the E, followed by a chord of multiple possibilities. Is its final member a B-flat, pointing possibly toward D major (ex. 2.1c)? No, it is an A-sharp, and the resolution is another apparent dominant, V6 of E (ex. 2.1d). Once more the obvious cadence is avoided. Measure 5 might seem to be pushing on one step further in the sequence, toward V of B (ex. 2.1e). That, however, is hardly likely; besides, at this point another

---

[12] It may be somewhat temerarious of me to return to this battleground. Some years ago the passage in question was the subject of a rather acrimonious exchange between Charles J. Smith and David Beach in the pages of *Music Theory Spectrum* [Smith, "The Functional Extravagance of Chromatic Chords," in vol. 8 (1986), pp. 94–139; Beach, "On Analysis, Beethoven, and Extravagance: A Response to Charles J. Smith," in vol. 9 (1987), pp. 173–85; Smith, "A Rejoinder to David Beach," also in vol. 9, pp. 186–94]. Although I cannot wholly agree with either of them, my own discussion will borrow freely from both; no doubt it will become obvious in which direction my sympathies lie.

memory from the first movement can come into play: the first climax in the development, on V of F, was approached by the same chromatic bass (F to D), and the same chord (augmented sixth on D-flat: mm. 110–12). So the initial F of m. 1 may be the governing tonic after all—and is confirmed as such in the cadence that follows (ex. 2.1f).

EXAMPLE 2.1 Beethoven, Sonata in C major, Op. 53, second movement

a. Recomposition of opening phrase

b. Measures 1–2

c. Recomposition of mm. 3–4

d. Measures 3–4

e. Recomposition of mm. 5–6

f. Measures 5–9

The foregoing sketch should indicate the extent to which not just hearing but also actual mishearing may contribute to musical meaning. The full significance of the passage can be grasped only by one whose ear is not only knowledgeable—recognizing all the allusions—but also willing—in this case, willing to be misled. The know-it-all who relies on his memory of previous encounters with the passage fails to receive the message of the progression, which depends on the unveiling of a mystery. But so does the neutral listener who, refusing to interpret the ambiguous situations as they arise, reserves all judgment until the outcome. No: the listener must participate in the music he hears. What I have called, from the composer's point of view, an intentional analysis, might equally well be called, from the listener's point of view, a participatory analysis, since it details the various memories, interpretations, misinterpretations, and reinterpretations, that constitute his own involvement with the music.

III

Enigmatic openings are a typical feature of nineteenth-century compositions. Examples abound in Beethoven—by no means restricted to the relative safety of an inner movement like the Adagio of Op. 53. They range from the indeterminate fifths that open the Ninth Symphony to the complex chromatic progression that introduces the String Quartet Op. 59 No. 3. Even the Fifth Symphony may suggest an ambiguity to an acute but unprejudiced ear, which may recognize in the opening a hint of the key of

E-flat. (That is a suggestion that Beethoven himself reinforced when he repeated the exposition. He further investigated it in one of his sketches.)

In this connection it is interesting to find Chopin, like Beethoven, puzzling the listener by using a classical opening formula in a subversive way. Such a reference is concealed in the introduction to the G minor Ballade. Its opening gesture is strikingly similar to those of Mozart's C-minor Piano Concerto K. 491, his C-minor Piano Fantasy K. 475, and even his C-major "Dissonant" Quartet K. 465. Whether intentionally alluding to Mozart or not, Chopin deceives the listener, for his ambiguous C minor turns out to be a subdominant.

Such openings are ambiguous because they invite multiple interpretations of harmonic functions, as we saw in the case of Beethoven's Op. 53. But the chord that concludes Chopin's introduction—provided that we accept E-flat as the correct reading of the questionable note—presents what we might call morphological as well as functional ambiguity: what precisely is the makeup of the chord? Is the nonharmonic member the notorious E-flat itself, or is it the D in the bass? In the one case the chord represents a I6/4 in G minor; in the other, a IV7 in G minor or perhaps a II7 in B-flat major. The entrance of the principal theme in G minor resolves the question of key; but the chord must await its return in m. 35 to be definitively revealed as a I6/4 (ex. 2.2).[13]

EXAMPLE 2.2   Chopin, Ballade in G minor, Op. 23, mm. 1–7 and the return of the m. 7 chord in m. 35

[13] Elsewhere I have discussed the opening of the Fourth Ballade as another example of Chopin's subversion. See my "Ambiguity and Reinterpretation" in the Chopin collection cited in note 6, pp. 140–42.

In Weber's Fourth Piano Sonata in E minor, Op. 70, is the first chord (m. 2) the 6/4 that it sounds like, or is the melody's E an appoggiatura resolving to D-sharp (ex. 2.3)? On the one hand, the E is consonant with every member of the chord and the D-sharp with none; on the other, the E resolves by step and the D-sharp is quitted by a leap. Not until the fourth measure is it revealed that the bass's E is also an appoggiatura, and that the underlying harmony, held in abeyance, is a diminished seventh resolving to a V6/5. This interpretation is confirmed by the second statement, at mm. 12–16, where the theme appears in the bass.

EXAMPLE 2.3   Weber, Piano Sonata in E minor, Op. 70, first movement, mm. 1–14

Schumann posed a question in mm. 80–81 of his *Fantasie* for Piano, Op. 17 (ex. 2.4). Is the first sonority in m. 80, a half-diminished seventh, the true harmony? Its soprano seems to resolve as an appoggiatura to E, producing a fully diminished seventh. But as the chord vanishes, that voice returns to F. Three fermatas in an Adagio offer ample time for the listener to contemplate the alternatives and to prepare for what may follow. Should one expect a continuation in F, or in a new key—and if so, which key? I believe that Schumann meant to bewilder us temporarily, and to startle us by a simultaneous change of key, range, dynamic, and tempo, in the subsequent passage. In retrospect we realize that the diminished seventh was the functioning harmony, and that the evanescent F was not a resolution but an anticipation, or an echappée.

EXAMPLE 2.4   Schumann, *Fantasie* for Piano, Op. 17, first movement, mm. 74–83

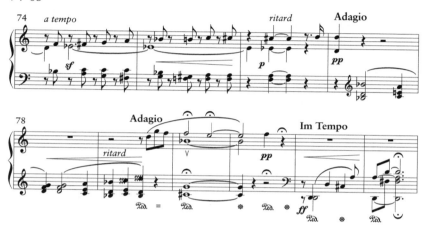

The most notorious example of the problematic appoggiatura is surely found in the Prelude to *Tristan und Isolde*. I have discussed the grammar of the opening motif elsewhere.[14] Here I wish to point out that to hear G-sharp on the one hand or A on the other as the principal melodic tone in m. 2 is to choose between two different progressions and therefore, to that extent, between two different compositions. The listener, by his disposition, completes the act of the composer. The conscientious one will try to determine the composer's intent and to hear the motif accordingly. The willful one will insist on his right to hear it as he likes. The lazy one will adopt no attitude at all; what he hears is therefore, in an important respect, an unfinished composition.

IV

The *Tristan* Prelude also exemplifies two techniques that demand further listener participation: postponement of resolution and transferal of func-

---

[14] I give a summary of my accounts of the passage in the introduction to *Music: A View from Delft* (see note 3).

tion. The two often occur in association. A chord that the listener has accepted, say, as a dominant seventh—because, in fact, it sounds like a dominant seventh—may fail to resolve immediately, either normally or deceptively. Instead, the hearer is required to shift his appropriate attitude to another apparent dominant—i.e., a chord that invokes a similar disposition although at a different harmonic level. Yet the first one should not be forgotten, for the transfer may not preclude but only postpone an ultimate resolution of the original dominant. That is exactly what happens in the Prelude. Through multiple transferal, the dominant of m. 3 (on E) is made to yield to two successive surrogates (on G and B, mm. 7 and 11). All are eventually resolved: B by the climactic return to V7 in m. 16, E by the deceptive cadence of m. 17, and G by the ensuing C major cantilena (ex. 2.5). A similar but perhaps even subtler program underlies the *Todesverkundigung* in *Die Walküre*, with its series of interlocking keys.

EXAMPLE 2.5   Wagner, Prelude to *Tristan and Isolde*, mm. 1–3, 7, 11, 16–20

Transferal also underlies Verdi's occasionally idiosyncratic use of the 6/4. Sometimes that chord, instead of being resolved, is followed by the corresponding chord in another key—as in "Il lacerato spirito" from the prologue to *Simon Boccanegra* (ex. 2.6a). Sometimes a foreign 6/4 intrudes into an otherwise normal progression, suggesting an incomplete tonicization—as in the "Kiss" motif that concludes *Otello* (ex. 2.6b, 13 measures from end).

EXAMPLE 2.6   Verdi's use of the 6/4 chord

F#: i⁶₄   A: V⁷   I⁶₄   F#: I⁶₄   V⁷   I

a. *Simon Boccanegra*, "Il lacerate spirito," p. 24, mm. 5–8

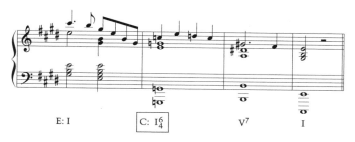

E: I   C: I⁶₄   V⁷   I

b. *Otello*, "Kiss" motif, 13 measures from end

Other examples of the technique may be found in Scriabin's late works. What I often hear there is a chain of constantly transferred quasi-dominants. Their tonics are never unambiguously stated; their ultimate resolutions are indefinitely—even perpetually—postponed.

Transferal and postponement do not require the highly charged chromatics of the later nineteenth century; they can work equally well in the simpler environment of Schumann's *Dichterliebe*. In the first two songs of the cycle the dominant of F-sharp minor is continually thwarted by transferal. Every occurrence of the harmony, both within each song and between them, leads to an authentic cadence in A major instead. Not until the final song of the cycle is the dominant of F-sharp definitively resolved: in mm. 20–27 a modulation to that key, based on the material of the opening song, must be meant to awaken the listener's memory and finally to satisfy his desire for the long-postponed tonic.[15]

When tendentious chords such as the dominant sevenths of the *Tristan* Prelude are left hanging in silence, how should the listener react? Wagner

[15] [See Edward T. Cone, "Poet's Love or Composer's Love?," *Music and Text: Critical Inquiries*, ed. Stephen Paul Scher (Cambridge: Cambridge University Press, 1992), pp. 172–92.]

himself has suggested at least one appropriate attitude. During the reprise toward the end of the Prelude, he inserts fillers that effectively ex-
tend the first two dominants [mm. 83–90]. He carries the process much
further during Act 1, at the moment when the lovers drink the potion
[pp. 90–91 of the Schirmer vocal score, mm. 9–44]: there the chords are
prolonged by elaborate cadenzas. In both instances Wagner exaggerates,
as it were, the listener's task. He is telling us that when a chord of suspense is left ringing in our ears, we are meant neither to resolve it mentally nor to forget it, but to savor it, think about it—even though we
cannot elaborate it as the composer does in his interludes.

It is true that sometimes when a dissonance is terminal, as in Schubert's
song "Die Stadt," one may be justified in supplying a mental resolution.
But when Schumann, in *Kinderscenen*, Op. 15, represents his "Kind im
Einschlummern" by a V7–IV cadence, surely he wants his audience to
fall asleep imaginatively on an unresolved chord. And how is one to take
Chopin's omission of the concluding half of the final phrase in the A-flat
major Mazurka Op. 41 No. 4? Perhaps it has become too soft to hear
because of the preceding diminuendo. A similar explanation may apply
to mm. 22–23 in the Scherzo of Beethoven's Piano Sonata Op. 106. Here,
and at corresponding points, the vacancy may represent a statement of
the principal motif too soft to be perceived. Unless one is very familiar
with the piece, it would be hardly possible to experience the passage thus
on its first appearance, but one might so construe its subsequent repetitions (ex. 2.7).

EXAMPLE 2.7   Beethoven, Piano Sonata in B-flat major, Op. 106, Scherzo,
mm. 19–24

V

One form whose proper apprehension has always required a specific exercise of memory is the variation pattern; its recognition and appreciation depend on what might be called thematic remembrance. Baroque
variations were typically constructed over a bass whose insistent reitera-

tion, in literal or slightly modified form, constantly confirmed the listener's memory. In contrast, during the Classical period, the dominant thematic role shifted to the melody. Its variations were, to be sure, much freer than the repetitions of the Baroque bass; but their similarity to the theme was usually sufficient to remind the hearer of their origin and to ensure his correct orientation. In the nineteenth century, however, the application of thematic remembrance tended to become more problematic. Variations often departed from their originals to the extent that simple memory needed further support. (Sometimes, to tell the truth, we have to take it on faith that what we are hearing is really a variation.)

Three examples from the Andante of Beethoven's C-sharp minor String Quartet, Op. 131 illustrate some of the difficulties. It takes a keen analytical ear to recognize the theme in the quasi-canonic dialogue of the third variation (m. 98), and to realize that in the sixth (m. 187) the theme is adumbrated in the cello and then moves into the inner voices. Between those two variations, the fifth (m. 162) requires not only memory of the theme but what might be called its imaginative auralization. The texture resembles that of an accompaniment. Indeed, its initial melody, such as it is, in violin I, is derived from the viola's line in the theme; and the whole suggests a hypothetical five-part arrangement from which the theme itself has been omitted. It is up to the auditor, then, to supply the missing part in his imagination. Beethoven goes even further in the thirteenth of the "Diabelli" Variations, Op. 120, where measures of silence leave mental reconstruction of the thematic material almost entirely up to the listener, with only occasional rhythmic punctuations to guide his memory.

Occasions for auralization are not confined to variations. Schumann explicitly recommended the exercise when he included an *innere Stimme* (inner voice), precisely notated but obviously not meant to be played, in his *Humoreske* Op. 20 [at the section marked *Hastig*]. I have discussed this passage in connection with the possibility of implied melodies in the music of Brahms.[16] In the present context I wish to point out that the listener's construction of the melody, in so far as it is possible at all, cannot depend on a specific memory, as in the Beethoven examples. It must rely, rather, on a general knowledge of style and on the memory of similar textures, as if one might ask oneself, "What kind of melody would suggest this kind of accompaniment?" A successful interpretation would be supported, this time explicitly, in a striking *sotto voce* passage that follows a noisy climax [at the return of the two-flat key signature]: "Yes, that is like the melody I imagined—or should have imagined!"—an identification confirmed by the continuation of the reprise in its original version. (The

---

[16] [See Edward T. Cone, "Brahms: Songs with Words and Songs without Words," *Intégral* 1 (1987): 36–37.]

concept of the *innere Stimme* might be applied to my original example from the "Moonlight" Sonata, the opening phrase being heard as the accompaniment of an "inner voice.")

At least once, Schumann seemed to imply an auralization derived from a previously stated theme. I am convinced that the peroration of the final movement of the *Fantasie* Op. 17 should be so interpreted. For the cantilena of the coda, after sinking from the right hand into the left [m. 127], apparently comes to a stop at m. 130 (ex. 2.8a). I believe that it does not really cease but simply ceases to be heard, drowned out by the increasingly insistent accompaniment. Yet the listener, drawing on his memory of its motivic structure, could be enabled by the accompaniment to imagine how it might continue (ex. 2.8b).

EXAMPLE 2.8   Schumann, *Fantasie* for Piano, Op. 17, last movement

a. Measures 129–32
b. Implied continuation of cantilena, mm. 130f

There are occasions, however, when melodic auralization is tempting but inappropriate. Beethoven, in a well-known passage, presents an accompaniment without its melody. That occurs at the opening of his Variations Op. 35, as well as at the corresponding passage in the finale of the Third Symphony. In each case the melodic component of the theme is withheld until the listener is thoroughly familiar with its bass and can accept the tune as the one that has been prepared and anticipated—but not revealed. This is an instance where memory suppression becomes important during repeated hearings. No matter how well one knows the work, one must resist the urge to recall the theme or to auralize it before its actual realization; otherwise the felicitous effect of its welcome entrance will be nullified.

In other situations, the listener may be called on to supply auralized accompaniments. Unlike the purely monophonic lines of plainchant, unaccompanied melodies in a tonal context are bound to suggest mental harmonizations. In imagining those, one must depend on what might be called generic memory: one's general knowledge of harmonic practice and stylistic conventions.

Such melodies are often ambiguous. The magical effect of the horn tune that opens Schubert's Great C major Symphony D. 944 depends on its suggestion of both C major and A minor—and our ability as listeners to entertain both possibilities. Without the belatedly inserted fourth measure[17] the composer may have felt the influence of A minor as too strong. As it is, the G of m. 4 points toward an outcome that we gratefully accept when the strings enter, confirming C major.

The somewhat similar opening of the Andante moderato in Brahms's Fourth Symphony, Op. 98 is often assigned to the Phrygian mode, but surely C major has at least an equal claim on our loyalty here. Without further clues, it is difficult to imagine what a Phrygian harmonization would be like, but easy and natural to supply one in C major. Moreover the implied contrast of C with the true tonic is touchingly effective when the chord of E major arrives. Returning to the passage in his coda [m. 113], Brahms demonstrates what the Phrygian harmonization might have been (a mixture with E major), but temporarily supplants it with a C major version.

Berlioz is another composer who obviously enjoyed the ambiguities arising from unaccompanied melodies. In his own fashion he too played with tonal and modal implications in the *Dies irae* of his Requiem, thereby effecting a startling reinterpretation that I have discussed elsewhere.[18]

Turning to *Roméo et Juliette*, we find that a purely tonal interpretation is called for by the solo line that introduces *Roméo seul*, opening the Second Part (ex. 2.9a). There the punctuating harmonies after each phrase keep the listener on track, except for a jolting F major chord in m. 13 that supplants the expected D minor. Has Berlioz intentionally misled us? At one time I considered the chord an example of what I called reversed resolution, a familiar Berliozian device whereby a chromatically raised note

[17] [See Maurice Brown, *Essays on Schubert* (London: Macmillan, 1966), P. 32.]

[18] [See Edward T. Cone, "Inside the Saint's Head: The Music of Berlioz, *in Music: A View from Delft*, p. 231.]

is deceptively resolved a half step downward (as in ex. 2.9a, mm. 8–9 and 12–13).[19] Now I am not so sure. That is the way it sounds to the unwary; but the sly composer may have been writing for a more sophisticated ear as well. An unusually sharp listener, taking the C-sharp of m. 12 seriously as a leading tone, could mentally hear it resolved at the beginning of m. 13. In that case the sounded F major of the plucked strings becomes transitional between an understood D major-minor and the melodically implied A minor of m. 14 (ex. 2.9b). One has but to play the missing chords to realize how wise Berlioz was to leave them unstated.

EXAMPLE 2.9   Berlioz, *Roméo et Juliette*

a. Second Part, mm. 1–17 (simplified)
b. Possible harmonization of mm. 12–14

Occasionally a melody may receive an incomplete harmonization. The listener may well be unaware of the deficiency until a reprise demonstrates what he was previously missing. Thus, at the beginning of *Vallée d'Obermann* Liszt withholds the bass that would explain the wandering harmonies of the theme; but he later explicitly reveals it when the passage

[19] [Ibid., pp. 228–30.]

is repeated [m. 34]. The sensitive listener reinterprets his memory: "So that is the real meaning of those progressions!" (Here again, note the importance of the suppression of memory on rehearing the piece, if one is to enjoy the full flavor of the contrast between the two presentations of the theme.)

Instances of that kind, soliciting completion by the auditor, are so frequent in nineteenth-century music that it is not surprising to find composers occasionally applying their talents for imaginative reconstruction to the works of others—as when Gounod added an obbligato to Bach's C major Prelude, or when Schumann provided piano accompaniments to Bach's works for solo violin and cello. Perhaps accepting what they construed as Bach's invitations, they were recording as composers what they had experienced as unusually active listeners.

VI

One type of memory required of the alert nineteenth-century auditor was closely associated with musical Romanticism. From Beethoven on, thematic recall played an important part in many typically Romantic forms, and it involved the listener in a special way. As I define it, recall differs from reprise or recapitulation in its independence of context. In recapitulation, as notably exemplified by the Viennese Classics, melody, harmony, and rhythm work together in theme, tonality, and form, to prepare for the return, to lead the listener to expect it, and to render it perceptible and appreciable as such. We find evidence of this process not only in every normal example but also in the exceptions: Haydn's false recapitulations proclaim themselves as such precisely because they have received only incomplete harmonic or rhythmic preparation. A true reprise is not just the return of a theme, but the prepared and expected return of a theme in context. Hence the listener does not depend on memory alone to recognize it. But when Beethoven recalls the opening of the Piano Sonata Op. 101 as he approaches the finale, or when Mendelssohn concludes his Piano Sonata Op. 6 with a return to its first movement, the themes are divorced from their original contexts. It is up to the listener not only to identify them but also to remember the circumstances under which they were formerly heard. Without that recognition of theme and memory of context the formal and expressive meanings of the passages are lost.

Composers may invoke a more subtle type of recall, such as we have already noted in the "Waldstein" Adagio, where the references to the preceding movement enrich rather than control the musical content. Their identification is not crucial. Sometimes, too, the composer aids the listener by preparing for the recall through thematic mediation. Schubert does that in the first movement of the Great C major Symphony: by the time the introductory theme returns in the coda [m. 662ff.]. It has been frequently and obviously foreshadowed.

In some cases a theme and its recalls may assume a formal life of their own, producing a pattern that from time to time interrupts and subverts the normal flow of the music. That happens when Schumann insinuates into his *Novellette* No. 8 what he designates as a *Stimme aus der Ferne* (voice from the distance), first as a coda to the second trio, next as a lyrical interlude [*Einfach und gesangvoll*], and lastly as a climactic outburst in the course of the finale [35 measures before the final return of Tempo I]. Schumann's words indicate that the design, musically convincing though it may be, is not purely musical in conception. It is partly determined by narrative or dramatic considerations. As Kofi Agawu has written of another Schumann composition, *Der Dichter spricht*, "What it succeeds in doing is loading the associative dimension in such a way that listener and performer are invited—indeed, compelled—to construct a metaphoric scenario or plot for the piece."[20]

The listener who takes a composer's intentions seriously must often come to terms with such extramusical references. Those who scorn specific verbal aids, even when supplied by the composer himself, must still "construct a metaphoric scenario or plot" if they are to appreciate the full import of his message. And in that respect there is little difference between explicit and implicit programs. In both cases the listener's imagination must supply the extramusical connotations at which the music itself can only hint. The words Beethoven assigns to his singers explain the dramatic motivation behind the recalls in the finale of his Ninth Symphony; the similar recalls in the last movement of Bruckner's Fifth Symphony dispense with words but require a corresponding interpretation.

A similar comparison can be made between the *idées fixes* of Berlioz's program symphonies and the motto theme of Tchaikovsky's Fifth Symphony. In the music of both composers the thematic repetitions pervade the texture of the more normal multi-movement structure, surfacing periodically. The designs they produce are musical, but also more than musical: their thematic techniques support a narrative or dramatic structure of extramusical connotations, whether verbally identified by Berlioz, or left unstated by Tchaikovsky.

Sometimes the composer's story requires him to quote the music or to imitate the style of another. Thus Mendelssohn introduces a chorale at the climax of his E minor Fugue Op. 35 No. 1 [29 measures from the

---

[20] [V. Kofi Agawu, *Playing with Signs* (Princeton, NJ: Princeton University Press, 1991), p. 142.]

end]—not, so far as I can discover, a specific hymn-tune, but an unmistakable stylistic pastiche. Liszt is more specific in his homage to Chopin's A-flat Polonaise in *Funérailles*. Schumann, in addition to his vaunted imitation of Chopin in *Carnaval*, refers on several occasions to Beethoven, especially to *An die ferne Geliebte*. The listener who is ignorant of the origin of such citations, or who refuses to take account of them, is as far from understanding the full import of the composition as one who fails to recognize the source of a Liszt transcription.

Verdi's motifs of reminiscence and Wagner's leitmotifs apply the technique of recall to music drama. Most listeners are willing to engage in elementary recognition and identification, but their responsibility does not stop there. Many operatic motifs, through their successive recalls, construct pervasive but intermittent musico-dramatic designs like those of program music. The symbolism conveyed by such patterns can be of primary importance. One who takes seriously the drama of *Der Ring des Nibelungen* must follow the Sword motif carefully—from its origin at the end of *Das Rheingold*, through its development in *Die Walküre* and *Siegfried*, to its apotheosis in Siegfried's funeral music and its mysterious farewell. Each appearance of the motif—each stage of its musical history, as it were—corresponds to a stage in the history of the object it symbolizes: from its inception in Wotan's mind; through its discovery by Siegmund, its failure to protect him, its rediscovery by Siegfried, and its triumphant use at his hands; to its final guardianship of his body. The motif thus creates a little music drama of its own—one of many such to be discovered in the *Ring* by acute listeners.

Stratagems of that kind have often been dismissed by purists as literary and therefore extramusical. They may indeed be extramusical, but they are not necessarily nonmusical. Like the techniques discussed earlier, these too invite the listener to take part in the musical action—not merely to contemplate it. And if, as Leonard Meyer puts it, "the increased size of the [nineteenth-century] audience was related to an overall decline in the level of its musical sophistication,"[21] its members could realize, through the aid of such obvious devices as programmatic or dramatic recall, a sense of participation otherwise denied them by the ever-growing harmonic complexity of the music.

VII

For a concluding example I turn to a tone poem from the end of the nineteenth century, Strauss's *Also sprach Zarathustra*. Even one who

---

[21] [Leonard B. Meyer, *Style and Music* (Philadelphia: University of Pennsylvania Press, 1989), p. 208.]

resolutely refuses to try to follow the pronouncements of its eponym through the complex symphonic structure must somehow deal with its notoriously ambiguous conclusion. How does one hear it? The ending is usually described in terms of two contrasting keys: the B of the immediately preceding theme, a tonality clearly stated but never cadentially resolved; and the C of the opening C–G–C motif—demonstrably the governing tonality of the composition. But it is possible to hear the dissonant chord (C–E–F-sharp) accompanying the motif as implying a resolution to B major (ex. 2.10a). In that case the C–G–C of the motif is merely an expansion of one element of the chord, and the three final lonely C's are unresolved neighbors. In a larger context, however, one can accept the B of the entire concluding section as a hugely expanded neighboring key to the overall C major. In that case, F-sharp is the dissonant member of the chord—a holdover from the B major episode—and the C–G–C motif attempts to reestablish the global tonic (ex. 2.10b). Or the listener can really go to work and shift allegiance from the one interpretation to the other. At first the C and E are dissonant members of the chord, resolved as it were on high by the B triad. But, aided by our memory of the importance of the primal motif, C gradually assumes independence, representing its own triad. After a doubtful vacillation, it finally assumes supremacy: B is now the neighboring chord to the tonic C. That is the way I try to read the conclusion, and if I were a conductor that is the interpretation I should try to project.[22]

EXAMPLE 2.10   *Also sprach Zarathustra*, ambiguous resolutions implied by final chord

a. To B Major

b. To C Major

[22] [For further discussion of this piece, see also the beginning of the next essay.]

The foregoing discussion has made no reference to a program, and Strauss has offered no specific interpretation of the ending. Yet I find that this enigmatic passage—like much of the rest of the work—cries out for at least a "metaphorical scenario"; and the way we interpret it—perhaps as a reference to Nietzsche's doctrine of eternal recurrence—determines the end of our story. At the same time, the way we hear it determines our understanding of its tonal role, hence of the entire tonal structure, and of the tone poem's *musical* form. I can think of no better illustration of the listener's responsibility—and power.

The Irrelevance of Tonality?

I

EVERYONE WILL AGREE that for a large body of music—the music we call functionally tonal in the classical sense—the key of a piece is one of its most important characteristics. That means that for an understanding of a tonal piece it is crucial to know, not only that a piece is in a key, but also just what key it is in. Let me make this absolutely clear by giving a familiar example—one in which the key is, or ought to be, self-evident, but one that is nevertheless often misinterpreted by audiences—whether because they are inattentive, or ill-trained, or just downright unmusical. It is the Tchaikovsky Fifth Symphony. I have often heard people clap [at m. 471 of the last movement]. But if they clap, they must think the piece is over. And if they think the piece is over, they have missed the point of the whole passage—maybe the point of the whole piece.

It is easy to laugh at such ignorance. But consider another traditional piece: the *Heilige Dankgesang* from Beethoven's A minor String Quartet, Op. 132. It is clearly in a key. But what key is it in? At the climax note the extremely long extension of the chord on C [mm. 189–201]. Is it a V or a I? I have heard arguments on both sides, and seen analyses that try to prove one side or the other. What I maintain is that one of the following statements must be true: A: the piece is in F; B: the piece is a failure. That is because the key of the piece is crucial to the conception of its form and its expression. If it is in the key of C, then the whole climax, standing interminably on C, is no longer a climax, since it is on a chord of resolution, not a V. If C is the tonic, the entire passage fails to produce the harmonic tension necessary to match the tension that everything else aims at: the melodic line, the contrapuntal and instrumental texture, the register. If on the other hand the passage is standing on the dominant, then it becomes a harmonic climax as well, and the final cadence is natural and satisfying.

The tonality here is just as crucial as it was in the Tchaikovsky. But I don't think we can laugh off the misinterpreters as we can in the case of the Tchaikovsky. Indeed, which are the misinterpreters? For there *is* an extended tonicization of V—the expansion of an idea inherent in the very conception of the piece, as we know. For Beethoven, Lydian could only mean F major with a persistent tonicization of the dominant C. The question is, not whether one can *analyze* the C as a dominant, but whether, in actual performance, its tonicization becomes so powerful (owing to the lack of a B-flat anywhere) that we cannot help *hearing* it as a tonic. And if that is the case, no analysis will make the F sound like a tonic for us. Here the progression might be I–V–I, but it might be IV–I–IV. In another case it might be V–II–V.

What I am saying is that for me, the sense of tonality is not only or even primarily a formal characteristic, but a phenomenalistic one. Or perhaps "experiential" is a better word. A tonic is not what can be analyzed as a tonic, but what is perceived as a tonic. Or felt as a tonic. Just what that means is one of the things I want to investigate.

A more extreme example may make my approach clearer: the end of *Also sprach Zarathustra*. This piece can be heard naively as a huge piece in C, followed by a short piece in B, followed by a reminder of C. But if we want to put these fragments into some kind of unified relation, if we want to hear the work as a single composition, we try to relate C and B. We can say, on the one hand, that the composition is in C, that there is a coda elaborating B as a neighbor, and that the neighbor is resolved by the reiterated C. Or we can say that the bulk of the piece, the huge expansion of C, is resolved at the end as a neighboring Neapolitan, and that the true tonic then becomes B, that the last C's are simply unresolved neighbors. Now suppose that the proponents of each view constructed elaborate Schenkerian analyses to support their view. These analyses could be exactly the same for the huge C section, and for the B coda. Their only difference would lie in the interpretation given to these two sections, which would in turn determine the interpretation of the last C's.[1]

How could one possibly decide between these two? If one analyst says that the length and complexity of the section in C makes it the tonic, the other could say that the final position of the section in B makes it the tonic. To which the first could reply that the bass C's are the last word, to which the other would respond that merely to state it, without further elaboration, in this context makes them neighbors. And so on. Now along comes a third party, who says: you are both wrong. Obviously the piece is in the key suggested by the juxtaposition of C major and B major: VI–V in E minor. And, purely analytically, nothing would have to be changed! Now if we try to analyze our *experience* of the piece—or what *I* hear, at any rate: there is a huge piece in C, but then C moves to B as N–I. Does this mean that the real key is B? I don't know. As the coda proceeds I become more and more comfortable

---

[1] [This piece is also discussed at the close of the preceding essay.]

in B, so that the bass C's sound like a neighbor to the prevailing B. But at the very end, I am able to hear it either way: I can hear C as continuing as a neighbor, or I can hear it as pulling B back to C as a tonic. This is the real tonal split of the ending—not just the superficial contrast of the B and the C, but the split in two ways of perceiving that contrast. This becomes then one of the few truly bitonal pieces that we have.

If you think the problem disappears with the advent of atonality or twelve-tone music, you are wrong. Consider Roy Travis's analyses of the second of Schoenberg's Six Little Piano Pieces, Op. 19 No. 2, and of the second movement of Webern's Variations for Piano, Op. 27.[2] In the first case, it makes a great deal of difference whether you hear the piece as he does, with a C tonic, or as I do, with a G tonic. In the second case, the entire sense of the piece is inverted if you hear it centered on A, rather than on B-flat/G-sharp as he does.

In the first case, I think Travis may have as good a case as I have. But I begin with my perception of the piece: I hear it in G. So then I ask why. Why do I hear G as I rather than V? I hear the opening as static; then the first phrase introduces some active elements—elements which are then elaborated: D-sharp–C in m. 3 returns as E-flat–C in m. 4; the chord in m. 5.1 is a neighbor between that of m. 2.4 and its return (new register) in m. 6.4. Measure 6, indeed, retrogrades mm. 2–3. The F-sharp now becomes the lowest note, resolved—along with the rest of its chord—in the last chord of the piece. In that chord I also hear a resolution of the C–E dyad that Travis takes as I.

But whereas I can imagine Travis as hearing the Schoenberg in C, I cannot imagine him hearing the Webern as his analysis indicates. For me, the piece is clearly, as Henry Weinberg[3] once remarked, "about resolutions." In every case, B-flat/G-sharp resolves either to A–A or to B–G, or to A–A through B–G. The one exception, m. 15, embeds the dyad in middle voices. The final B-flat/G-sharp is in fact resolved when the section is repeated. I hear A as again expected. That makes the entrance of E-flat in the third movement doubly effective: it is unexpected, but it is at the same time equally a symmetrical resolution of B-flat/G-sharp. Note too that when the first phrase of movement three is repeated at m. 5, it takes off again from E-flat, the two E-flats now making an octave, completing the symmetry in register as well as in note.

---

[2] [Roy Travis, "Directed Motion in Schoenberg and Webern," *Perspectives of New Music* 4, no. 2 (1966): 84–89.]

[3] [A composer, now living in New York, who studied at Princeton.]

Now let us look at another sort of piece. It is, I think, more problematic, but I still think the experiential approach must be observed to avoid gross error. In the third of Roger Sessions's piano pieces *From My Diary*, I have heard or read at least four different interpretations of key: B minor, E-flat major, C minor, and even D major. Sessions considers it to be in B minor, hence the signature, which apparently misled Allen Forte, who puts it in D major.[4] I myself hear the piece in E-flat, taking the original and final sonority as including the bass as root—a major-minor third. Sessions takes the same sonority, but interprets it as a B without root, the G being a neighbor. But he also admits C minor, taking the F-sharp as a neighbor. Sessions was dissatisfied with the original version, and added the middle line in the right hand—ostensibly to clarify the tonality! I believe that his ear is supplying a missing root—perhaps even a missing line, and that an unprejudiced hearer would accept E-flat. What about Forte? His analysis tries to show that the piece *can* be construed in D major—but nowhere does he indicate that the *effect* of the piece is D, or in what sense it could be *heard* in D. For him, D is a pure abstraction. Note that any of his lines, which assign D as the center, would work equally well if he had assigned D-sharp—even better in the bass.

But there is another important point illustrated by this piece—a point that explains the title of this article. The question of tonality in this piece is not crucial; it may even be considered irrelevant. For the form can be the same no matter which of the tonal centers is chosen (even D), since the form is really independent of the tonality. It consists of the fairly firm and static establishment of a given linear-harmonic level, with a characteristic sonority, followed by a rise to a climax, and finally a fall back to the original level and sonority. The climax is higher, louder, more dissonant than the beginning and end, and there is a clear sense of return. These characteristics persist regardless of the chosen key.

Why could we not say the same of the Beethoven quartet movement? Because there the climax, on a consonant chord, can under one interpretation be heard as a tonic. If it is V, it is a point of tension; if it is I, it is not. But with Sessions, no matter what we choose as tonic, or even whether we choose a tonic, the climax remains the point of highest tension. The movements of the piece, low–high–low, static–moving–static, less–more–less dissonant, all reinforce one another regardless of the choice of tonic. It is like a graph whose shape remains the same regardless of what axes may be superimposed.

[4][Allen Forte, *Contemporary Tone-Structures* (New York: Bureau of Publications, Teachers College, Columbia University, 1955), pp. 48–62 and Sketches 21–29.]

II

It was in order to cover cases of this kind that I coined the term *normal* to mean a sonority "to which all others are implicitly compared."[5] I went on to state further: "Without a final statement of such a sonority no composition can sound complete—indeed, hardly a phrase." Speaking of classical tonality, of course the normal is the triad; and further, "the normal form of a normal is a triad in root position"; and "there is a hierarchy of normals, the one we call the tonic being the normal of normals."[6] But in later music, "[l]ike consonant normals, dissonances may be established at the outset."[7] In the case of the Sessions, the normal can be construed as the opening sonority, or as I prefer, that sonority plus the E-flat bass. Or, perhaps one might say that the minor ninth in general is the normal sonority for this piece. In the hierarchy of ninths, the F-sharp–G is supreme, and is to be construed as an incomplete sonority of which D-sharp is the bass. (You will note that this can be converted into quasi-tonal terms for C minor, B minor, and E-flat major, but not for D major).

As we know, in the nineteenth century and later more and more pieces failed to end on the normal. Examples are Chopin's F major Prelude, Mahler's *Das Lied von der Erde*, Mussorgsky's *Boris Gudonov*, and many of Liszt's late pieces. And when we add that fact to the admission of dissonant normals, new problems arise. Consider Debussy's piano piece *Voiles*, from the first book of Preludes. The form is easily comprehended: ABA, characterized by whole-tone on B-flat, pentatonic resolving to a 6/4 on E-flat minor, and back to B-flat whole-tone. One *can* hear the whole-tone as a quasi-V and the 6/4 as a quasi-I. But in that case could one also hear the piece as quasi I–quasi-IV–quasi-I? Suppose we use the terminology of normals, avoiding the issue of tonality. Then the possibilities are:

1. The whole-tone scale is the normal. In this case the normal is the "more dissonant" chord than its contrast—although the contrast is not totally consonant. But if whole-tone is normal, do we still stick by our definition of the normal as a cadential chord of resolution?

2. The 6/4 chord is normal. In this case, the normal is "less dissonant"; but the normal does not end the piece and no longer appears to be the sonority to which all others are implicitly compared.

---

[5] [Edward T. Cone, "Sound and Syntax: An Introduction to Schoenberg's Harmony" (*Perspectives of New Music* 13, no. 1 [1974]), reprinted in *Music: A View from Delft* (Chicago: University of Chicago Press, 1989), p. 250.]

[6] [Ibid.]

[7] [Ibid., pp. 261–62.]

In other words, are the two functions of normality—as a standard and as a chord of resolution—becoming separate? This suggests some additional queries. How would it affect our decision if in the middle part *Voiles* came to a root-position E-flat minor triad? Suppose it gave us an authentic cadence in B-flat minor? To what extent is our knowledge of the date of composition important? Suppose the piece were written in 1850? In 1950?

I raised these questions in the Schoenberg article but refused to give general answers: "Must the normal always be a chord of relative resolution? Must it be among the characteristic sonorities of a composition? Must it always be stated? More drastically, must every composition have a normal?"[8] In other words, how should we redefine the term in order for it to be most useful in dealing with twentieth-century music? Certainly one can say that, historically, normal as stated resolution and normal as standard were once equivalent. But during the nineteenth century the two functions separated more and more—in Wagner, Strauss, Debussy. The tension between the two is resolved in certain twentieth-century music in favor of the normal as standard but not stable: for music in which the concept of resolution is no longer relevant, but in which there is still a certain harmonic consistency—e.g., much twelve-tone music. But what happens in between?

Let us consider some possibilities. To avoid preconceptions, we will adopt the terms "stable" [resolved], "nonstable" [unresolved], and "final" [closing the piece]. We begin with two functional classes:

Class I: The final is a stable triad (or portion thereof) in a functional context. Then we accept the final as *the* normal, as in classical tonality. But there are problem pieces. What we accept as normal for *Zarathustra* depends on how stable we hear the final. In Chopin's Second Ballade, I think we should have to say that A minor is, or has become, the normal. But in Mahler's *Das Lied von der Erde*, is the final chord (a major triad plus added sixth) the normal, or normal plus—a variation of normal? Or are we now verging on dissonant yet stable finals? Let us call a stable final of this kind a functional tonic.

Class Ia: If the tonic occurs only at the end, though triads are standard, as in Brahms's B-flat Intermezzo, Op. 76 No. 4, by definition the tonic is still the normal. But suppose that triads are not standard, in the sense that resolutions are constantly avoided, as in Scriabin's Fourth Piano Sonata? Again, by definition, the tonic is normal [it ends on an F-sharp major triad]. Even here, triads could be considered standard as always present by implication, by directionality.

[8][Ibid., p. 263.]

But suppose that such a piece *never* came to a tonic? This suggests the possibility of:

> *Class II*: The normal is still a stable triad [in a functional context], but it is no longer the final. There are compositions that can still be heard as functional, but as not arriving at the tonic: e.g., Scriabin's *Désir*, Op. 59 No. 1, which though it closes with a dissonance, ends with a strongly implied resolution to a C major triad, suggesting what might be the (absent) normal. But suppose it didn't? Would we still imagine the major triad as normal? Or would some form of dominant be normal?

To these can be added two nonfunctional, yet tonal, classes matching the first two:

> *Class III*: The normal is final, tonic, stable, and triadic; but the harmony is nonfunctional—for the most part, voice leading determines the directionality: e.g., Debussy's *Pas sur la neige* from the first book of Preludes.
>
> *Class IV*: This is similar to III, but now the normal is not final: e.g., Debussy's *Brouillards* from the second book of Preludes, [where the normal is C major but the piece ends with a B diminished triad]. But note that here a new possibility again opens up: perhaps the final is indeed normal? Can normal be divorced from stability? I think not, *if* there is contrasting stability available, as there is here (and even in *Désir*). For that reason, we should say that the piece is still in C [at the end]. But what of Liszt's late piano piece *Nuages gris*? Here the contrasting stability is very tenuous, not very stable. (This is similar to the problem with *Voiles*.)

Should there be a *Class IIIa*, corresponding to *Class Ia*, for pieces that avoid a stable final for most of their length? Are there such pieces in the nonfunctional area? The problem is illustrated by Debussy's *La Puerto del Vino* from the second book of Preludes: what is normal, the D-flat major triad plus B (C-flat), or the D-flat triad with acciaccatura with which the piece ends? Or in a somewhat different but related case: what is normal in Debussy's *Feux d'artifice* from the same volume? Are we arriving at a separation of normal as standard from normal as final, or do we hear the voice leading as affording enough directionality to accept the final as normal?) This brings us to a further possibility:

> *Class V*: The normal is stable, triadic, and no longer final, as in II and IV, but it is also no longer standard. Returning to Scriabin, let us take his dominant functionality one step further. His mystic chord sometimes seems to function as a perpetual V, moving in sequences instead of resolving. In that case, we can construe one of two possibilities: the normal as still stable and triadic, but also nonstandard (indeed, it is never stated) and nonfinal, the standard becoming the mystic chord, which is also final. Or, on the other

hand, we can refuse in the Scriabin to accept a normal that is never stated and instead insist that the mystic chord itself is normal, the normal becoming unstable and nontriadic, but standard and final. In these last two cases, then, we can no longer insist that the normal must always be standard, stated, or stable!

But in such cases our terminology becomes problematic. In what sense is a chord *unstable* if there is no stable normal implied? Consider Scriabin's Piano Etude Op. 65 No. 2. Is the form in this piece perhaps pure convention, so that it could continue to move in the same restless fashion infinitely? Perhaps that is its meaning—constant striving. In that case, we would have a normal that is a quasi-V rather than a quasi-I. Or are all chords now tending toward neutrality—neither stable nor unstable?

Or consider two much more successful pieces by Scriabin, the Piano Sonatas Nos. 9 and 10, Op. 68 and Op. 70. In each, two forms of the mystic chord are employed. In both cases, one of the two definitely sounds like a resolution, and hence comparatively stable. But both sonatas end as they begin, with the more unstable chord. How do we construe these? Here we see the *Voiles* syndrome again: the form is unstable–stable–unstable. But the stability is not so secure that one can insist that it be taken as normal. One really wants to ask the forbidden question here: what did Scriabin intend? Does he perhaps mean to reverse our sense of the two functions? In Sonata No. 10, at the entrance of the first theme [m. 39], and in the theme itself, could the F-like chord be heard always as resolving to a more V-like chord? And in the appearance of the [F-like] chord at the climax [m. 221], is this meant to be a moment of stability or the reverse? This takes us to the next and final step:

> *Class VI*: a frankly dissonant normal, but one that is no longer necessarily unstable. We can certainly find examples of this in Bartók, where the normal is dissonant but stable, and thus functions as final; or where it is a simple unison and thus not dissonant, for example in his Improvisations Op. 20 Nos. 1, 2, 3, 5, and 7. But compare the "Night Music" movement from the *Out of Doors* Suite, where there is ironic juxtaposition of two kinds of normal, one dissonant and the other not, or also in the Finale of the Fifth String Quartet. And is the dissonant normal that closes "Night Music" stable or unstable, or is it not rather completely neutral?

III

We can now turn to some more problematic post-tonal examples. An interesting case is provided by Sessions's *From My Diary*. In the third and fourth piece, the normal is dissonant, final, and relatively stable. Here, then, there are no problems. But what about the first piece? Sessions hears it in C minor, and made some analysis toward that end. But is that the relevant point? The return to the theme is certainly not in C minor, and the key is in fact given short shrift after the first page. But what is made clear is that the static chord [mm. 7–9] is heard as the expansion of a quasi half cadence, not a stable cadence. Thus it is not a "tonic," since it is not stable. And although the first phrase begins on the C–E-flat third, and the third ends on C–E, I question whether this is enough to justify giving C major-minor normal status. So either the piece has no normal, or an unstated normal, or an incompletely stated normal, or an unstable normal, or a neutral normal. Similarly, in the second piece the octave opening contrasts with the dissonance that follows, as it does in its repetition [m. 3] (with the octaves supported by fifths in the left hand), and again at the close. The final statement is closely preceded by alternating chords from which a C minor chord could be extracted; so is this the normal? At any rate, the closing sonority is again not stable (i.e., it is unstable or neutral). In both No. 1 and No. 2, we might say that the only relevance of a possible tonic is to separate normal from stability—to create a beautifully tentative close (neutral?) in No. 1 and a restless sense of incompletion (unstable?) in No. 2. And note the connections among the four pieces: possibly "IV–V" going from Nos. 1 to 2; then a shift [up chromatically] of the ninth from Nos. 2 to 3 (is this possibly why Sessions considers C minor as a possible tonic for No. 3?); and finally the definitive resolution of the low D-sharp to D in No. 4.

Turning to twelve-tone examples, I must confess that much twelve-tone and post–twelve-tone music sounds to me harmonically neutral—that is, neither stable nor unstable. But that need not be the case—as we have seen in the second movement of Webern's Variations. Let us now look at Dallapiccola's *Quaderno musicale di Annalibera* No. 1. One might be tempted to say it is in A minor, since the first and last phrases end on the triad. But their beginnings equally suggest E-flat; and the A minor chord is in a sense a happy accident—in any event, one more example of the irrelevances of the strictly tonal concept. But we can discern here an analogy to tonality in the harmonic area defined by the original chords, from which we depart and to which we return. It is true that the triads implied by the last three tones as the row goes through its various transpositions, marks out a progression related to A (A minor, E minor, C major, E major, F-sharp minor, D major, A minor [mm. 5, 8, 14, 17, 25–27, 37–38, 46–47]); nevertheless, to single these out of the total nonfunctional texture would be unjustified. Rather, we must take the total area defined by the row statement as a unit: As I wrote of Schoenberg's twelve-tone music, we can have a "normal that depends, not on a single chord or tone, but on a succession"; also, "for Schoenberg, at least, the standard twelve-tone pattern is analogous to the standard tonal pattern: statement of normal, departure from normal, return to normal." And although I insisted that in Schoenberg "there is always a normal to be found, and to be heard," I must admit that I find it much easier to hear them in Dallapiccola, and even in Webern.[9]

In *Annalibera* No. 9, for example, Dallapiccola exploits phrases that end with relatively mild dissonance and which form a quasi-tonal progression. The first phrase [mm. 1–4], which presents the row in original form, ends with a triad and mild dissonance; and the second [mm. 5–7], while it has a transposed retrograde of the row, ends similarly (quasi sharp-VII–I in A minor). But then a tritone [E-flat] is added [m. 8], forming a transition to phrases three and four, two shorter two-measure groups in sequence [mm. 9–10, 11–12], based on the inversion and hence ending with triads, but now in the bass (the F-sharp [G-flat] and E major triads forming a quasi VI–V). In contrast, the last phrase [mm. 13–19] begins triadically because it is based on the retrograde inversion, and ends with a strong tritone dissonance [E–B-flat in the left hand], which is hence nonnormal.

In closing, I return briefly to Webern's Variations. In the first movement, phrases two [mm. 8–10] and four [mm. 15.3–18] are relatively stable, as indicated by their metrical regularity. Thus I consider the inversion, on which these phrases are based, to be normal, and in opposition to the original and retrograde, from which the first and third phrases are derived [mm. 1–7 and 11–15.1]. But the return to this section [m. 37] is not at the same level; and it does not even remain at the new level, nor does metrical regularity prevail in its last phrase. Hence the music is unstable and ends with a nonnormal.

In the third movement, the role of E-flat at the beginning has already been mentioned. This sets up a stable opening area, from which the movement then diverges, only to return to the area at the end [m. 56], where palindromes are used to help create finality. There is a very skillful use of E-flat, G, and C in the bass [mm. 56–64] to give an almost chordal feeling at the end. (Webern is supposed to have said, "We need twelve-tone in order to learn to write tonally.")

At this point one might well say that all of the pieces we have been considering are really tonal after all: not tonal in the classical sense, so that we can say that they are in the key of C major, or E-flat major, or B-flat minor; but in a wider sense, in which any musical sound—a single note, a certain chord, in orchestral music even a special tone color—can act as a center, from which the piece grows, about which it revolves, and to

---

[9][Ibid., pp. 264, 265, 266.]

which it normally returns. That is why I call such a sound a normal—avoiding the more specific word tonic, which refers only to the older conception of tonality. So if one should ask, don't all these pieces have, if not tonics, at least normals, I should reply, yes, they have. And in that sense they all exhibit something at least corresponding to tonality. I do not wish to claim that *all* music written today can be heard in those terms. But a great deal of music that on the surface is atonal and very puzzling, not only can but ought to be heard in those terms. And in that broader sense tonality is just as relevant as it ever was.

Hearing and Knowing Music

I

LET ME APPROACH my subject in a roundabout way—through a discussion of symbolism in music. When we say that music is a language we mean that music is a symbolic utterance. But the utterance that constitutes a musical composition is, as we might expect, more like a poem than like a piece of expository prose. The purpose of the expository prose, like the purpose of most everyday speech, is to convey meaning; once that meaning has been conveyed its job is done. But the job of a poem is not done once it has conveyed a meaning; indeed, at that point its job has just begun. For only then can we begin to read the poem with full understanding and enjoyment. I can put it more strongly: a poem has no meaning. It may have a meaning, or several meanings, but no meaning. That is, there is no piece of intelligence that it is the function of the poem to communicate, such that, once the intelligence has been communicated, the poem's function has been discharged.

In the same way, I insist that music has no meaning. But this is a disability that it shares, not only with poetry, but with all art. Parodying Stravinsky, I should say: I consider that art is by its very nature essentially powerless to *mean* anything at all. *Meaning* has never been an inherent property. That is by no means the purpose of its existence. What, then, is the purpose of its existence?

Let us approach this question again by way of poetry. Archibald MacLeish, in a famous poem, "Ars Poetica," states a point of view similar to mine, but in a neatly paradoxical way. He begins with a number of similes:

> A poem should be palpable and mute
> As a globed fruit
>
> Dumb
> As old medallions to the thumb

and so on. But his conclusion is a general statement that seems to bring the validity of the whole poem into question:

A poem should not mean
But be.[1]

If a poem should not mean anything, then is it not an artistic error for it to state that it should not mean anything? The answer is, of course, that the final statement is not *the* meaning *of* the poem; it is only *a* meaning *in* the poem. The poem communicates through a series of relationships. True, meaning is involved in these: relationships between the sound and the sense of the words, among the various similes, and between the similes and the general statement, and so on. But the total *import* of the poem—to use a word that conveys simultaneously a sense of communication and the significance of that communication—is not a meaning. It is a relationship among relationships. It is what we mean when we say, loosely, that context arises from the interaction of subject matter and form. And the purpose of the poem is to allow us to experience that import, and at the same time to adopt a certain attitude toward it, or to accept a certain evaluation of it. We might even say that the purpose of any work of art is to cause us to have a special kind of experience, an essential part of which is an acute realization of our attitude toward it and our evaluation of it, both of which are controlled by the work of art itself.

Returning to music, there is, to be sure, a certain sense in which all music, like all other art, is symbolic. Music, being an art of tones moving in time, is primarily and preeminently symbolic of human activity in every possible sense of the word—activity real or imaginary; purely temporal or also spatial; physical, mental, emotional, or moral. But most purely instrumental music is what Susanne Langer calls an "unconsummated symbol." As she says,

> music has all the earmarks of a true symbolism, except one: the existence of an *assigned connotation*. It is a form that is capable of connotation, and the meanings to which it is amenable are articulations of emotive, vital, sentient experiences. But its import is never fixed. . . . *[M]usic at its highest, though clearly a symbolic form, is an unconsummated symbol. . . .* The actual function of meaning, which calls for permanent contents, is not fulfilled; for the assignment of one rather than another possible meaning to each form is never explicitly made.[2]

Yet there are numerous examples of music that attempt to employ symbols in a more precise sense, to turn musical motifs into what we

---

[1] [Archibald MacLeish, *Collected Poems, 1927–1982* (Boston: Houghton Mifflin, 1985), pp. 106–7.]

[2] [Susanne K. Langer, *Philosophy in a New Key* (Cambridge, MA: Harvard University Press, 1948), pp. 195–96.]

may call Proper Symbols, symbols that act—again in Langer's words—as *"vehicles for the conception of objects."*[3] (She means objects in the sense of specific objects of thought—which may or may not be a concrete object in the ordinary sense of the word.) Some of these symbols are perfectly obvious and very familiar; but others, the more interesting ones, present real problems of perception and comprehension.

II

Let me begin by contrasting two proper symbols, both from familiar compositions. The first is in the finale of the *Fantastic Symphony*, where Berlioz uses the familiar melody of the *Dies irae* to symbolize first the funeral of the beloved, and then the parody of the funeral rites performed by the demons of the witches' Sabbath [m. 127ff.]. This is an example of what I call a manifest symbol. There can be no question that a symbol is involved: the use of the traditional tune; the orchestration, with its bells (and originally a serpent—a traditional funeral instrument); finally, the gradual transformation of the dirge into a kind of jig—all these are perfectly obvious.

But now listen to Saint-Saëns's use of the same material in the *Danse macabre*. Here the symbol is by no means manifest; many listeners, indeed, may be unaware of the source of the tune. In fact, Saint-Saëns has laid a trap for the unwary. The quotation occurs in the development section [m. 173ff.], and indeed it could be construed as a transformation of a motif from the first theme to fit the rhythm of the second—a covert internal allusion. Moreover, what Saint-Saëns is using here is not just the *Dies irae*: he is specifically using Berlioz's transformation of the *Dies irae*. At this point we realize not only that the symbol itself is veiled, but that its meaning is subtle and ambiguous. For those who recognize it, the quotation not only parodies the hymn, but also indicates a connection that Saint-Saëns felt between his music and that of Berlioz, a composer whom we know Saint-Saëns deeply admired. Perhaps, Saint-Saëns is saying that without Berlioz and such works as the *Fantastic Symphony*, his own tone poem could never have been written. So the quotation becomes symbolic of a recognition of kinship, of influence, and of an act of homage.

This is an example of what I call covert symbolism: symbolism that is masked in its presentation, and possibly also in its meaning. It may in fact pass unnoticed—and I think it is meant to be unnoticed by the superficial listener. I might call your attention here to Schumann's famous

---

[3] [Ibid., p. 49.]

quotation of the "Marseillaise" in the first movement of *Fasching-schwank aus Wien*, Op. 26 [mm. 293–300]; here the tune is made intentionally unrecognizable—at least to the Viennese censors. As in the case of the *Danse macabre*, there is a strong element of play, of joke, involved—and in fact I wonder whether there is not always some playfulness, or whimsy, or fantasy at work in cases of covert symbolism.

In each of the foregoing examples the symbol was itself well known: it was borrowed from a familiar source, not invented by the composer. Symbols can indeed be invented, but most invented symbols are neither manifest nor covert. They belong, instead, to a third type, somewhere midway between the other two (and indeed the gradations among the three types are by no means always clear). I call the third type *emergent*: a symbol whose meaning—and indeed, whose very status as a symbol—only gradually becomes clear as the musical work proceeds. As an example I should like to cite a familiar passage from Wagner's *Ring des Nie-belungen*. In *Das Rheingold*, the first we hear about the power that accrues to one who makes the gold into a ring is when in the first scene Wellgunde sings, "Der Welt Erbe gewänne zu eigen, wer aus dem Rhein-gold schüfe den Ring" ("He who forges the Ring from the Rheingold will inherit the world") [pp. 41–42].[4] It is set to music that seems almost parenthetical and hardly of prime importance. But that passage gains in significance when it is repeated, in slightly different form, by Alberich, "Der Welt Erbe gewänn' ich zu eigen durch dich?" ("I could inherit the world for myself through you?") [p. 47]. Already a keen listener will recognize that the motif must have symbolic significance—it is, in fact, on the way to being transformed into a true leitmotif, that of the Ring itself. That comes definitively at the end of the scene when it is stated complete and in isolation [p. 53]. But no sooner is it stated than it in turn is transformed—gradually—into Walhalla, which is what we see (are supposed to see) when the curtain rises on the second scene [pp. 53—55]. And thus the casual theme of the Rhinemaiden's indiscreet announcement has emerged as the source of the two chief dramatic symbols of power in the tetralogy: the Ring and Walhalla.

III

All the above examples display a characteristic that seems to me essential to proper musical symbols: all attempt to convey a meaning that is to some extent independent of their immediate musical or verbal contexts (or both). That is immediately clear in the case of the borrowed symbols,

---

[4] [Page references to the *Ring* refer to the Schirmer vocal scores.]

which did indeed have a prior life of their own, independent of the new use to which the composers put them. That is why the manifest symbols are immediately manifest: the listener, recognizing the motif, recalls its standard associations and brings them to bear on his understanding of the motif in its new context. Other examples abound; the use of chorale melodies, whether in Bach's chorale preludes or Berg's Violin Concerto; or Berg's quotation from *Tristan* in the *Lyric Suite*. In every case the principle is the same: a familiar melody brings with it a set of connotations from an earlier context. By the same token, it is familiarity that makes the covert symbol work too: if we did not ultimately recognize the "Marseillaise" in *Faschingsschwank* or the *Dies irae* in *Danse macabre*, how could either be said to function as a symbol at all, except possibly as a private symbol known only to the composer and those to whom he reveals the secret?

For this reason I find analyses of Bach's or Berg's numerology basically irrelevant and uninteresting. In both cases what seems to be involved is a kind of covert symbolism that, whatever its significance and usefulness to the composer may have been, was probably meant to remain secret and hence is of no real aesthetic importance. But unlike those, the covert symbols we have been discussing are meant to be discovered by the discriminating listener. But when, and how? Does he come to his realization as he listens? Or only later, as he thinks about what he has heard? Or perhaps, only when he has read about it—or heard a lecture about it? Here, on a simple level, arises the distinction between hearing and knowing music—knowing it, that is, in the sense of fully comprehending it.

Both manifest and covert symbols, then, are almost always borrowed from some prior source. In contrast to these, however, the invented symbol is most frequently emergent, for not until its second or even later appearance can we be sure that a symbol is involved. There are, of course, exceptions. Schumann, who was probably the most versatile of all musical symbolists, could not only create an emergent symbol out of borrowed material—e.g., his use of Beethoven's *An die ferne Geliebte* in the first movement of his Fantasy, Op. 17—but apparently even tried to make invented symbols manifest on first hearing—e.g., the "Stimme aus der Ferne" ("voice from the distance") in the eighth of the *Novelletten*, Op. 21. Nevertheless, the successful execution of such a feat is at best very rare indeed—a fact that creates problems for the composer who wants his symbol to be recognized as such from the outset. Suppose that Berlioz had not furnished us with a program for the *Fantastic Symphony*. Would we in that case have recognized the theme of the beloved as being symbolic in the first movement? Would we not rather have taken it to be what in fact it is—the first theme of a sonata form? Only as it appeared in new contexts would we realize its symbolic force.

Or take a case in which the composer, so far as I know, has avowed no specific program, yet in which he has certainly imbued an *idée fixe* with symbolic value: I refer to the opening motto of Tchaikovsky's Fifth Symphony. Certainly by the end of the work we realize that the theme is a symbol—representing, say, destiny, or man's reactions in the face of it. Be that as it may, it is obvious in the case of Berlioz and justifiably inferential in the case of Tchaikovsky, that the theme is meant to be heard at the outset as a manifest symbol. But in fact it can only be so heard retrospectively—if one thinks about it after hearing the work—or proleptically—if one hears the work again after having become familiar with its outcome.

The same problem must be faced in numerous operatic overtures and preludes. Does the Overture to Mozart's *Don Giovanni* remind us of the awful fate awaiting the hero after a life of licentious pleasure? Only if we already know the opera. Does the Prelude to Wagner's *Lohengrin* symbolize the vision of the Holy Grail? Only to one familiar with the hero's third-act narrative. Such preludes, then, would seem really to make complete sense only when performed as postludes—as we can all experience for ourselves every time we hear the *Leonora* No. 3 played as an entr'acte.

But of course we do know what happens to Don Giovanni, and we do know about the Holy Grail. Even if we have never heard the operas we have all been stuffed with information from books and program notes. But here we again face the question: Are these symbolic functions something we really hear, or rather something we know?

In the above, fairly simple cases, the answer is fairly clear: we do not in fact forget what we have previously learned about a composition each time we hear it, and in a sense none of us today ever hears the *Fantastic Symphony* or *Danse macabre* or Tchaikovsky's Fifth or *Don Giovanni* or *Lohengrin* for the first time: the world knows these works, and we are part of that world. And so we accept these symbolic meanings both retrospectively (from what we remember) and proleptically (from what we know is to come) and find it natural to do so. We say to ourselves "Ah, the Stone Guest" and "Oh yes, the Grail"—almost subconsciously, as when we recognize a well-known face. The effectiveness of all borrowed symbols relies on just such prior knowledge on the part of the listener. What I want to suggest now is that it is not always possible to combine what we know and what we hear in this simple way.

In the late works of Wagner, the interplay among symbols becomes so concentrated that only a close analysis can uncover all the embedded implications. I shall mention only one short, well-known example: Brunnhilde's touching phrase "Ruhe, du Gott" ["Rest thou, o God], in her immolation scene from *Götterdämmerung*. The passage is based first of all on a reminiscence of the Rhinemaidens' paean to the Gold in *Rheingold* [p. 326].[5] But this motif, simple as it is, has two predecessors here. First of all the motif of Bondage, given here with the highly dissonant harmonization that is peculiar to this music-drama and is associated with Hagen's destructive work [mm. 3—4]; this motif, melodically G–F-sharp, a descending half step, moves down and becomes the whole step, F–E-flat, of the Rhinemaidens. But before that happens, the curse is interposed [mm. 11–13]. That motif normally ends with another harmonization of Bondage, on a dominant minor ninth. This time, however, the minor motif becomes major: the first chord of the Rhinemaiden's Cry, to which the Curse now gives way [mm. 14–15]. But now that motif in turn is transformed, to a completely consonant form—the extended conclusion of the fully developed Walhalla motif of Scene 2 of *Rheingold* [m. 16]. But this conclusion itself is interrupted—its V–I alternation is broken by a minor IV, on which is played, in the bass, the motif of the Gods' Distress [mm. 17–18], which dies away into the final beneficent glow of the cadence sometimes called Hail to Walhalla [mm. 19–20]. But we must note in passing that the Gods' Distress motif itself had a history: it was long ago developed from a minor form of the all-pervading Rhine motif, a form of that motif further associated with Erda.

I need not go into all the possible symbolic interpretations of this motivic interweaving: I leave that as an exercise for the reader. But it is clear that a sense of the dramatic concepts invoked is as important as a comprehension of the purely musical connections for a full appreciation of the significance of the simple words "Ruhe, du Gott."

But we are not done yet. The passage we have been considering is, in its entirety, a condensed recapitulation of a crucial moment in Waltraute's narrative to Brunnhilde in *Götterdämmerung* Act I. There she describes how Wotan revealed his one source of hope: that Brunnhilde might restore the Ring to the Rhinemaidens. But that statement did not lead to the cadence: D-flat major turns to minor, and a restless modulation follows. So an adequate understanding of the "Ruhe, du Gott" passage involves, not only grasping the musical and dramatic interrelationships that we have already observed, but also remembering the connection of this passage with that of the Waltraute scene in Act 1 [pp. 104–5], with the realization that what was musically incomplete there (representing Wotan's last hope) is now fulfilled (as Brunnhilde prepares to restore the Ring).[6]

[5] [The paean to Gold first appears in *Rheingold*, Scene 1, p. 33 of the vocal score.]

[6] [The recapitulation involves the following motifs, all at the same pitch: Bondage (p. 104, mm. 7–8), Rheingold and Walhalla conclusion (p. 105, mm. 22–23 and 24–27). The turn to minor begins on p. 106, m. 1.]

Again: how much of this can be heard during an actual performance? Especially, how much can be heard if at the same time we try to follow what most of us consider the more basic vehicle of expression, the purely musical structure?

IV

One can argue that the entire symbolic structure is irrelevant; music is not meant to employ what I call proper symbols; it must be content with being what Langer calls an unconsummated symbol. But such a view ignores much of the history of music, from the ethos of Greek modes, through the Augenmusik of the Renaissance and the Figuren of the Baroque, to the problematic examples we have been discussing. The tradition is a long one, and including as it does such figures as Ockeghem and Josquin, Bach and Handel, Schumann and Wagner, an honorable one. What did these composers think they were doing? Perhaps one should retreat to a less comprehensive rejection, and take the position that symbolic techniques are admissible and can even prove advantageous so long as they are not too complex to be apprehended during actual performance. On this view, the examples we have been discussing represent an overcomplication—a historical aberration that it has been the task of our own century to correct.

The position I wish to defend is different from both of these. Implicit in the condemnation of complex symbolism is the belief that music should be completely comprehensible in performance. I don't mean that it must be completely comprehensible to one who is hearing it for the first time, or the second, or even the tenth. But it must be comprehensible to someone hearing it at some time. No matter how difficult a composition is, if we get to know it, really to know it, then we can listen to it and really hear it—really hear all of it, in all of its complexity. I suggest that this view is mistaken. I happen to think that it is mistaken about all art—but I cannot argue that point here. Let me restrict myself to those arts that have to be perceived in time, like music and the drama. Can we adequately comprehend the totality of a play of Shakespeare, for instance, both sensuously and intellectually, during any performance, no matter how familiar we are with the play, and no matter how profoundly conceived the performance may be? Here is R. P. Blackmur expounding a single word from Horatio's line in *Hamlet*, describing the appearance of the ghost "in the dead vast and middle of the night."

Vast is of course the focal word, and it should be said at once that it appears in this form only in the first Quarto. In the second Quarto and the first Folio it

was *wast*, and in the second, third, and fourth folios it was *waste*. My contention . . . is that no matter which way the word is printed the effect of all three
is evident and felt, with a strong possibility of a fourth sense, that of *waist*, as
well. The accident of the recorded variations in printing forces the attention
upon the variety of meanings bedded down to sleep in this single syllable. Let
us read the line in the middle spelling: "In the dead wast and middle of the
night," and do we not have all at once in the word the sense of the vast void
of the night, the stretching and useless waste of the night, and the waist or
middle and generative part of the night as well? And do we not have, finally, a
kind of undifferentiated meaning . . . which can only be less defined the more
deeply it is experienced?[7]

The fact that we accept and even welcome such verbal analysis is evidence that we tacitly acknowledge that the total effect of *Hamlet* is not
delivered in performance; for how could a member of the audience mentally catalogue the various forms of the word, much less their interre-
lated meanings, without losing the thread of the dialogue? And in a play
of *Hamlet*'s texture this would be happening not once but continually.
And if this applies to single words, it applies more importantly to the
concepts, the themes, and the symbols evoked by them. In plain words,
we accept the fact that a play is something to think about as well as to
watch—or even to read; for the purpose of reading such a play is precisely to be able to take it at one's own speed, in one's own order—that
is, to think about it as we go along. The result is that when one thinks
Hamlet, one does not think through any performance one has seen, or
even any imaginary ideal performance; one obviously cannot unroll the
play in one's mind every time one summons up the concept. Rather, one
thinks of the play as if it were a familiar object, almost a spatial object,
which one can examine at leisure and knows, or can come to know, in
all its detail; one can relate these details to one another as they form
characters, concepts, themes, symbols, and as these in turn compose
larger forms and finally the entire play itself. It is the memory of this
kind of mental activity that informs every intelligent hearing of the play
in actual performance: what one hears is shaped and controlled by what
one knows.

To return to our example, I do not need to rehearse the exegesis of the
word "vast." If I have done my homework, the word will produce an effect that is the resultant of all its meanings together, a single charged moment of expression that I can savor without remembering each component, but that I can savor only because I have once recognized each
component. That, I believe, is what Blackmur means when he says, as a

7[R. P. Blackmur, *Language as Gesture* (New York: Harcourt Brace, 1953), pp. 17–18.]

final comment on our problematic word, "And do we not have, finally, a kind of undifferentiated meaning . . . which can only be less defined the more deeply it is experienced?"

Is this not the solution to "Ruhe, du Gott" in *Die Götterdämmerung*? The total effect of the passage will depend on our knowledge of the motifs and their prior history, yet will also depend on our ability to transcend that knowledge and to let it work subconsciously as it were. If we have done our homework, what we know will profoundly affect what we hear—and we shall recognize that passage as the moment of resolution of the entire quadruple music-drama, the rest being coda.

Let me make an important point here. The last time I actually heard *Götterdämmerung* was over five years ago. And I arrived at the realization of the effect of "Ruhe, du Gott" only long since then. But this new appreciation illuminates in retrospect every performance of the *Ring* I have ever heard. It has become a part of the work—and simply through my thought about the work. If I hear *Götterdämmerung* again, I shall hear it in a different way. So: even those symbolic relations that cannot be heard in actuality do affect the way we hear a piece, and in that sense *can* ultimately be heard, not actually, but ideally.

For some, all this intellectual activity will simply confirm their sweeping opinion: music has no business concerning itself with symbolism at all. It is an art of pure form. If all art aspires to the condition of music, all music aspires to the condition of absolute music, free of words or program of any kind. In reply, I insist that the difficulties we encounter with symbolic structures are equally present in purely musical form. Absolute music presents the same problem: relationships that function profoundly in the structure of a composition may yet prove to be unhearable in actual performance.

One common example is afforded by the familiar pattern of theme-and-variation. Some variations, it is true, remain so close to the parent theme that we can hear that theme beneath the variation, so to speak. But some variations move so far from the original that it is no longer recognizable—to the unaided ear alone, that is. Think for a moment of Beethoven's Piano Sonata Op. 109—not the last movement, a frank theme and variations, but the first. How many listeners, even after a number of hearings, realize that the second theme of this unique movement consists of a theme plus a variation [mm. 9−11 + 12−15]? What sounds like a fantastic improvisation is strictly modeled on the preceding phrase—both in the exposition, and perhaps even more fantastically, in the recapitulation [mm. 58–65].

Let us go a bit further. In the last movement—the avowed theme and variations—the second half of the second variation introduces a strange foreign note—a D-natural—that is presumably an alteration of the

D-sharp of the bass of the theme at that point [m. 25]. At any rate, it so alters the harmonic direction that, even though we know this must be a variation, we must take that fact on faith; and although later analysis will show how the variation "works," it is impossible, during performance, to hear the theme behind the passage. But this D-natural has more than just local importance. It returns in several later variations, most notably in the last. And now, finally, we can understand its significance. Here, then, is the climactic version of the second half of the theme—a version incorporating the D-natural of the second variation, which was an alteration of the D-sharp in the bass of the theme [m. 17]. But, as if these connections are not enough to take in, Beethoven reveals another: the passage is at the same time a recapitulation of the second theme from the first movement! This connection is basic to the organic unity of the entire sonata: yet can one really hear such a complex network of relationships?

In all these cases, there is a complicated interchange between hearing the music and knowing the music—just as there was in the cases of symbolism. It is not enough to know *that* passage x is a variation or a derivation; that is knowing *about* the music. No, we must know passage x *as* a variation or derivation. And that means that we must be able to think the music—to think through it. And that thought can be available only to one able to hear the music on his own terms, at his own speed, in any kind of order, independently of any performance. And that, I fear, means that we must either read or memorize the music! I am sorry to have to arrive at such a conclusion, yet I see no way out. If we are adequately to hear music, we must have some way of recovering it in order to think through it. For the music that we can think *through* is the only music that we can really think *about* in any relevant way; the music that we can think about is the only music that we can really know; the music that we know is the only music that we can adequately hear. So if it is true, and I believe it is (some seem not to!), that one must first hear a composition in order to know it, it is equally true that one must know the composition in order to hear it. That is why it is completely wrongheaded to use the word "cerebral" as a term of critical opprobrium, or to accuse a performer of having an "intellectual" approach. Rightly to appreciate music of any profundity at all is a highly intellectual activity.

As a final example, let us look at a passage from that paragon of lucidity, Mozart—an instance of a very common situation in his works. Mozart often presents us with unbalanced periods—4:6, say, or 4:8. And when he recapitulates them, he often unbalances them in a different way—4:6 may become 4:8, or 4:8 may become even 4:16. When we hear a period, we compare the second phrase with the first in order to grasp its tonal and temporal relationship. And when we hear a recapitulation, if we are to appreciate its role, we must compare it with the original statement. But that means we may have to make four complex comparisons at once: if a phrase formally organized as A^1B^1 is recapitulated by A^2B^2, we must first of all compare B^1 with A^1. But in the recapitulation, we must compare A^2 with A^1, B^2 with A^2, B^2 with B^1, and A^2B^2 with A^1B^1. In the Clarinet Quintet, K. 581, the second theme of the first movement affords a beautiful instance—not really a period, but a statement followed by an extended variation in the minor. The phrases of the first statement are proportioned 7:16 [mm. 43–49; 50–65]! The recapitulation is 7:14 [149–55; 156–69]. Adequately to hear the consequent in the recapitulation, we must be conscious that it is both longer than the antecedent (just twice as long) but also shorter than its model in the exposition! But that is not all: each time, remember, the consequent is an extended minor variation of the antecedent. But in the recapitulation, the consequent is at the same time a variation on the consequent in the exposition. Thus it must be compared simultaneously with two models that it varies.

At this point one is tempted to agree with the idealist position: the real work of art is the one we think about, the one we construct in our mind. I do not go that far: I still want to hear my music, see my pictures, watch my plays. But we cannot spend our lives listening to music, or looking at pictures, or seeing plays—most of us can't, at any rate. It is fortunate that the work of art can live in our minds, live vividly and vitally—ready to be summoned up whenever we wish, to be examined or rehearsed as we like. I may never get to Athens again: that does not prevent me from right now experiencing the Parthenon as a great building. I may never hear another performance of *Götterdämmerung*; I can enjoy it now, as I suggested, in a way that I never could when I actually heard it.

A piece of music, like any work of art, is first of all a construction of the mind, communicated through the senses to other minds. And though it must be perceived through the senses, it can be understood only by the mind. Perhaps the test of a great work of art is whether it can become an object of contemplation. Now, one can contemplate a spatial work—a picture, a statue, a building—while actually observing it. But one can contemplate temporal works—literature, drama, music—only in retrospect. That is the way we can grasp their unique control of great complexity through organic unity. Paradoxically, then, a composition becomes great not as it is heard, but as it is known and thought about.

PART II

Opera and Song

CONE'S IDEAS ABOUT opera and music, and in general music's relationship to text, influenced many other scholars, perhaps most notably his younger colleague the music historian Carolyn Abbate (formerly at Princeton). In developing the notion of music's "persona," or its "voice," and applying it to a wide range of musical situations, Cone raised a number of far-reaching questions that opened up a range of new issues related to vocal music. For example, just whose music does one hear in opera: the composer's, the character's, or that of music itself? And with what effect is it heard? These three essays, which develop this complex and multifaceted project, represent Cone's final thoughts on the subject.

"Mozart's Deceptions" takes as its example two of Mozart's best-known operas, *Così fan tutte* and *The Marriage of Figaro*, posing the question: how does a composer write convincingly beautiful music for operatic characters who are clearly deceitful? Cone effectively argues that, in the world of opera, all characters are always treated as consummate actors and are thus equally at home—and musically prescient— whether stating truths or falsehoods. But Cone is also at pains to note that one must understand the specific nature of the character's deceit: is what he or she is singing understood as deceitful by all the characters present or only by some? And what is the character's own understanding of what he or she is singing?

The Wagner essay, "Siegfried at the Dragon's Cave," the longest of the unpublished writings, deals with opera's voice in more general terms but confines itself to a single compositional technique: the Wagnerian leitmotif. With frequent reference to Wagner's writings as well as his own (especially *The Composer's Voice*), Cone probes such matters as when, and in what combination, particular leitmotifs appear; how and why they relate to one another; how and to what purpose they develop; whether of not they are invented and recognized by the characters who sing and hear them; and the different roles played by orchestra and voice in projecting them. This essay is especially useful for its revision of Cone's earlier views about operatic assertion, providing a valuable summary of his final thoughts on the topic.

The third essay, "Schubert's Heine Songs," deals with the six settings of poems by this poet in the composer's *Schwanengesang* cycle (songs 8–13). Although it does not treat opera, it deals with similar musical-textual issues. Almost half of this essay was reworked to form one of Cone's last published works: "'Am Meer' Reconsidered: Strophic, Binary, or Ternary" (1998).[1] The focus is quite different, however, as here emphasis is placed on the musical-poetic integrity of the Heine group as a whole, rather than on a single song. It includes, along with that of

---

[1] *Schubert Studies*, ed. Brian Newbould (Aldershot, England: Ashgate, 1998).

"Am Meer," relatively detailed analyses of "Der Atlas," "Die Stadt," and especially "Der Doppelgänger," as well as commentary on the other Heine songs. The essay's sole musical example is taken from a related article, "Repetition and Correspondence in *Schwanengesang*."[2] That essay, however, while incorporating some material from this essay's second half, deals with the entire cycle, not just the Heine settings; and unlike this one, it focuses on formal and rhythmic matters, especially repetition. Not only different in detail, it also omits much that is included here.

[2] *A Companion to Schubert's Schwanengesang*, ed. Martin Chusid (New Haven, CT: Yale University Press, 2000).

Mozart's Deceptions

I

MANY YEARS AGO I read a discussion of *Samson et Dalila*. According to the critic, Saint-Saëns faced a dilemma in composing "Mon coeur s'ouvre à ta voix" ["My heart opens to your voice"]: if he tried to set the words as a supposedly sincere love lyric, the result would be untrue to Dalila's character; if he emphasized her hypocrisy, the song would not be convincing to Samson.[1]

Similar comments are often applied to the roles of the duplicitous men in *Così fan tutte*. Referring to the quintet of farewell, Alfred Einstein typically wondered: "What was Mozart to do at this point? The two young ladies were weeping real tears, while the officers knew that there was no occasion to do so." His answer was ambiguous: "Mozart raises the banner of pure beauty, without forgetting the old cynic in the background, 'laughing himself to death.'"[2]

Both critics might have profited from a visit to Greensboro (North Carolina) High School in the 1930s, where Miss Sarah Lesley was teaching fourth-year Latin. (In those far-off, benighted days, it was not uncommon for public high schools to offer four years of Latin.) Miss Lesley worshipped Vergil and every year successfully communicated her enthusiasm for the *Aeneid* to some two dozen students. I particularly remember her appreciation of the mendacious tale by which Sinon, the apparently renegade Greek, persuades the Trojans to bring the wooden horse into the fortified city. "Sinon's narrative is so artfully composed," said she, "that I find myself believing it every time I reread it. I can fully understand how the Trojans were deceived." Sinon was depicted as an accomplished actor, one who played his part so perfectly that his story was accepted by the Trojans as truth; and Vergil had portrayed Sinon's character and composed his tale so successfully that Miss Lesley, engrossed in the narrative of the epic, was equally compelled to accept the story every time she read it.

---

[1] I had thought that the author of the critique was Gustav Kobbe, but a search through his various books on opera has proved fruitless.

[2] Alfred Einstein, *Mozart, His Character, His Work* (London: Oxford University Press, 1945), p. 446.

To be sure, Miss Lesley could have gone further. She could have pointed out that in believing Sinon's tale she was tacitly assuming the reliability of Aeneas's narrative, in which the Sinon episode is embedded—and the reliability of the entire poem as well. This is not to say that she took the *Aeneid* as veridical; but she did recognize its artistically constructed world as one governed by the same law of logic and consistency as our own. It is within that world that concepts such as Aeneas's reliability and Sinon's hypocrisy apply. (Every successful example of storytelling constructs such a world. It is one that we must accept whenever we read a novel, see a play, or hear an opera, if we mean to take its story seriously. But this excursion into literary theory was one Miss Lesley did not pursue—not, at any rate for the benefit of her high-school seniors.)

Returning now to Saint-Saëns's dilemma, with what we might call the Sinon effect in mind, we find that it turns out to be no dilemma at all. In the world of Saint-Saëns's operatic fiction, Dalila, like Sinon, is a consummate hypocrite; and she has the requisite histrionic ability to support her duplicity. Naturally she would exert all her wiles to ensnare Samson, and of course the composer would supply her with the most enticing melody at his command. The result is an aria that captivates Samson and audience alike.

As for Guglielmo and Ferrando, they too are actors in *Così*. They are men of honor who have paradoxically sworn to do their best to play deceptive roles. Whether they are representing themselves in the feigned sorrow of a long farewell, or whether they are making love in the guise of their Albanian alter egos, they must strive to be as convincing as possible; and Mozart has granted them the musical ability needed to guarantee their success. The banner that, according to Einstein, Mozart raised in his quintet of farewell was one of beauty that was by no means pure. Four voices share similar musical material, despite the fact that two of them are dissembling. Moreover, the orchestra, with its subdued coloration, accepts the situation at face value—leaving Don Alfonso as a detached and amused outsider who interjects his own rhythmic motif in order to laugh quietly to himself. But he must sometimes conceal his true feelings: when he joins the ladies in the trio "Soave sia il vento" ["Gently blows the wind"], his expression is apparently as heartfelt as theirs. He too is a good actor, as he boasts immediately afterward.

II

The Sinon effect in *Così* thus involves all three men. But Don Alfonso's part in the intrigue is special. In addition to his talent as a deceptive actor he demonstrates his ability as an author-director, for the success of his scheme depends on the effective staging of what might be regarded as his own play-within-the-play, a didactic comedy whose aim is to instruct the young men—although at the cost of deceiving their paramours. The author-director has composed its general outlines, but in commedia dell'arte fashion he has left the details to his principals. Let us examine its structure.

The farewell scene may be considered the first of five acts arranged by Don Alfonso. At this point the young men have not yet assumed their new guises but are playing their real selves, although in a fictive situation. They vividly imagine their reactions as matching those expressed by their deluded lovers, and from that point of view they are behaving sincerely—like "method" actors, as it were. That is why the quintet is so affecting.

In complete contrast is the burlesque of Don Alfonso's second act, which includes the introduction of the young men in Albanian disguise and their faked attempt at suicide. The audience of a burlesque remains untouched by the emotional life of the portrayed characters. Instead of crying with them it laughs at them. From Don Alfonso's point of view, the episode is a plot device to trick the ladies into entertaining the two strangers, and it performs the same function on the level of the Mozart and da Ponte play. Mozart cleverly supports both the mummery of the young men and the naive response of the women by the exaggeration of conventional musical effects: string tremolos, rushing scales, and chromatic lines. If we wonder how, realistically, Fiordiligi and Dorabella can be taken in by such nonsense, we must remember that these are the same two who earlier claimed to prefer death to separation. They have lived in a state of emotional unreality and hence are ready to be unconscious actresses in Don Alfonso's play. He can cynically depend on their reactions: grief at their lovers' departures, horrified interest in the attempted suicide of two strangers, and eager acceptance of their incredibly quick recovery.

He can depend equally on their behavior in his third act, which encompasses the Albanians' increasingly impassioned lovemaking. In Don Alfonso's second act the young men's performance was an example of what might be called external simulation: they were feigning what they had presumably never felt, in a situation that was obviously false. Now, however, they are engaged in thorough dissimulation. They are still disguised; but they are now assuming mental states with which they can empathize and can even to a certain extent—again like good "method" actors—accept as their own. The resulting emotional reality of their lovemaking explains, if it does not excuse, the responses it evokes.

That is what Don Alfonso is depending on. He expects that the women will eventually give in; hence he prepares the mock wedding of his fourth act. He foresees that their eagerness to believe in what is happening around them will prevent them from recognizing Despina's crude impersonation of a notary—just as it has earlier led them to accept her in the role of a doctor. What he does not foresee, however, is Guglielmo's failure to carry out his part in the wedding canon. Some time ago I wondered "whether Ferrando, by joining in with the two ladies (musically as well as verbally), expresses his acquiescence in a situation that he has hitherto deplored—or perhaps has only seemed to. One has the suspicion that Ferrando has enjoyed the whole charade and might not be averse to the change of fiancées! Is this really the case?"[3] I failed to give a direct answer to the question, referring to Mozart's subtlety and ambiguity. Now I am willing to be more straightforward. We have no reason to believe that Ferrando wishes to make the swap. All we know from this episode is that he is a better actor than Guglielmo. He can carry out his part to the end, whereas Guglielmo finds himself unable to remain in character at a crucial moment. If we, like Fiordiligi, believe in the sincerity of Ferrando's attitude, we are yielding to the power of the Sinon effect.

Don Alfonso's fifth and final act, which follows without a break near the opera's end, is the denouement. Now undisguised, the young men are nevertheless expressing emotions they do not really feel: delight on the occasion of the early return, followed by angry astonishment. At this point their music reverts to the exaggerations of the previous scene of external simulation, although only briefly. As for the ladies, their first admission of guilt cleverly (or with unconscious irony) reminds the two men of their own happy greeting: singing "il mio fallo tardi vedo" ("too late I see my error"), they echo their lovers' earlier "ritorniamo, di gioja esultanti" ("we return exultant with joy"), examples 5.1a and 5.1b.[4] Only when the whole truth is at last revealed do they honestly come to terms with themselves and their lovers. That is a change of heart too quick to be realistically acceptable, but nevertheless convincing when expressed by the affecting duet "Idol mio, se questo è vero" ["My idol, if this is true"]. After that, anyone who insists that it is immaterial which pairing now obtains, or even claims that the original pairing is now impossible, is taking Don Alfonso's play too seriously—and Mozart and da Ponte's not seriously enough. Indeed, once the men have shed their costumes, the disguised lovers no

---

[3] [Edward T. Cone, *The Composer's Voice* (Berkeley: University of California Press, 1974), pp. 38–39.]

[4] [Page numbers for *Così fan tutte* refer to the Schirmer vocal score.]

longer exist. It is thus the second pairing, not the first, that has become impossible.

EXAMPLE 5.1   Mozart, *Così fan Tutte*

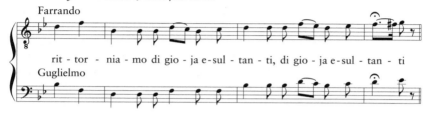

a. "Ritorniamo, di gioia esultanti" (p. 342)

b. "Il mio fallo tardi vedo" (p. 349)

There is one participant in Don Alfonso's play of whom we have so far taken no notice. Despina's two roles in that play are of course pure burlesque. They are meant to provide moments of hilarity for the audience, but at the same time they have a more serious illustrative function: they point up the frailty of the two heroines—not just their gullibility but their obvious willingness to be deceived. It is instructive to contrast the depiction of Despina's impersonations with those of the two heroes. Despina's natural vivacity is indicated in her arias by her lively melodic lines and by the perky 6/8 meter to which she is partial. As doctor and notary, both her melodic flexibility and her rhythm are restricted. In the first instance she takes her cues from Don Alfonso; in the second, her singing is gradually reduced to mere formula. Despina, then, is merely "play-acting": her own personality disappears. Guglielmo and Ferrando, on the other hand, play their roles not as denials but as extensions of themselves. Like many professionals, they seem able to express themselves more freely on the stage than in real life. That is the psychological truth that permits the success of Don Alfonso's deception—and that makes *Così fan tutte* a more believable opera than is usually acknowledged.

III

Così fan tutte is not the only opera of Mozart that relies on deception perpetrated by its characters. *Le Nozze di Figaro* depends on the ability of its principals to display counterfeit emotions and to assume actual disguises. The Sinon effect, however, does not operate here: we are never in doubt as to their genuine feelings. Thus when Susanna agrees to an assignation with the Count, she makes sure that we in the audience are not taken in. During their Act 3 duet she plays a double role. For the Count, she is the willing object of his desire: "Se piace a voi, verrò" ["If it pleases you, I will"]. At the same time her asides try to excuse her lies. So although her melody matches that of the Count's amorous outburst, her words are directed elsewhere: "Scusatemi se mento, voi che intendete amor" ["Forgive me if I lie, you who understand love"]. Presumably the Count, excited by his own passion, gladly accepts her musical agreement but fails to hear, or to pay attention to, the words that we in the audience hear. The ambivalent role that Susanna must play is cleverly underlined by her mistakes in replying to the Count's insistent questions. Twice she is confused in her alternation of "si" and "no"—slips of the tongue, by which her subconscious reveals her true intentions.

Susanna's talent for deception of a peculiarly subtle type is revealed in what is perhaps the most specifically operatic scene in *Le Nozze*: her recitative and aria in Act 4, "Giunse alfin il momento. . . . Deh vieni, non tardar" ["The moment has finally arrived. . . . Do come, do not delay"]. I call the scene specifically operatic because at this point da Ponte's libretto develops a theme independently of Beaumarchais's original play. For how could such a moment be realized in spoken drama? Susanna is indulging in a soliloquy—long a conventional medium for representing a character thinking or talking to herself. But this one is an overheard soliloquy—in fact, an intentionally overheard soliloquy, as Susanna has made clear: "Diamogli la mercè de' dubbi suoi" ["Let's give him the benefit of his doubts"]. Figaro, then, must be close enough to Susanna to recognize her voice and to distinguish her words, but too far away to realize (in the dim light) that she is disguised as the Countess. Thus the stage is set for Susanna's deception: an impersonation, but an impersonation of herself. The real Susanna, obviously deeply in love with Figaro, pretends to be a false Susanna, in love with—or at least infatuated with—the Count.

Susanna's ability to play this role is in part a result of expert coaching. When the Countess dictated Susanna's letter in Act 3, she taught her the suave 6/8 meter and the flowing three-measure phrases that Susanna now exploits on her own. The connection between the two numbers is made obvious by the prominence of the flute and bassoon, which in both cases weave concertante melodies, often in octaves, around the voices. Even the keys, B-flat and F, delicately suggest a close relationship.

Susanna's duplicity works on a deeper level as well. The song that she hopes Figaro will overhear and take as an invitation to the Count is in reality addressed to Figaro himself. For the motif (let us call it *x*) which she calls upon to express her longing (ex. 5.2a[5]) is one familiar from her opening duet with Figaro in Act 1 (ex. 5.2b). There it first appeared, in the tonic G major, as she tried on her hat, "sembra fatto in ver per me" ["it truly seems to be made for me"]. It was answered in the dominant by Figaro, forced to turn his attention from floor-measurement: "fatto in ver per te" ["it is truly made for you"]. Finally they sing the theme together, once again in the tonic as if in acknowledgment of Figaro's surrender to Susanna's captivation: "che Susanna ella stessa si fè" ["that Susanna made it herself"]. So when Susanna invokes motif *x* at "Deh vieni, non tardar," she is recalling a moment of simultaneous delight—albeit one in which she subtly triumphed.

EXAMPLE 5.2 Mozart, *Le Nozze di Figaro*

a. Finale, Act 3 (p. 307)

b. Opening duet, Act 1 (pp. 9–10)

Figaro overhears the words and reacts as Susanna expects. Does he recognize the tune? Very likely, as we shall see. If so, his attitude is, no doubt, "She's singing *our* song—for *him*!" In any case Susanna has her little revenge, comforting herself at the same time by the security of her love.

She is thus successful in her deception of both the Count and her fiancé—so long as she maintains her identity as Susanna. Her impersonation of the Countess, however, is far from perfect. In her later colloquy with Figaro, in the Finale, not only does she forget to disguise her voice,

---

[5] [Page numbers for *Le Nozze di Figaro* refer to the Boosey and Hawkes vocal score.]

but she also appropriates his melodic line, her "ma vendicarmi vo'" ["but I wish to avenge myself"] quoting his "toccar io vi farò" ["I will have you touched"], examples 5.3a and 5.3b. Both musically and verbally the passage is uncharacteristic of the Countess. Even if Figaro fails to penetrate her vocal disguise, he can still see through her motivic usage.

EXAMPLE 5.3   Mozart, *Le Nozze di Figaro*, Finale, Act 3 (p. 330)

toc - car io vi fa - rò, toc - car io vi fa - rò,

a. "toccar io vi farò"

ma ven - di-car - mi vo', ma ven - di-car - mi vo'.

b. "ma vendicarmi vo"

At this point he proves himself Susanna's match in deception. For when the tables are turned and he pretends to be enamored of the supposed Countess, he adopts a transformation of motif x, strongly suggesting that he did indeed recognize it in Susanna's aria. Musically, it well accords with his plan, "Two can play at this game." The motif in question finds its place in Figaro's feigned love song, as the completion of a chromatic line that has an interesting derivation of its own. The chromatic melody is first adumbrated in the orchestral bass line during the enchanting Larghetto that ironically surrounds Figaro's vision of Venus, Mars, and Vulcan, example 5.4a. Shortly thereafter, in the ensuing Allegro molto, it is presented by the orchestra in rapid diminution, as Figaro approaches the supposed Countess—and perhaps its introductory rising fourth is the source of Susanna's exclamation: "Ehi Figaro! tacete!" ["Hey Figaro, be silent!"], example 5.4b. That orchestral form reappears in the dominant, B-flat, when Figaro recognizes Susanna, but now the sustained version is given to Susanna, who has her own ideas of revenge: "L'iniquo io vo' sorprendere" ["I wish to surprise the wicked fellow"], example 5.4c. The return to the tonic at last allows motif x to answer the chromatic line, as Figaro's apparently impassioned appeal to the "Countess" unites pretended retaliation with actual love in an extended melody (a complete double-period) that sets a text of delightful ambivalence:

"Ecco mi a vostri piedi" ["Here I am at your feet"], example 5.4d. Figaro symbolically satisfies his anger at the Count by feigning love for the Countess; and in so doing he teasingly arouses Susanna's jealousy while at the same time expressing his real love for her. When it subsequently returns, that melody promises still further expansion by Figaro ("Date mi un po' la mano"; "Give me your hand a bit") but it is thwarted by Susanna's outburst of temper: "Servitevi, Signor!" ["Serve yourself, sir"], example 5.4e. Her interruption prevents our hearing what might have been a lovely Mozartian development. We shall never know, for Figaro's next and last statement of the melody returns to its original form (with "o schiaffi graziosissimi" ["O most delightful smacks"]—recapitulating "Ecco mi a vostri piedi") [mm. 6–8]. This time Susanna, instead of interrupting, sings in antiphonal counterpoint that answers Figaro's motif *x* with a version of her own, answering Figaro's tonic with her subdominant (ex. 5.4f). The motif of complete accord has become the vehicle of a lovers' quarrel. When the couple unite to bring the Allegro to a tonic close, it is on the same cadential motif that they have used at several points throughout the movement to express their desire for vengeance— from Figaro's "Toccar io vi farò" and Susanna's "ma vendicar mi vo'" (see ex. 5.3) to her later "Poi so quel che farò ["I'll know just what I'll do"] and "che smania, che furor!" ["What agitation, what furor!"]. Susanna now turns the phrase against Figaro ("a fare il seduttor" ["to play the seducer"]), who, delighted with this turn of events, willingly supports her, "o mio felice amor" ["O my happy love"], example 5.4g.

EXAMPLE 5.4   Variations of Descending Chromatic Line and Motif *x* in *Le Nozze di Figaro*, Finale, Act 3

a. With orchestral bass line (p. 329)

b. With orchestral line (p. 329)

c. Page 331, mm. 5–10

d. Page 332, mm. 12–18

e. Page 334, mm. 8–14

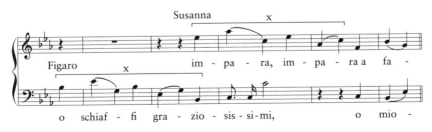

f. Page 335, mm. 14–18

g. Page 336, mm. 4–9

One last charade remains to be enacted: the deception of the Count, the opportunity for which occurs when he unknowingly interrupts the scene of the lovers' reconciliation. Their melody at that point is initiated by a chordal motif that displays a brief family resemblance to motif *x*, example 5.5. It is amusing to hear the Count enter singing the same vocal melody as theirs to the words "Non la trovo e girai tutto il bosco!" ["I don't find her and I've been all over the woods!"]. He is searching everywhere for Susanna, and she is standing directly before him. Perhaps the thematic reference is an intentional bit of irony on Mozart's part.

EXAMPLE 5.5   *Le Nozze di Figaro*, Finale, Act 3 (p. 336, mm. 13–16)

Taking advantage of this situation, Figaro returns to his amorous pursuit of the supposed Countess. But this time Susanna knows the truth; only the Count is taken in. The scene is played out for him to misinterpret; nevertheless, the love duet is sincere. For although Figaro's initial approach is exaggerated ("Si, madama, voi siete il ben mio!" ["Yes, madam, you are my beloved"!]), he and Susanna soon come together for a reprise of their music of reconciliation ("Ah, corriamo, mio bene" ["Ah, let's run, my beloved"]). The Count misinterprets the lady's identity but not the couple's sentiments.

A reappearance of motif *x* appropriately occurs at the moment when the personal reconciliation of the Count and the Countess is accepted by all. As the assembled company voices its approval of the outcome, "Ah tutti contenti saremo così" ["Ah, thus we'll all be happy"], the violins inject a commentary developed from the motif, example 5.6a. The key is G major, recalling the duet in which motif *x* first appeared. Perhaps the motif is also subtly implied in the climax of the ensemble as well, example 5.6b. Certainly it is echoed during the concluding Allegro assai, "di capricci e di follìa" ["of caprices and madness"], turning to minor to reflect the capricious madness of the day just past, example 5.6c. And in a final gesture, it is inverted to confirm the triumphal D major ("corriam tutti" ["let's all run"]), example 5.6d—and to remind us of the original D major of the Overture.

EXAMPLE 5.6   Voices of Approval Near End of *Le Nozze di Figaro*, Finale, Act 3

a. Susanna and Countess (pp. 346–47)

b. Susanna and Countess, and Marcellina, Cherubino, and Barbarina (p. 347)

c. Tutti (p. 349)

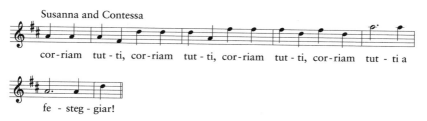

d. Susanna and Countess (p. 352–53)

What of the Countess's part in this tangle of intrigue? Narrowly considered, her deceptiveness is short-lived. Her pretense at being Susanna is hardly tested. In that role her most extensive colloquy is with the amorous Cherubino. As she repulses his advances, she does so in both verbal and musical terms that sound more like herself than like Susanna (e.g., her "Arditello," "You little rascal," sung against a descending octave in the violins, ex. 5.7); but presumably the ardent Cherubino does not notice the inconsistency. When she is approached by the Count, her replies to him are brief and punctuated by asides that he is obviously not meant to hear. Soon she disappears from the scene, returning only when she can reveal herself.

EXAMPLE 5.7   *Le Nozze di Figaro*, Finale, Act 3 (p. 312, m. 3)

From a broader point of view, however, the Countess's deceptiveness is much more complex, for it controls the whole pattern of double identities that permeates the last act of *Figaro*. It is she who plans the scheme whereby she doubly stoops to conquer: by impersonating Susanna and by allowing Susanna to impersonate her. When she composes Susanna's letter, she is expressing her own desires in the pretended voice of Susanna—an act of duplicity that will be repeated more obviously when she assumes Susanna's guise.

This kind of duplicity is matched by a related type that is indulged in by Susanna and Figaro: the pretense that one's genuine desires are directed elsewhere than toward their true object. Whereas the Countess's letter assigns its true feelings to a false source, Susanna's aria expresses her true feelings, but toward a double object—one feigned and one real—with an ambiguous purpose: to arouse Figaro's jealousy while revealing her love for him. But at the same time the Countess is present in spirit—and not just in Susanna's costume. For does Susanna not add a further complication: the suggestion that she is trying to impersonate the Countess in song as well as in dress, and that as the Countess she is hopefully addressing the Count? If, as I have suggested, her aria is a continuation and completion of the letter, the idea of such an additional complication is not outlandish.

Similar ambiguous doubleness characterizes Figaro's wooing of the supposed Countess. Here the twofold object of his affection—ostensibly the Countess, actually Susanna—is paired with a twofold object of deception—at first Susanna, and later the Count. Even though absent, the Countess is thus a central figure: she is present in Susanna's pretense and in the Count's inflamed imagination. This constant virtual presence is what makes her actual appearance at the denouement so effective.

IV

In comparison with the multiple deceptions of *Figaro*, the frank role playing of *Così* seems relatively simple and straightforward. And although in each opera the impersonations are controlled by a character who works as a script writer and stage manager, only in *Figaro* is that character personally affected by the ensuing action. The Countess takes a crucial role in her own play; and when that play develops a course that she does not foresee, she is able in the end to turn it to her advantage. Don Alfonso's personal feelings, in contrast, are not touched by his play— except for the satisfaction of winning his bet and proving his theory correct.

From another point of view, however, that of the attentive and sympathetic auditor, *Figaro* turns out to be the simpler of the two. We know that the Countess, Figaro, and Susanna, however false their immediate positions may be, are fundamentally expressing real feelings directed toward their proper objects. Consequently, we can empathize wholeheartedly with each in turn. In *Così* we are confronted by emotions that, in the case of the women, are true but shallow; in the case of the men, presumably false. Where are our sympathies to lie? Or are we to play Don Alfonso and watch the proceedings as a game?

The answer, I believe, lies in a renewed consideration of the Sinon effect. Earlier I cautioned against yielding to its deceptiveness; now I wish to suggest that in so doing we enable ourselves to appreciate more fully the complexity of the dramatic situation. By recognizing the validity of the music Mozart has assigned to the young men we can understand and hence forgive the behavior of their paramours. Indeed, such is the persuasiveness of the music that while it lasts we may well find ourselves, like Fiordiligi and Dorabella, convinced of the sincerity of their disguised lovers. We may suspect that the men are performing so wholeheartedly that they have come to believe in their false roles. In this case, Mozart's deceptiveness operates on two levels: that of the duped characters, and that of the bemused audience. If his strategy is successful—if, as a result, we find ourselves accepting as true the protestations that we ought to know are false—it is because Mozart has made his Sinons so convincing that we in the audience, like Miss Lesley long ago, cannot resist being taken in.

Siegfried at the Dragon's Cave: The Motivic Language of *The Ring*

I

W HEN S IEGFRIED BLOWS his horn at the entrance of Neidhöhle [*Siegfried*, Act 2, Scene 2, p. 184[1]], he pretends to be seeking "ein lieber Gesell." Those words are obviously ironic; his true purpose, as disclosed in his previous colloquy with Mime, is to arouse the dragon and to challenge him to combat. That message is conveyed, not by words but by the fanfare of the horn itself. From a narrowly realistic point of view, the job is done by the penetrating voice of the instrument. Musically, however, the power of the utterance depends on the aggressive, increasingly persistent character of the melody. Whether expression of that kind is thought to be natural or conventional, it is generally accepted, for musico-dramatic purposes, as being available to all operatic characters—even to Siegfried, the child of nature, and to Fafner, the hermit-dragon. But the fanfare also exemplifies another kind of communication that is specific to the music dramas of the *Ring*, for it depends on the cycle's leitmotivic vocabulary. "Hear my horn! I am Siegfried. I am armed with my father's sword." That, as generally agreed, is the motivic meaning of Siegfried's message. But is it a true message? To what extent is it intentional on the sender's part and comprehensible to the recipient?

As we know, the characters in Wagner's music dramas sing and act their way through a complex web of orchestral sound. Within the resulting vocal-instrumental texture, the most prominent musical strands—those easily recognizable because of emphasis and repetition—have come to be called leitmotifs and have been named—sometimes appropriately, sometimes less so—according to the characters, objects, situations, or motivations dramatically associated with them. Specific interpretations—such as the "translation" suggested above—may differ from commentator to commentator, but the principle of leitmotivic identification is almost universally accepted.

The leitmotivic system is sometimes loosely called a language. In some ways it does resemble a language, although a very rudimentary one,

[1] [Page references to the four operas of the *Ring* are to the Schirmer vocal scores.]

restricted to a combination of nouns. (The fanfare, for instance, utilizes three, denoting the horn-call, Siegfried himself, and the Sword.) The language analogy is relevant, moreover, because the motifs do convey information—to a knowledgeable audience. But only to that audience? Do the motifs constitute a code whereby the composer communicates with his listeners over the heads, so to speak, of his characters? To adopt the terminology developed in my book *The Composer's Voice*,[2] are the motifs primarily or even exclusively the vocabulary of the composer's persona, and therefore of its closest representative, the orchestral persona? True, the motifs are by no means restricted to the orchestra; many, indeed, are of vocal origin. Yet the fact that a character sings (or blows) a motif does not prove that he or she is intentionally using it in a language-like way—that is to say, as a means of expression or communication based on knowledge of its denotative significance.

Here arises a crucial question for one who is determined to take the motivic system seriously as a musico-dramatic device, and who also wishes to impute to the characters that intentionality of thought and action essential to their full dramatic reality. To what extent, if at all, can we construe the characters as being aware of the denotative significance—nay, of the very existence—of the motifs they employ? That query in turn may lead to others. For if the characters are so aware, how did they come by that knowledge? How did they learn the motivic melodies and their meanings? To what extent do they hear and understand the motifs presented by the orchestra? To answer these questions is to define the rules, so to speak, by which Wagner operates. That is the problem on which Siegfried's defiant blast may throw some light.

All leitmotifs can be classified in each of two ways: (a) as either vocal or instrumental, and (b) as either realistic or symbolic. Moreover, each of these classifications may vary as it is applied to the original or to the subsequent appearances of the motifs.

When distinguishing between vocal and instrumental motifs I grant primacy to the voice. That is to say, I count any sung motif, even when orchestrally doubled, as vocal. Motifs originally vocal may be subsequently assigned to instruments alone, but instrumental motifs are turned over to voices much less frequently. Indeed, motifs predominantly chordal in effect, such as the "Tarnhelm,"[3] are inappropriate for vocal use.

Realistic motifs are those employed in situations utilizing actual musical sound; all others I classify as symbolic. The "Cry of the Valkyries" is

---

[2] [Edward T. Cone, *The Composer's Voice* (Berkeley: University of California Press, 1974).]

[3] I have placed the names of all motifs in quotation marks in order to distinguish the motifs from their referents.

originally a realistic vocal motif; so is the Rhinemaidens' ecstatic "Praise of the Gold." Like all other realistic motifs, they may be said to represent themselves; that is, they *are* just what they signify. The motif of the "Valkyries' Cry" *is* the Valkyries' cry; the motif of "Praise" *is* the Rhinemaidens' praise. However, when those motifs are later used instrumentally, they perforce become symbols that metonymically suggest the Valkyries or the Rhinemaidens. (At least one realistic motif that is originally instrumental, however, retains its realistic character even when it is given to the voice: the "Song of the Forest-Bird.")

Symbolic motifs can be highly descriptive—of the storm at the opening of *Die Walküre*, or of the Valkyries' ride—but, unlike realistic motifs, they do not represent themselves. In cinematic terms, they present "background" rather than "source" music.[4] The "Nibelung Forge" is an interesting borderline case. Its initial presentation by the full orchestra [*Rheingold* 2, p. 113] is symbolically descriptive, but it gradually yields to a purely rhythmic statement by anvils alone. As heard temporally, the new version is derived from the preceding; but considered conceptually, it is the realistic original from which the orchestral version was derived. (The same strategy introduces Mime's hammering at the beginning of *Siegfried*.)

Turning now to the motifs of Siegfried's fanfare, we find that the most prominent one can likewise be referred to as having what might be termed a proleptically realistic origin. Although it is often called simply—and quite properly—"Siegfried's Horn-Call" (ex. 6.1a), that is not the way it is introduced. It is announced symbolically by the orchestra, to characterize the hero as he makes his entrance in *Siegfried* [Act 1, Scene 1, p. 11]. A little later, however, Siegfried himself explains its origin [p. 14]: "Nach bess'rem Gesellen sucht' ich, als daheim mir einer sitzt; im tiefen Walde mein Horn liess ich hallend da ertönen: ob sich froh mir gesellte ein guter Freund? Das frug ich mit dem Getön'!" ["Seeking better companions than the one who sits at home, I let my horn sound in the deep forest: is there a faithful friend to accompany me? That I asked with sound!"] At that point, in consonance with his memory of the incident, a single orchestral horn realistically sounds the motif. (Siegfried's memory of the motif also influences his vocal line at "liess ich hallend da ertönen.")

The other two motifs of the fanfare are entirely symbolic. Directly contrasted with the "Horn-Call" is the motif associated with Siegfried himself (ex. 6.1b). Of the three themes in question, it is the only one of

---

[4]See Alicyn Warren, "The Camera's Voice," *College Music Symposium* 29 (1989): 66–74. As any reader of that essay will realize, I am indebted to it for a number of helpful ideas.

vocal origin: Brünnhilde sang the melody when she announced to Sieglinde the conception of her son [*Walküre*, Act 3, Scene 1, p. 226]. (*How*
Brünnhilde knew of the impregnation we are not told.) The third motif
is the "Sword." Initially stated by the trumpet in the last scene of *Das
Rheingold* [p. 213], it is stubbornly instrumental in character. (I believe
that it is never sung in its entirety.) In the fanfare it is restricted to a single statement that adopts a version, first heard in *Siegfried*, Act 1 [p. 44],
combining "Sword" and "Horn-Call" into a single phrase (ex. 6.1c).

EXAMPLE 6.1 Three Principal Motifs of Siegfried's Horn Fanfare, *Siegfried* Act
2, Scene 2 (pp. 184–85)

a. "Siegfried's Horn-Call"

b. "Siegfried Guardian of the Sword"

c. "Sword" and "Horn-Call" combined

The fanfare is important to an understanding of the motivic aesthetic
because it represents what I call motivic emergence: the process by which
a symbolic motif emerges into the realistic world of actual sound, although still retaining its symbolic character. The specific symbolic component of Siegfried's message is communicated, not in the abstract music
of the orchestra, not through the convention of operatic singing, but by
the fanfare of an actual horn, blown by a living personage of the drama.
That is why the passage raises, in a peculiarly vivid fashion, our basic
question: How much do the characters understand?

II

In the broadest terms there are three possible interpretations of the leitmotivic convention, each related to (although not entirely dependent
upon) a specific view of operatic convention in general. The simplest, or
the most simplistic, position with regard to opera is that of reductionism:
operatic singing (except when it imitates realistic song) is pure artifice.

The characters are entirely unaware of their musical environment; their dramatic existence is verbal, not vocal. According to the most restrictive interpretation of this view, the music is to be heard as merely decorative—as I once wrote, "contributing formal elegance to an artificial dramatic construct and at the same time affording the audience added sensuous delight."[5] A broader interpretation, however, would allow the music to be "a mode of representation through which a character is realized . . . , which controls our perception of the character . . . , yet which is fundamentally external to the character. . . . According to this theory, the music, proceeding entirely and directly from the consciousness of the composer's persona, could be dramatically appropriate and highly expressive, yet outside the represented world of the character, and hence totally unperceived by him."[6] The leitmotivic system supported by either hypothesis is just a code by means of which Wagner comments on the drama for the benefit of the audience; it has no subsistence in the dramatic world of the characters. Of course, even such a know-nothing view would have to allow characters to be aware of realistic motifs. Siegfried consciously blows his horn, consciously employing his typical call.

But what of the other two motifs? How did they get there? On this view, they are there for the composer's purposes only: to spell out a message to his audience. From the point of view of the drama and its protagonist, they are purely accidental: Siegfried has improvised a fanfare, by chance hitting upon the two symbolic motifs.

The reductionist position is not entirely untenable; but when applied to the passage in question—and to many others as well—it yields an improbably jejune and undramatic result. Much less rigid is the alternative I put forward in *The Composer's Voice*, recommending that "we conceive the contrast between the verbal and the vocal as a symbolic parallel to the contrast between the conscious and subconscious components of the personality. . . . [I]t is natural for us to accept the music as referring to a subconscious level underlying—and lying under—whatever thoughts and emotions are expressed by the words."[7] True, such a position does not entail that the characters are necessarily affected by the motivic significance of their music; but it does allow for that possibility, "for a musical idea may often be taken as representing the subconscious component of a vocal character's thought."[8]

Convincing as I once considered that position to be, I now find it difficult to apply it to passages of emergence such as the one that now con-

[5] [*The Composer's Voice*, p. 32.]
[6] [Ibid.]
[7] [Ibid., pp. 33–35.]
[8] [Ibid., pp. 112.]

cerns us. The theory of *The Composer's Voice* neatly divides the verbal from the vocal aspects of Siegfried's singing. To put it very roughly, his words express conscious thoughts; his music reveals his subconscious attitudes. But how does his horn-blowing fit in? Here there is nothing to correspond to the contrast of verbal and vocal; all lies exposed on the surface of the music. The process of emergence places the realistic motif embodying the horn-call and the symbolic motif representing Siegfried himself on the same footing: they are heard as successive manifestations of a single conscious effort of the will. To whatever level of Siegfried's psyche we ascribe his power of musical expression, the emergence of his symbolic motif into the realistic setting of the fanfare must signal his full awareness of its significance. The evidence for that position is even stronger in the case of the "Sword," which is inextricably combined with the "Horn-Call."

Such passages of emergence thus throw doubt on the general validity of the theory of *The Composer's Voice*, at least so far as it relates to Wagnerian practice. I have revised that theory, however, in a later essay, "The World of Opera and Its Inhabitants," which describes characters who "naturally express themselves in song—song of which, in the peculiar operatic world they inhabit, they are fully aware" because "the musically communicable aspects of their personalities have been brought to full consciousness."[9] That, I now believe, is what it means to be an operatic character.

Wagner himself offered support for this view when he described his own characters' medium of expression as "verse-melody" (Versmelodie), which conjoins "not only verbal speech (Wortsprache) with musical speech (Tonsprache), but also what those two media express—namely, the absent with the present, the thought with the emotion. . . . The poet's verse-melody actualizes the thought, or the absent emotion, recalled by memory into a present, actually perceptible emotion."[10] Furthermore, when he stated his principle of restricting passages of independent orchestral music to "moments . . . for which the complete ascent of verbal thought into musical feeling on the part of the dramatic characters is not yet feasible," he implied (although in negative fashion) that his characters were normally equally aware of both the verbal and the musical components of their verse-melody. If a Siegfried of that description states a motif—whether by voice or by horn—we can assume that he does so consciously, in full awareness of both its musical shape and its emotional

[9] [Edward T. Cone, "The World of Opera and Its Inhabitants," in *Music: A View from Delft*, ed. Robert P. Morgan (Chicago: University of Chicago Press, 1989), p. 133.]

[10] [Richard Wagner, *Oper und Drama*, in *Gesammelte Schriften und Dichtungen*, 2nd ed. (Leipzig, 1887), vol. 4, pp. 181–83. Subsequent quotations from Wagner's essays refer to this edition. The translations are evidently by Cone himself.]

expressiveness. Taking one more step, with what I believe to be Wagner's sanction, we can envisage a Siegfried who understands the symbolic significance of the motif as well.

The revised theory of "The World of Opera" thus permits a third interpretation of the leitmotivic system: it is a quasi-language with which the characters are familiar, and of which they consciously avail themselves as a means of musico-dramatic expression. This hypothesis of what might be called motivic comprehension may not be provable, but it allows us to make dramatic sense of passages of emergence.

On this view, then, Siegfried intentionally constructs his fanfare as a sequence of motifs that will announce his arrival—even though Fafner, in his isolated ignorance, fails to grasp the message. His "Wer bist du, kühner Knabe?" ["Who are you, brave youth?," pp. 190–91] reveals that it is lost on him. But a similar message is not lost on Brünnhilde when, at the end of *Götterdämmerung* Act 1, Scene 3, she hears an approaching horn. She identifies Siegfried's own motif immediately, even before that of the "Horn-Call" [p. 117]; and that recognition increases the shock of her confrontation with the supposed Gunther. Here, perhaps, lies the reason for her exclamation, "Verrath!" ["treachery," p. 119]. The apparent stranger has already tried to seduce her through his deceptive use of Siegfried's themes.

Hunding's motif [*Walküre* Act 1, Scene 2, p. 17] is another that emerges into the actuality of a horn-call. That occurs when its rhythm is adopted by the relentless *Stierhorn* that signals the pursuit of Siegmund (ex. 6.2). Sieglinde first hears it—or imagines it—in *Walküre* Act 1, Scene 2 [p. 16], recognizing it as Hunding's. So does Siegmund, when he hears the approach of his enemy.

EXAMPLE 6.2 "Hunding" and Stierhorn motifs, *Walküre* Act 1, Scene 2 (p. 17) and Act 2, Scene 5 (p. 174)

In *Götterdämmerung*, the motif associated with Gutrune, first heard in *Götterdämmerung* Act 1, Scene 2 (ex. 6.3a), emerges as what Wagner called a "Hochzeitsruf" at the end of Act II (ex. 6.3b), which, according to his directions, "Siegfried und die Männer blasen auf ihren Hörnern" [Siegfried and the Vassals blow on their horns]. In Act 3, Scene 3 that

"Wedding-Call" adds to the pathos of Gutrune's anxiety. It is coupled with an incomplete, distorted version of Siegfried's own "Call" played by an orchestral horn sounding from afar [p. 307]. That represents what Gutrune imagines; the "Wedding-Call," what she actually hears. She responds to both in the same way: "War das sein Horn? Nein!"

EXAMPLE 6.3   Relationship of "Gutrune" and "Wedding-Call"

a. "Gutrune," *Götterdämmerung* Act 1, Scene 2 (p. 68)

b. "Wedding-Call," *Götterdämmerung* Act 2, Scene 5 (p. 230)

The descending octave employed by Siegmund in *Die Walküre* Act 1, Scene 3, first to appeal to his father for the promised Sword (ex. 6.4a), and later in this scene to give that Sword its name (ex. 6.4b), may be considered too simple to enjoy leitmotivic status. Nevertheless, "Nothung" is easily recognized; and its symbolic status is confirmed in *Siegfried* Act 1, Scene 3, when Mime uses it to impart the name to Siegfried (ex. 6.4c). The latter delightedly appropriates both name and motif as he sings in support of the blowing of the bellows. Here is a passage of emergence effected by the voice; for "Nothung," having achieved symbolic motivic status, is now embedded in a realistic song (which Wagner labels as a "Gesang").

EXAMPLE 6.4   Three Versions of "Nothung"

Siegmund

Wäl - se!   Wäl - se!   Wo   ist dein   Schwert?

a. *Walküre* Act 1, Scene 3, Siegmund's descending octave (p. 38–39)

Siegmund

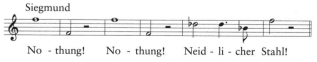

No - thung!   No - thung!   Neid - li - cher Stahl!

b. *Walküre* Act 1, Scene 3, Siegmund's descending octave (p. 72)

No - thung! nennt sich das neid - li - che Schwert!

c. *Siegfried* Act 1, Scene 3, Mime's descending octave (p. 106)

The same scene reveals another possibility opened by the hypothesis of motivic comprehension. When Siegfried demands to know the name of the Sword, he demonstrates the power of the word: really to possess the Sword as object, he must know its name. Only thus can he experience a sense of identity with the father for whom the Sword was originally created and who bestowed its name. If the Sword symbolizes the strength bequeathed him by his father, its name symbolizes his recognition of that strength. How much more vivid does that realization become when the verbal "Nothung" is supported by the musical! Like the word, the musical figure is a motive in a double sense: as a symbol to be recognized (leitmotif) and as a motive for action. As an object of recognition it confirms and enhances Siegfried's knowledge of his heritage; put to use in the ensuing song that accompanies the blowing of the bellows, it releases his energies and directs his powers.

Knowledge and power: those attributes, commonly associated with the use of words, accrue in increased measure if characters can take full advantage of the leitmotivic language as well. Their motivic comprehension can widen their range of voluntary action and go far toward establishing their autonomy as individuals. Lacking such understanding, they are in danger of losing all apparent initiative as dramatic figures and hence of being reduced to mere instrumentalities of the composer's will, helpless in the continuous flow of his overwhelming music.

III

Those, then, are the advantages of the hypothesis of motivic comprehension; but a number of questions remain to be answered. Where do the motifs come from? How do the characters learn them? How much do they hear and understand of what is going on in the orchestra?

Motifs of realistic origin present few problems. Whether vocal or instrumental, they arise in response to situations calling for music; as sound-signals they are heard and understood by all. As we have seen, that is the case with "Siegfried's Horn-Call." Symbolic motifs of vocal origin are more complex. According to the theory of "The World of

Opera," such a theme would be composed by the character who first voices it; but how is it transmitted—not just to those who may actually hear its proclamation but to those who may be generations in the future? In some cases of vocal origin we can devise a literal explanation. "Nothung" was invented by Siegmund. When he redeemed the Sword, Sieglinde heard the word and the associated melody. She could have revealed that connection to Mime, who was thus able to pass on the information to Siegfried when he demanded it. A similarly neat account, pedantic though it may be, is available for Siegfried's own motif. Brünnhilde composed it when she revealed Siegfried's conception to Sieglinde in *Walküre* Act 3, Scene 1. Again, Sieglinde would have imparted it to Mime along with Siegfried's name; and, indeed, Siegfried and Mime imply just that when they share the motif during their conversation in *Siegfried* Act 1, Scene 1 [pp. 39–40]:

> SIEGFRIED. Jetzt sag': woher, heiss' ich Siegfried?
> MIME. So heiss mich die Mutter, möcht' ich dich heissen . . .
>
> [SIEGFRIED. Now tell me: who named me Siegfried?
> MIME. Your mother told me to call you that . . .]

Reliance on such pat explanations leads to absurdity in other cases, however. When Siegmund seizes the Sword in *Walküre* Act 1, Scene 3, he invokes the motif called—erroneously, I think—"Renunciation of Love" (ex. 6.5a). How did he come by it and why does he use it? Let us trace its history. First enunciated in Scene 1 of *Rheingold*, by Woglinde [p. 43], the motif is truncated by Alberich as he seizes the gold ("so verfluch' ich die Liebe!") ["thus I curse love," p. 50]; and orchestral versions precede and follow the theft [pp. 48 and 53]. We next hear it from Loge in Scene 2, as he recounts what has happened: "Weibes Wonne und Werth" ["Woman's delight and worth," p. 86]. That is the end of it so far as *Rheingold* is concerned (although its echo can be heard in the minor transformation of the "Golden Apples" that marks Freia's absence, ex. 6.5b). In *Die Walküre*, two occurrences of the motif frame the principal action: Siegmund's vocal statement in Act 1, Scene 1 [p. 71], and the orchestral statement in Act 3, Scene 3 that accompanies Wotan's farewell embrace of Brünnhilde, its restatement turning into "Weibes Wonne und Werth" (ex. 6.5c). Now, Siegmund *could* have learned this motif from his father, Wotan-Wälse, who *could* have remembered it from his conversation with Loge, who *could* have heard it from the Rhinemaidens. Or, less precisely but more simply, the motif, along with its verbal associations, might have become an element in a well-known tale, long familiar to all the inhabitants of the world of the *Ring*, Siegmund among them. But by what convoluted thought processes would he have summoned up such a motif from the depths of his memory at a crucial moment?

EXAMPLE 6.5   Three Versions of "Renunciation of Love"

a. *Walküre* Act 1, Scene 3 (p. 71)

b. *Rheingold* Scene 2 (p. 107)

c. "Renunciation of Love," becoming "Weibes Wonne und Werth," *Walküre* Act 3, Scene 3 (p. 297)

IV

We can arrive at a more flexible solution of this problem of motivic transmission through a lesson from literature. The first messenger reporting disaster to Job concludes thus: "I only am escaped alone to tell thee." When the second and third messengers exactly repeat those words, we do not inquire where they learned them. We do not think of them as "learned" at all. Each messenger is ignorant of the others' words, yet employs the same locution as the expression of a similar reaction to a similar situation—the result, to be sure, of an artful stylization by the author. Again, when Macbeth's "So foul and fair a day I have not seen" unconsciously echoes the Witches' "Fair is foul and foul is fair," we do not ask how Macbeth could have hit upon the same conjunction of opposites. We accept that coupling as a resource of the language, equally available to the Witches and to Macbeth, and appropriately used by each. Macbeth, while fully aware of the significance of his own words, does not realize their connection with those of the Witches; the irony of the speech would be lost if he did. Like the messengers, Macbeth recomposes a "verbal leitmotif" in the act of using it.

In an influential essay, Caroline Spurgeon developed this point still further, suggesting that "recurrent images play a part in raising, sustaining and repeating emotion in [Shakespeare's] tragedies, which is somewhat analogous to the action of a recurrent theme or 'motif' in a musical fugue or sonata, or in one of Wagner's operas."[11] Thus, to return to *Macbeth*, she points out how the image of ill-fitting clothes is used by one character after another to depict the inappropriateness of Macbeth's new honors. Other images interwoven throughout the texture of the play are those of sound reverberating through space, light against dark, and sin as disease.[12] Shakespeare's characters *think* in images; that is their natural language. So when a number of the characters in turn invoke pictures of "borrowed robes," "strange garments," and the like, they are not imitating one another. Responding naturally in their imagistic language to similar situations, they are inventing, or reinventing, similar images—producing, as they do so, what Spurgeon rightly sees as something that resembles a Wagnerian leitmotif.

V

The elements of Shakespeare's imagistic system might be described as verbally pictorial. Those of Wagner's system are musically pictorial. For Wagner's characters think in music. Like Shakespeare's, they invent and reinvent motifs—but musical motifs. That is a principle by which we can explain Siegmund's "recall" of the misnamed "Renunciation of Love" in *Walküre* Act 1, Scene 3. He does not recall it; he recomposes it.

That is not the first time he has shown his talent for such re-creativity. Earlier in the same scene, as he muses on the promised Sword—"Ein Schwert verhiess mir der Vater, ich fänd' es in höchster Noth" ["My father promised me a sword, which I would find in my greatest need"], example 6.6a—his vocal line is derived from Wotan's original invocation of the Sword at the end of *Das Rheingold*: "So grüss ich die Burg, sicher vor Bang' und Grau'n!" ["Thus I greet the castle, safe from fear and dread"], example 6.6b. Although far apart in dramatic space and time,

---

[11] Caroline F. E. Spurgeon, *Leading Motives in the Imagery of Shakespeare's Tragedy* (London, 1930), p. 3. See also her later book *Shakespeare's Imagery and What It Tells Us* (Cambridge: The University Press, 1935), which further develops this line of thought.

[12] [Ibid., pp. 18–26.]

two related concepts are clothed in almost identical melodies by father and son.

EXAMPLE 6.6 Siegmund's Recompositions of Wotan

Ein Schwert ver-hiess mir der Va - ter, ich fänd' es in höch - ster Noth.

a. *Walküre* Act 1, Scene 3 (p. 37)

So grüss' ich die Burg, si - cher vor Bang' und Grau'n!

b. *Rheingold* Scene 4 (p. 213)

Wäl - se ver - heiss mir, in höch - ster Noth fänd' ich es einst.

c. *Walküre* Act 1, Scene 3 (p. 70–71)

Siegmund summons the phrase once more, both verbally and musically, as he prepares to draw the Sword: "Wälse verhiess mir, in höchster Noth fänd' ich es einst" ["Wälse promised me, I would find it in my greatest need"], example 6.6c. This time the process of recomposition continues, as, seeking help, he calls on the sacred name of Love. It is not the Renunciation of Love but the Power of Love that links this episode thematically with the theft of the Gold. But there is a renunciation here, too—of the laws of hospitality and marriage—which, like the earlier renunciation, will have dire consequences. The motif that Siegmund recomposes here cannot be given a simple name: it applies to situations that connect the recognition of Love's power with a fateful resolution involving a tragic renunciation. That interpretation is confirmed by the reappearance of the motif as Wotan, putting Brünnhilde to sleep, renounces, not love itself, but the object of his deepest affection (see ex. 6.5c). Here the motif is linked with a similar one celebrating the power of love: Loge's "Weibes Wonne und Werth," from *Rheingold* Scene 2 [p. 86].

According to the principle of recomposition, a character's use of a previously stated motif does not necessarily imply memory on his part, nor does it require some mechanically obvious linkage between the two statements. Yet the character is not unaware of the motif's meaning; indeed, by recomposing it, he in a sense reinvents its meaning. What he may well be unaware of is its history. That is why Siegmund's use of "Renunciation of Love," like Macbeth's echo of "foul and fair," can be heard as significantly ironic. We in the audience know, as Siegmund does not, what that motif has meant in the past and what evil it foretells.

The concept of recomposition may not seem so outlandish if we view it as the basis for a Wagnerian convention analogous to that of simultaneous singing in more traditional operas. There we accept it as normal that characters—or even entire choruses—express unity of purpose or of emotional reaction by singing identical or mutually supportive melodic lines at the same time. The principle of recomposition asks us to hear a comparable identity at work in passages separated by extended periods of time.

Even when literal transmission is traceable, as in the case of Siegfried's familiarity with his own motif, recomposition may offer a less adventitious source of that knowledge. The motif, after all, is not a label like the name Siegfried. It stands for a certain conception of the hero's personality. That is how Brünnhilde proposed it, and that is how Wotan, at the end of *Die Walküre*, accepted it. If Siegfried, at the opening of his own drama, has arrived at the state of his development when his self-perception matches Brünnhilde's prophecy, it is natural that he should adopt the same musical imagery, although in ignorance of its history. That is exactly what he does when he recalls his encounter with his own reflection in the stream: "Da sah ich denn auch mein eigen Bild" ["There I saw my own image," p. 33].

VI

Another cluster of problems concerns the role of the orchestra, which not only appropriates vocal motifs but also invents its own. Wagner, by insisting on the orchestra's "power of speech," its "capacity to communicate the ineffable,"[13] by dwelling on its "ability to awaken presentiment (Ahnung) and recollection (Erinnerung)," and by describing passages where it might "express itself independently,"[14] seems to have had in mind what, using the vocabulary of *The Composer's Voice*, could be called an orchestral persona. He revealed the extent of his attribution of consciousness to the orchestra by a significant comparison: "[The orchestra] will enter into approximately the same relationship to my kind of drama as the tragic chorus of the Greeks bore to their dramatic action. That chorus was always present; before its eyes the motives of the ongoing action were laid bare; it sought to fathom these motives and

[13] [Oper und Drama, p. 173.]
[14] [Ibid., p. 191.]

therefore to formulate a judgment on the action."[15] I suggested another comparison when I wrote of orchestral utterances that might be "best understood as subsisting in a kind of universal world-consciousness so vividly personified in the *Ring* by the figure of Erda."[16] Erda, as she herself proclaims in *Das Rheingold*, knows all things: "Wie alles war weiss ich, wie alles wird, wie alles sein wird seh' ich auch" ["I know how everything was, and also see how everything becomes, how everything will be," p. 193].

In theory Wagner was sometimes more restrictive, insisting that the orchestra's "expressive moments" must "always direct our feeling toward the dramatic character alone and to whatever pertains to or proceeds from him. We may not perceive these melodic moments of presentiment or recollection except when we can experience them as a completion of the utterance of the character, who at the moment will not or cannot reveal to us his full emotion."[17] In practice, however, the orchestra often reveals facts concerning past, present, and even future that are unavailable to the characters on the stage. In *Walküre* Act 1 it informs us, through its reference to "Walhalla," that the vanished Wälse was actually Wotan [p. 67]. When the disguised Siegfried confronts Brünnhilde at the end of *Götterdämmerung* Act 1, it reminds us that they are victims of Hagen's magic potion [p. 119]. As for the future, when Mime attempts to teach Siegfried the meaning of fear in *Siegfried* Act 2, Scene 2, the orchestra foretells Siegfried's discovery of Brünnhilde, when he *will* experience fear [p. 151].

Moreover, the orchestra seems to divine all thoughts, spoken (i.e., sung) or silent. Wotan's words to Erda in Act 3, Scene 1 of *Siegfried* come to mind: "wo Hirne sinnen, haftet dein Sinn" ["where brains think, your mind grasps them," pp. 246–47]. When Siegfried arrives at the Hall of the Gibichungs as *Götterdämmerung* Act 1, Scene 2 begins [pp. 61–63], a succession of motifs refers to hidden as well as overt thoughts. The motifs pertaining to Siegfried, to the Gibichungs, and to Grane (the "Ride") underline the actual colloquy; but the music gives equal prominence to unspoken ideas through the "Curse," "Hagen's Perfidy," and "Brünnhilde." Most interesting is the treatment accorded the "Curse," which underlies Hagen's hypocritical "Heil! Siegfried, theurer Held!" ["Hail Siegfried, true hero!"]. When Siegfried imitates that vocal phrase, "Du rief'st mich Siegfried" ["You called me Siegfried"], the "Curse" cunningly recurs. As Siegfried innocently echoes Hagen's greeting, the orchestra makes explicit what is in the villain's mind: a plot to turn his father's malediction against

---

[15] [Richard Wagner, *Zukunftsmusik*, in *Gesammelte Schriften*, vol. 7, p. 130.]
[16] ["The World of Opera," p. 138.]
[17] [*Oper und Drama*, p. 200.]

the hero. Hagen's reply, in contrast, is accompanied by Siegfried's own theme. The ironic juxtaposition of the two motifs reveals each to be a parody of the other (ex. 6.7). (This coupling calls to mind the well-known passage in *Das Rheingold* where the "Ring" is transformed into "Walhalla" [pp. 54–55]. Each of the two couplings suggests an important motivation of the subsequent action.)

EXAMPLE 6.7   Ironic coupling of "Curse" and "Siegfried" motifs, *Götterdämmerung* Act 1, Scene 2 (p. 62–63)

Wagner's orchestra, then, penetrates the minds of all. Its power in that respect is indicated by its continuous presence from beginning to end of each act. In earlier opera we hear the accompaniment of each discrete number as "belonging," so to speak, to the singer or singers whom it is supporting. We can conceive of the operatic characters as controlling those accompaniments, even as composing them along with their vocal lines. Wagner's musico-dramatic characters, in contrast, participate in the pervasive and perpetual flow of an orchestra that, as its own master, produces an elaborate texture to which they can contribute but which they do not control.

To what extent do they penetrate the mind of that orchestra? How much do they hear, and how much of that do they comprehend? The foregoing examples prove that sometimes, at least, they do not hear, or fail to understand, what goes on there. On the other hand, Siegfried's employment of the "Sword" in the course of his fanfare demonstrates his familiarity with a symbolic motif that is definitively instrumental. In an attempt to discover how he might have come by that knowledge, let us trace the history of the motif.

Musically, the motif is born simultaneously with its associated concept: Wotan's image of the Sword as a symbol of the heroic race that he would father. The birth of the motif is typical in that regard; although instrumental motifs may subsequently lead independent orchestral lives, at the outset they are usually associated with ideas in the minds of one or more characters. The exceptions are such elemental motifs as the "Rhine" and the "Gold," which, despite their obvious initial connection with the Rhinemaidens, are better construed as timeless representatives of the eternal natural order. In other cases, as I wrote, "Wagnerian leitmotifs . . . seldom represent persons or objects. . . . Usually a leitmotif corresponds to a character's unspoken attitude toward himself, another character, an object, or a situation. It presents a mental, not a physical image."[18] The physical Sword may be prefigured by the motif, but it is Wotan's concept that is immediately signaled. That is a possible reason why Wagner ultimately decided against having Wotan pick up an actual sword left behind by the Giants.[19]

If the concept of the Sword is Wotan's, why not its musical image as well? As I pointed out above, Wagner's characters do not normally determine the course of the orchestra. But when the trumpet announces the "Sword" in splendid isolation [near the end of *Rheingold*, p. 213], it breaks out of the orchestral web. Could that sally not represent a unique motivic moment? As I have suggested, "The dramatic situation becomes more vivid, and the intensity is heightened, for an auditor who conceives the 'Sword' motif as occurring to Wotan at the same time as the image of the object itself."[20] Perhaps, then, the "Sword" presents an exceptional case. For once the orchestra hears an instrumental motif as a character's thought. Instead of creating the motif, the orchestra reflects it. Wagner's own stage direction can be read as supporting that interpretation: Wotan, silent during the first statement of the motif, is directly enjoined to sing "as if seized by a great idea, very decisively."

If one character can invent an instrumental motif, another can reinvent it. The theory of recomposition could be invoked to explain how such motifs can arise in minds that did not originate them. But that ex-

[18] [*The Composer's Voice*, p. 113.]

[19] [See Carl Dahlhaus, *Richard Wagner's Music Dramas*, trans. Mary Whittall (Cambridge: Cambridge University Press, 1979), p. 115.]

[20] ["The World of Opera," p. 137.]

planation, applied to the complex series of references to the "Sword" in *Walküre* Act 1, Scene 3 [pp. 36–46], would be as pedantic as the reliance on a literal explanation of the transmission of certain vocal motifs. We can stipulate a Siegmund and a Sieglinde, each independently reinventing a motif long ago conceived by Wotan; but that is not necessary.

VII

Much more flexible is the concept of discovery, which we can substitute for that of recomposition in cases where we can adopt "the assumption of what might be called orchestral accessibility."[21] Every motif, whether vocal or instrumental, realistic or symbolic, once enunciated enters the consciousness, as it were, of the orchestral persona. The repertory thus formed becomes a kind of universal memory, a collection of musical archetypes to which all can contribute. According to the hypothesis of accessibility, that repertory is potentially available to all as well. When aware of their orchestral environment, characters discover and rediscover those archetypal forms of expression, which they appropriate for their own uses; by developing them they enrich the repertory still further. The world-consciousness that I have ascribed to the orchestra thus plays a quasi-Jungian role. As I wrote, "Wagner's orchestra has sometimes been compared to a 'collective unconscious,' in which each character participates according to his own knowledge and ability."[22] Wagner's own suggestive metaphor sees the orchestra as "the soil of endless, universal feeling, out of which the personal feeling of the individual actor is enabled to grow to completion. . . . It resembles the earth that gave Antaeus new, undying vigor as soon as his foot touched it."[23]

In *Walküre* Act 1, Scene 3 we can share Siegmund's experience of that renewal as he gradually recovers and appropriates the "Sword" motif. "Recovers" rather than "discovers" because both Siegmund and Sieglinde must have discovered the motif long before—Siegmund presumably on the occasion of his father's promise, and Sieglinde on her wedding night. But whereas for Siegmund the motif has become a dim memory, for Sieglinde it has probably remained vivid because of the constant presence of the Sword itself. At the end of Scene 2 [pp. 35–36], the threefold statement of that theme, accompanying Sieglinde's meaningful gaze on the

---

[21] [Ibid.]

[22] [*The Composer's Voice*, p. 36.]

[23] [Richard Wagner, *Das Kunstwerk der Zukunft*, in *Gesammelte Schriften*, vol. 3, p. 157.]

ash-tree, obviously reflects her own knowledge of the weapon buried there; Siegmund apparently neither hears nor understands. Yet the motif remains in the orchestral mind, so to speak, ready to inspire Siegmund at the beginning of Scene 3. There, as if gradually coming to light from the depths of Siegmund's memory, the motif is three times adumbrated in the lower strings before it is stated in full, though halfheartedly, by the bass trumpets [p. 37]. That the recovery of the motif is Siegmund's as well as the orchestra's is made clear by his first words: "Ein Schwert verhiess mir der Vater" ["My father promised me a sword"].

The multiple statements of the motif that subsequently accompany the gleam of the Sword in the firelight are doubly significant [p. 39ff.]. We in the audience can make out the hilt (as indicated by the stage direction, "auf die Stelle an der man jetzt deutlich einen Schwertgriff sieht" ["at the spot where one can clearly see a sword hilt"]); Siegmund sees only its glow, which he poetically associates with Sieglinde's glance. From a literal point of view, the orchestral development of the motif depicts the actual weapon as we see it. At the same time, Siegmund's unspoken thoughts are still centered on the promised Sword. His awareness of the motif is indicated at the outset by the arpeggio he borrows from it to sing "Was gleisst dort hell im Glimmerschein" ["What glimmers there brightly in the gloom," p. 39]. A little further on, he makes the connection between the gleam of the metal and the glance of the woman by another arpeggio at "Ist es der Blick der blühenden Frau?" ["Is it the glance of the blooming woman?," p. 40]. Not until Sieglinde's narrative are object, word, and motif connected, as she explains the history of the Sword [pp. 45–46]. Only much later, when he discloses his identity, does the hero take full possession of the motif, adapting it to his own purposes [pp. 70–71]. At that point his recall of "in höchster Noth" ["in greatest need"] indicates his realization of the source and the significance of the actual weapon, which is now his to possess. "Ich fass' es nun!" ["Now I grasp it!"] thus applies to both motif and object.

In Act 1, Scene 1 of *Siegfried*, we are present at the very moment when Siegfried, newly discovering the motif, makes it uniquely his own. Although hitherto apparently incurious about his parentage, Siegfried has now forced Mime to tell him the truth. As evidence, Mime produces the pieces of the broken Sword. Two orchestral statements of the motif accompany the action [p. 43]. Siegfried seizes upon the musical idea and attaches it to his "Horn-Call," musically binding the "Sword" to himself as he demands that Mime forge the weapon anew for him [p. 44]. That motivic form—"Sword" plus "Horn-Call"—is what he is to utilize at the Dragon's Cave [see ex. 6.1c]. When he does so, a phrase combining a symbolic and a realistic motif emerges into actuality; yet its musical shape must have been conceived at the moment in Act 1 just described. It therefore constitutes an important bit of evidence for the theory of orchestral accessibility and motivic availability.

Despite its explanatory value, accessibility must not be assumed to be unlimited. As we know, characters are not necessarily aware of all the music around them. We accept that they hear all sung motifs, even though they may not fully comprehend their symbolic significance. More puzzling is the extent to which they hear and understand their fellows' orchestral accompaniments—or even their own. Whether they are deaf to certain motifs, or whether hearing, they fail to understand them, it is not always possible to decide.[24] In Scene 2 of *Götterdämmerung* Act 1, when Gunther tells the intoxicated Siegfried of the maiden surrounded by fire [p. 73], the orchestra envelops their colloquy by the "Fire" motif, which can easily be construed as heard by both. But the "Bird-Song," which suggests a slight stirring of Siegfried's memory, is either unheard by Gunther or meaningless to him. Earlier in the same scene, we have already noted the "Curse" that accompanies Siegfried's response to Hagen's greeting. Here we must assume that Siegfried fails to hear the motif that projects Hagen's thoughts—or else that he is totally ignorant of its significance.

VIII

Such complexities may well lead one to doubt Wagner's consistency in the deployment of his leitmotifs; nevertheless, despite disparities in detail, I believe that one can derive from the composer's practice a few general principles governing motivic comprehension and orchestral accessibility. I suggest the following as a rough guide:

1. Characters are responsible for the musical content of their own vocal lines and hence are aware of the motifs they sing.
2. The extent of the characters' understanding of the symbolic meaning of those motifs is less clear. It depends on the limits of their general knowledge and on the specific circumstances of each situation.
3. Characters are not necessarily aware—or fully aware—of the motivic content, musical and symbolic, of their orchestral environments. Clues to the extent of that knowledge are the relative salience of the orchestral motifs and, more importantly, their influence on the vocal lines they accompany.

---

[24] On the question of one character's awareness of another's accompaniment, see the interesting discussion by Peter Kivy in "Opera Talk: A Philosophical 'Phantasie,'" *Cambridge Opera Journal* 3, no. 1 (1991): 63–77, especially pp. 73–77.

4. In conversation characters may or may not recognize the motivic references of their colleagues' vocal lines and accompaniments. The extent of their recognition is indicated by their own responses and accompaniments.

5. Orchestral interludes are not necessarily perceived or understood by any of the characters.

With these principles in mind, let us examine a final case: the relations of Siegmund and Sieglinde to "Walhalla." One thing is clear in *Walküre* Act 1: whether or not either twin is familiar with the motif, neither realizes its connection with Walhalla. That is privileged information from *Das Rheingold* that the orchestra shares with the audience. The protagonists, insofar as they hear the motif at all, can at most associate it with the figure they know as Wälse. But to what extent do they hear it?

Siegmund, at the outset, shows no cognizance whatsoever of the motif, for it plays no part during the narration of his exploits with his father in Scene 2. But while he silently ponders his father's disappearance, the motif is intoned as an orchestral aside, by trombones in E major (ex. 6.8). (Both the key and the brass coloration will prove to be typical when the motif returns in Scene 3, although horns will then predominate.) The passage not only reveals to the audience Wälse's identity, as I have previously suggested, but also underlines Siegmund's ignorance.

EXAMPLE 6.8   "Walhalla," *Walküre* Act 1, Scene 2 (p. 26)

Sieglinde's narrative in Scene 3 stands in contrast. When she describes the stranger's arrival at her wedding, the horns of "Walhalla" evidently represent a vivid memory; for as the orchestra expands the motif, her vocal line moves constantly in arpeggiation or simple harmony with its E major tonality [pp. 44–45]. The same is true when the motif returns at the end of her story, as she recounts her moment of recognition: "Da wusst' ich wer der war" ["Then I knew who he was," p. 47]. There is an interesting orchestral distinction between the two passages, however. In the first, which focuses on the appearance of the stranger himself, horns predominate, in accordance with the motif's typical brass coloration. In the second, which describes Sieglinde's own reaction, horns are replaced by strings. Is this a subtle indication that Sieglinde recognizes a kindly father rather than a fierce god? (Limited though her knowledge is, her connection of the motif with her father at this point proves that she, like Siegmund, failed to hear the orchestral aside in Scene 2; otherwise she would have guessed her brother's identity much too early for dramatic purposes.)

Siegmund's reaction to "Walhalla" develops through several stages. They reflect his increasing familiarity with a musical idea that is, we must assume, new to him, since it calls forth no sign of recognition. I believe that his growing musical control of the motif symbolizes a gradual realization of the identity of the figure associated with it by Sieglinde. The first indication of Siegmund's aroused interest occurs after the Spring Song in the shape of a new musical idea, one that seems to have little relation to "Walhalla." Sung to the words "denn wonnig weidet mein Blick" ["as blissfully my glance feasted"], it might be called "Siegmund's Joy" (ex. 6.9). Its C major tonality suggests an important association, for that is the typical key of the "Sword," established by its inception in *Das Rheingold*. When that motif returned to inspire Siegmund's soliloquy early in Scene 3 [p. 39], so, too, did its key. The connection of tonality and character is now reestablished with the emergence of "Siegmund's Joy." The key, then, is Siegmund's, but the motif is not his alone. Its orchestral development, supporting Sieglinde's reply, reveals an unsuspected connection with the rhythm and contour of "Walhalla" [pp. 63–64]. Sieglinde seizes upon this. As the orchestra turns overtly to that motif and its typical key, her memory once again awakens: "Ein Wunder will mich gemahnen" ["A wonder wants to arouse my memory"]. Siegmund's understanding, however, is still hazy, for his own motif effects a return to C as it supports his "Ein Minnetraum gemahnt auch mich" ["A love-dream also reminds me"].

EXAMPLE 6.9 "Siegmund's Joy," with Accompanimental Suggestions of "Walhalla," *Walküre* Act 1, Scene 2 (p. 63)

Somewhat later Sieglinde reverts once more to her recollection of the old man, stronger than ever as she compares his glance with Siegmund's: "Deines Auges Gluth erglänzte mir schon: so blickte der Greis grüssend auf mich" ["His burning eyes already saw me: the old man looked at me greetingly," p. 67]. (Here again, as horns yield to strings, we may perhaps infer Sieglinde's affectionate view of her father.) This time Siegmund suggests a recognition of kinship. When he answers her query as to his real name, a version of his own motif now closely echoes the "Walhalla" that accompanied her recollected recognition of her father. Compare his "nun walt' ich der hehrsten Wonnen" ["then I experienced the most exalted joys," p. 68] with the accompaniment of her previous "An dem Blick erkannt ihn sein Kind" ["From the glance he recognized his child"], example 6.10. This citation of "Walhalla" is not yet definitive, however, since it remains on the subdominant side of the characteristic E major.

EXAMPLE 6.10   "Walhalla"-related Accompaniment of Sieglinde's "An dem Blick erkannt' ihn sein Kind," *Walküre* Act 1, Scene 2 (p. 67) and Siegmund's "nun walt' ich der hehrsten Wonnen," *Walküre* Act 1, Scene 2 (p. 68)

Only after a conclusive reference to his own motif, one that reaches an authentic cadence in F ("den Namen nahm' ich von dir!" ["the name I take from you!"]), does Siegmund confirm his grasp of "Walhalla" and its significance. Thematic material, key (E), and instrumentation (horns) underline his own reference to the gleam of his father's eye, when he compares it to Sieglinde's: "Doch dem so stolz strahlte das Auge wie, Herrliche, hehr dir es strahlt" ["Yet so proudly gleamed his eye as exaltedly and nobly shines your own"], example 6.11. Once again a modulation to C ensues, as he reveals the name of Wälse. Perhaps his own key—which is also that of the "Sword"—affords him a more vivid memory of his father. Thus the last reference to "Walhalla" in Act 1 is not allowed to reach its own cadence, and Siegmund's acceptance of the motif is not wholehearted. It represents Sieglinde's view of their father, not his own.

EXAMPLE 6.11 Accompanimental Reference to "Walhalla," *Walküre* Act 1, Scene 2 (pp. 68–69)

Despite that reservation, Siegmund has gradually achieved some comprehension of the musical shape of "Walhalla" and its symbolic meaning—but only insofar as the latter relates to the figure the twins know as Wälse. What, then, is Siegmund to make of the association of the motif with Brünnhilde's appearance in Act 2, Scene 4? The exact point at which he recognizes the motif—if indeed he does—is not clear. "Walhalla," as it accompanies Brünnhilde, is represented by harmonies associated with the D-flat of *Das Rheingold* rather than the E major that Siegmund would find familiar [p. 153]. Moreover, the motif is fragmentary, lacking its characteristic opening and dwelling on a cadence familiar to those of us who remember *Das Rheingold*, but not to Siegmund. He himself concentrates on the motif usually identified as *Todesverkündigung* ["The Announcement of Death"]. Originally orchestral, this theme might better be termed "Siegmund's Doom." It is first stated as Brünnhilde gazes at the hero, who is as yet unaware of her presence [p. 152]. During the colloquy that follows, he appropriates the motif with increasing control as he questions Brünnhilde more and more intently. (Note his extension of the motif as he inquires about Sieglinde's destiny [pp. 157–58].)

Brünnhilde bases her replies on the closely related "Fate" (indeed, the source motif of "Siegmund's Doom") and increasingly on "Walhalla." Like Sieglinde, she demonstrates her familiarity by an arpeggiated vocal line that closely follows its harmony. But only when Walhalla is named as Siegmund's future home is the motif stated in full, and in the key of E [p. 155].

At this point Siegmund may recognize both theme and tonality; for his questioning turns, first indirectly and then directly, to the possibility of finding his father. Significantly, his query "Fänd' ich in Walhall Wälse, den eig'nen Vater?" ["Would I find Wälse, my own father, in Walhalla?"] ends on a dominant seventh in E, inviting a positive answer [p. 156]. Brünnhilde replies evasively. The key changes deceptively to C, and Brünnhilde's cadence ("der Wälsung dort" ["the Wälsung there"]) echoes Siegmund's revelation of his father's name in Act 1, Scene 3 ("Wälse genannt" ["named Wälse," p. 69]), example 6.12. At any rate, when Siegmund at last finds himself accompanied by "Walhalla," as the motif supports the rising sequence by which he renounces Walhalla, Wotan, and Wälse in turn, he still has no idea of his father's identity (ex. 6.13). He invokes the motif only to disclaim it.

EXAMPLE 6.12 Brünnhilde's "der Wälsung dort," *Walküre* Act 2, Scene 4 (p. 156) as echo of Siegmund's "Wälse genannt," *Walküre* Act 1, Scene 3 (p. 69)

EXAMPLE 6.13 Siegmund's "Walhalla"-related Accompaniment, *Walküre* Act 2, Scene 4 (p. 158)

A simpler interpretation of the scene is also possible. After all, Siegmund's grasp of "Walhalla" is tenuous. Perhaps, then, the motif, which
is here primarily associated with Brünnhilde, pertains to her consciousness alone. Siegmund's vocal line in the passage just cited is in no way
derived from the motif; on the contrary, the motivic sequence in the orchestra can be heard as reflecting the ascent of the voice. It could thus
represent an image in Brünnhilde's mind responding to the successive re-
jections by which Siegmund refuses to accept the heritage of which he remains pathetically ignorant.

IX

Some of the conclusions reached in the course of the foregoing analyses
may seem forced. Indeed, as I have admitted, Wagner's utilization of his
own system may not always be as consistent as it is here made out to be.
Nevertheless, I believe that sensitivity to a character's motivic comprehension—to its extent on the one hand and to its limitations on the
other—enables one to arrive at an appreciative understanding of the
character's intentions and of the tragic or ironic aspects of his or her dramatic situation. For those of us who wish to take the cycle seriously as
drama, and its characters seriously as persons, that understanding is
crucial.

Schubert's Heine Songs

SCHUBERT'S LAST SONG CYCLE, *Schwanengesang*, has occasioned more than one controversy. In the first place, is it really a cycle? It consists of two disparate sequences: seven settings of poems by L. Rellstab, followed by six settings of Heinrich Heine. The entire group is concluded by a setting of a poem by J. G. Seidl. Do the Rellstab and Heine songs belong together as a unit? They are certainly copied together in Schubert's manuscript. But what of "Die Taubenpost," the final song? Its status is equivocal: it is bound in at the very end of the manuscript, but it is not clear whether that was Schubert's intention.

Now, I happen to have a rather strong opinion on the question of the unity of the entire cycle, but what interests me more now is another question that has arisen in recent years. That concerns the ordering of the individual Heine songs. In the autograph, and hence in all the standard editions, "Der Atlas" is followed in turn by "Ihr Bild," "Das Fischermädchen," "Die Stadt," "Am Meer," and finally "Der Doppelgänger." These are all based on poems from Heine's *Heimkehr*, but they are drawn, apparently in random order, from different portions of Heine's own poetic cycle.

In 1972 a German scholar, Harry Goldschmidt, proposed a different ordering for the songs, based upon their position in the Heine cycle.[1] Doing so, he believed, strengthened both musical and poetic connections among the songs. His proposal has recently been seconded by Richard Kramer, who tried to reconstruct possible reasons why Schubert might have eventually decided against the original arrangement, which in Kramer's opinion was more cogent.[2] Kramer outlines the plot revealed by this ordering: "Das Fischermädchen," the beginning of an affair; "Am Meer," the consummation and end of the affair; "Die Stadt," much later, the lover visits the beloved's hometown; "Der Doppelgänger," he stands before her house; "Ihr Bild," he remembers her image in a dream; "Der Atlas," he realizes the futility of the whole affair. And Kramer supports

---

[1] [Harry Goldschmidt, "Welches war die ursprungliche Reihenfolge in Schuberts Heine Liedern?" *Deutsches Jahrbuch der Musikwissenschaft* (1972): 52–76.]

[2] [Richard Kramer, *Distant Cycles: Schubert and the Conceiving of Song* (Chicago: University of Chicago Press, 1994).]

his version by an analysis purporting to show a single linear and harmonic progression uniting the cycle.

I do not find this reconstruction convincing. Most obviously, from my point of view, it deprives "Der Doppelgänger" of its commanding position at the end. Beautiful as it is, "Ihr Bild" can only prove to be a letdown. And the rhetoric of "Der Atlas," quite different both musically and poetically from anything in the other songs, appears as an unmotivated coda.

But the relative isolation of "Der Atlas" makes sense if it is placed, not as a coda, but as an introduction. This, according to my own hypothetical story, is the way the protagonist claims to see himself now. But that attitude is shown up by the following songs as a pose. Reminded by a vivid dream, he relives crucial moments in his affair and its aftermath, ending with his confrontation of his former self and his realization that the long-buried affair is still very much alive in his memory.

The introductory position of the song makes sense musically, too, for it states boldly and unequivocally in various guises, in both voice and piano, the musical motif that will bind the entire sequence of songs together (ex. 7.1).

EXAMPLE 7.1 Motivic Connections among the Six Heine Songs from Schubert's *Schwanengesang*, D. 957

a. "Der Atlas"

b. "Ihr Bild"

c. "Das Fischermädchen"

d. "Die Stadt"

e. "Am Meer," mm. 2–4 and 23–25

f. "Am Meer," mm. 14–17 and 35–38

g. "Der Doppelgänger"

Schubert's setting of "Der Atlas" has been adversely criticized for, among other things, its distortion of Heine's poem by its textual repetitions. The ultimate return of the first two lines makes of the song a convincing musical structure—an ABA—but that is only the most extensive of the many verbal repetitions to which Schubert subjects Heine's poem. However, I find that treatment justified by the poet's own rhetoric, which depends on constant verbal linkages within and among lines:

"Ich unglücksel'ger Atlas . . . glücklich sein, unendlich glücklich . . . "
"Eine Welt. / Die ganze Welt . . . "
". . . muss ich tragen, / Ich trage Unerträgliches. . . ."
"Das Herz im Leibe. / Du stolzes Herz . . . stolzes Herz . . ."
". . . ja, gewollt. / Du wolltest . . ."
". . . unendlich elend . . . bist du elend."

Schubert's textual reduplications produce the space needed to build his musical form—one equally based on insistent repetition. Its principal material is the pervasive motif noted above—let us call it *x*. Announced (for the cycle as a whole as well as for this song) by the octave bass of the introduction, *x* proceeds to generate a vocal melody [mm. 5–8], calling forth an answering phrase *y* [mm. 9–14]. A modulation now leads to the contrasting second stanza. So far, the vocal melody has been freely doubling the bass, but now it strikes out more independently as the protagonist turns to address his "stolzes Herz" ["proud heart," m. 23]. At the same time, a pulsing reiteration of *x*—a symbol of the heart?—continues to control the bass line. A return to the tonic heralds the reprise [m. 39ff.]. It is by no means literal, for it temporarily sets voice and piano at odds. Continuing to assert its independence, the voice recalls a version of *y* against the piano's insistence on *x* [mm. 40–43]. Not until the answering phrase are the two united as before [mm. 44–48], perhaps because the hero only belatedly remembers that the "stolzes Herz" which he was excoriating is, after all, his own. Now voice and accompaniment coincide once again, as if to synchronize thought and feeling in time for a last outburst.

The next two songs of the cycle, "Ihr Bild" and "Das Fischermäd-chen," are likewise in simple ternary form (ABA). Since their poems consist of three stanzas each, they can be set straightforwardly without the necessity of a textual repetition. Their stanzas correspond to the respective divisions of the musical form. I should like, however, to concentrate on the final three songs, "Die Stadt," "Am Meer," and "Der Doppelgän-ger," which are bound together in a triple unity of increasing intensity. The "Fischermädchen" reenacted a courtship. "Die Stadt" and "Der "Doppelgänger" recount an event that occurs much later: the protagonist's return to the scenes associated with his lost love. Those two frame a memory invoked by the journey: for "Am Meer" describes a fateful event—probably the end of the affair—and its consequences.

The poem of "Die Stadt" is obviously adaptable to the ternary mold ABA. In the first and last of the three stanzas, the poet views the fateful town; in the second, he describes the boat-ride that brings it into sight. In Schubert's version the journey is characterized by a monotonously re-iterated musical gesture: the pianistic elaboration of a diminished seventh over an octave tremolo. This famous arpeggiation seems to arise from nowhere to create an atmospheric prelude, it recurs as the accompaniment of the central contrasting section, and it dies away to nothing in a postlude. Despite its connections with other songs in the cycle, in its immediate context it is unprepared and unresolved, as if depicting a journey that has no beginning and no ending.

The overall pattern of the song can accordingly be shown as an ABA in which the accompaniment figure of B serve both as introduction and as coda. Thus: b–ABA–b. But that schematization does not indicate the contrast between the first and third stanzas. Both of them are declaimed against a starkly rhythmic chordal accompaniment, but the *pianissimo* of a misty dusk in the first is replaced by the *forte-fortissimo* of a sunrise in the third. The melody, also, is varied. Its two cadences, on iv (m. 10) and i (m. 14), are circumspectly approached by stepwise motion in the first stanza; in the third both are intensified by upward and downward leaps [mm. 30–31 and 34–35]—the only occurrences in the song of vocal intervals greater than a third. Their parallelism suggests a symbolic relationship between the illumination of the sun ("leuchtend vom Boden empor" ["shining up from the shore"]) and the acute realization of loss ("wo ich die Liebste verlor" ["where I lost my beloved"]). Equally as striking is the alteration of a normal supertonic sixth to a Neapolitan in order to create a special accent: "und zeigt mir *jene* Stelle" ["and reveals to me *that* place"], m. 32, my emphasis. The rays of the rising sun have fallen on just *that* place with its associations of loss and grief.

"Am Meer," which follows in the traditional ordering, begins with one of the most famous motifs in the song literature, two mysterious chords which, as introduction and postlude, set off the rest of the song. This introduction has been convincingly placed in musical and historical perspective by Joseph Kerman, who also appreciatively discusses its expressive potential. Praising the motif's "unforgettable, enigmatic solemnity, which seems to plumb infinite marine and spiritual depths," he claims that "from the Romantic point of view it suggests everything—everything in the world that is inward, sentient, and arcane."[3] That may be an extreme description but I do not find it an exaggeration. What is excessive, however, is Kerman's insistence on what he calls the introduction's independence: "It does not signal ahead to a later event in the song. . . . It simply recurs."[4] This, as we shall see, is not quite the case. Nevertheless, the introduction does stand in a certain isolation. That is a source of its uncanny effect. But by the time it returns as a coda, it is charged with a meaning derived from the song itself, both music and text.

Even at the outset the isolation is not complete. Whether one accepts the ordering of the Heine songs proposed by Goldschmidt or whether one wishes to preserve the traditional succession, the opening of "Am Meer" can be heard as arising from a reinterpretation of the final sonority of the preceding song. In the first instance, it (enharmonically) transforms the final A-flat major triad of "Das Fischermädchen," which, by the addition of a dissonant F-sharp, is turned into an inverted augmented sixth. The resolution accordingly introduces a change of key. In the second and more familiar case, the diminished seventh of "Die Stadt" is altered by the substitution of one note for another: A-natural for A-flat. This time the resolution changes mode—minor to major—but not key. I myself feel the latter connection to be the more mysteriously evocative, throwing new light on the unresolved conclusion of "Die Stadt."

Looking ahead, one realizes that the introduction has at least a registral connection with what follows. It prepares for the mellifluous piano sound that characterizes the accompaniment of the first stanza. That sound, a favorite of Schubert's, is produced by a right-hand melody in octaves, assigned to the warmest range of the piano and further colored

---

[3] [Joseph Kerman, "A Romantic Detail in Schubert's Schwanengesang," in *Schubert: Critical and Analytical Studies*, ed. Walter Frisch (Lincoln: University of Nebraska Press, 1986), p. 52.]

[4] [Ibid.]

by intervals within the octave—predominantly thirds and sixths. Examples abound in the composer's piano works: the openings of the late Piano Sonatas in B-flat and G, the development of the first movement of the unfinished 1825 Sonata in C ("Reliquie"), the *Moments Musicals* Op. 94 No. 2. In accompaniments, it is found in the introduction and coda of "Das Wirtshaus" from *Die Winterreise*, at the phrase that concludes each strophe of "Des Baches Wiegenlied" from *Die schöne Müllerin*, and in Mignon's song "So lasst mich scheinen," Op. 62 No. 3.

Is it a coincidence that all of the songs are about death, but at the same time solace? In the present instance the music seems to depict the dying day, whose sunset still offers solace by illuminating sea and shore—a metaphor, perhaps, for the lingering sweetness of a love affair that is now dying. But there is also the possibility of a more direct musical symbolism. Voice and piano present two parallel melodies of equal weight. The piano melody is doubled at the lower octave, and the vocal line is doubled by the inner part of the piano's right hand. What might the unusual strictness of that parallel motion suggest about the relations between the two implied characters of the poem? On the one hand, propinquity, as the thoughts of both follow the same path. On the other hand, distance: parallels, after all, never meet. Perhaps Schubert was reading two meanings into Heine's word "alleine" ["alone"]. The lovers, sitting alone—that is, just the two of them—are physically close to each other and separated from the rest of the world. At the same time each, individually, is emotionally alone.[5]

In the next stanza of the song the calm sea gives way to a stormy one [m. 12ff.], and the picture of the two quiet lovers yields to that of the restless gull. A single gull may be strange from a naturalistic point of view; but it is symbolically important here, as the second half of the stanza suggests. There the woman is weeping—because of a vision of her lover's flight "hin und wieder" ["here and there"]. The identification of gull and lover will be reinforced in the next strophe; but what is already obvious is the replacement of the single couple, alone but together, by two utterly lonely individuals, the gull and the weeping woman. The music reflects the shift simply but vividly. The rising storm is depicted by piano tremolos, above which the vocal line, now a quasi-recitative instead of a lyrical cantilena like the opening, indeed flies back and forth, with key changes. Now, as the poetry focuses on the weeping woman, the mood of the first stanza returns [m. 19ff.]; but here voice and piano are independent of each other, both melodically and rhythmically. The unity of togetherness-in-loneliness has been broken. And so, when, as

[5] Compare Schubert's somewhat similar use of parallelism in the song "Sei mir gegrüsst." There the lovers are together in spirit, apart in actuality.

before, the piano marks the end of the stanza by repeating the last measure, it is a mere echo, *ppp*, an octave below [m. 23].

That measure is the half cadence that marks the end of the first full strophe and prepares for the repetition of the opening musical material. The second strophe, consisting of the second pair of stanzas, parallels the first. Whereas the first ends with the woman weeping, as if alone, the second begins by bringing the two once more together by the man's acknowledgment of her tears and by his tender, if sentimental, reaction. The music accordingly returns to the glow of the opening theme, suggesting a moment of renewed affection [m. 24ff.]; but it is followed, as before, by the tremolo-accompanied recitative [m. 33ff.]. The association of this passage with the protagonist's own life confirms our earlier interpretation of the image of the restless gull. This time, in the final section, it is the protagonist who is alone. His bitter memory of the tears recalls the corresponding music [mm. 40–43], now altered so as to achieve a perfect cadence and to permit a return of the introductory chords.

Jack M. Stein takes a dim view of Schubert's Heine settings, especially of this one. He claims that the quasi-strophic setting "negates the main effect of the poem," because it divides the stanzas two by two, instead of the three plus one that the time-division of the poem demands.[6] But Stein fails to take into account the role of performance. Although superficially, the periodic structure of Schubert's music would seem to insist on a parallel AB–AB, a performance can emphasize the unity of ABA—a closed section representing the past, followed by a reminiscent return to B, as a coda representing the stormy life that followed the narrated event.

Note, too, that the approach to the final cadence contains an important alteration of the original. When the poet refers to "das unglücksel'ge Weib," that "unfortunate woman," the composer heightens both the melodic and the harmonic tension. The vocal climax clashes against the accompaniment, and a fifth is left emptily ringing as the voice rests after "Weib" [m. 41]. Schubert's "unglücksel'ge Weib" is not Heine's woman, who seems to have caused more misfortune than she suffered. Nor is Schubert's protagonist the same as Heine's: his attitude is one of sorrowful regret rather than of anger. Still, the unusual musical treatment of "Weib" darkens the succeeding measure as well, so that the dissonances once pathetically associated with the falling tears now sound harsher when ironically applied to their poisonous effect. Those tears, Schubert's protagonist no doubt feels, must have been as bitter for the one who shed them as they have since become for himself.

---

[6] [Jack M. Stein, *Poem and Music in the German Lied from Gluck to Hugo Wolf* (Cambridge, MA: Harvard University Press, 1971), p. 87.]

The final perfect cadence is succeeded by the real coda: the return of the enigmatic chords of the introduction. We are now in a position to appreciate their relation to the song as a whole, both musically and dramatically. At the outset the dissonance (an augmented sixth) and its resolution can at most suggest a key. They offer a range of possibilities—like a wide but incompletely defined landscape within which a specific scene is to take shape. That occurs, verbally and musically, when the first words symbolically associate the image of the sea with the B-flat key of the opening phrase, actualizing the tonal potential of the introduction. In the song, as opposed to the poem alone, the memory of that sea, glowing "im letzten Abendscheine" ["in the last rays of evening"], pervades the narrative; for the music never moves far from the tonic. But the sea, too, is symbolic. Its meaning is confirmed by the musical association of the stormy waters with the protagonist's own vicissitudes. Key and sea coalesce in what I fear must be identified by that hackneyed phrase, "the sea of life."

Thus, when the introductory chords at last return, they do so within a context that has established their tonality. They can also now be heard to refer motivically to the body of the song. Most obviously, they can be connected with the two measures of accompaniment that punctuate the close of each of the odd stanzas [mm. 10–11 and 31–32]. Echoing V7–I cadences, those brief piano interludes recall the texture and the register of the introduction and look forward to the postlude.

Here, especially, we realize the difference between Heine's poem and Schubert's: Heine's concluding tone of bitter resentment has given way to Schubert's mood of calm acceptance. We feel that the poisonous tears are at last absorbed, and with them both love and anger—because that is what happens in the music. The postlude receives and assimilates all that has occurred, whether musically or dramatically. The chord succession is not like that of the perfect cadence that preceded it, for its dissonance is not so much resolved as dissolved. The augmented sixth melts into its surroundings. The introduction-postlude, surrounding the song, embeds it in a kind of transcendental tonality from which everything arises and into which everything ultimately sinks: the manifestation, as it were, of a permanent environment subsisting not before and after, but outside the time of the song that it surrounds.

The final song in the traditional ordering, "Der Doppelgänger," is also the most celebrated. I think its position as the final song is confirmed by its introduction, which states a form of the pervasive motif more clearly than we have heard it since the beginning of "Der Atlas" (see ex. 7.1). Thus four songs in which the motif assumes a subsidiary role are flanked by two that not only give it prominence but are musically based on it. For the "Doppelgänger" is a kind of chaconne or passacaglia—that is, a form in which a constantly recurring ostinato melody or chord progression is heard beneath a series of variations. (The introduction presents half of that ostinato [mm. 1–4].)

What is so interesting here is that, at every level, the music forecasts the image of doubleness that emerges at the climax of the poem. At the outset, the four-measure introduction exhibits several dimensions of duplication. To begin with, the outer voices double each other in parallel octaves around a constant pedal on the dominant; indeed, the entire chordal texture is doubled. Then, the descending half step of the first pair of measures is exactly transposed in the next pair. More than that, those two measures present a melodic and harmonic retrograde inversion of the first two. Schubert's hero is haunted by the concept of doubleness from the beginning.

When the voice enters, the piano repeats its four measures, but it extends them to produce what will be the eight-measure chordal ostinato of the chaconne [mm. 5–12]. But that extension at the same time conceals another duplication: its bass [G–F-natural–B-flat–A, mm. 9–12] is a slightly varied form of the introductory motif. In the last two measures of the ostinato, the right hand prepares for the introduction of a new pianistic voice (mm. 13–14). That supports one more reduplication: an echo of the vocal line [mm. 11–12].

Duplication now arises on a higher level, as that entire ten-measure section, which covers half of the first stanza [mm. 5–14], is repeated for the second half of the stanza (mm. 15–24). The repetition is exact in the piano and only slightly varied in the voice. It is succeeded by an even more comprehensive duplication, when the pattern of two complete ostinati is repeated for the second stanza (mm. 25–42). That repetition, however, is compressed. As the hero draws nearer to his goal, the ten-measure units of ostinato plus echo are reduced to nine, the echo being suppressed in favor of a one-measure extension of the final chord (mm. 33 and 42). That chord is expressively modified each time by an alteration of the dominant seventh (the first time it becomes a French sixth, the second time a climactic German sixth), marking the first occasion in the entire song when the omnipresent dominant is forsaken. The approach to the climax is of course shared by the voice. Unlike the static melody of the first stanza, that of the second steadily rises. As before, the second half of the stanza is a variation of the first, but this time a variation that increases the tension. Instead of the high F-sharp that was the goal of the first phrase (over the French sixth), it substitutes one a step higher (over the German sixth): G [m. 42].

The final section of the song is heralded as the German sixth resolves back into the French. Here, at the confrontation of hero and Doppelgän-

ger, the music apparently gives up the ostinato and its insistence on duplication. But does it? The passage begins with a static two-measure
fragment in the voice (mm. 43–44), followed immediately by a varied
repetition. The piano supports this reduplication by a steady rise, effected by two successive inversions of the initial half-step motif. Now the
voice, too, begins to rise, expanding the range of its motif in two more
variations (mm. 47–50). The harmony is based on a shocking modulatory shift to sharp-iii, D-sharp minor, supported by full triadic sonorities, i–V in that key. Here the top voice of the piano reverts twice to a descending form of the half step [mm. 47–50]—the most immediate and
boldest reiteration in the entire song. Surely the hero and his double are
face to face! A wrenching German sixth (m. 51) effects a return to the
tonic B minor by way of a resolution to i6/4. In so doing it recalls the
earlier German sixth on C [mm. 41–42], copying both its striking sound
and its half-step resolution G–F-sharp. An important connection is heard
in the voice, whose high F-sharp over the i6/4 of m. 52 at last resolves
the voice's climactic G of mm. 41–42. In so doing it initiates a vocal
phrase that closes at last on a tonic supported by a perfect cadence.

It is important to recognize that the final vocal phrase is the only one
in the song that is not stated twice. True, it is doubled by the piano—but
conventionally, in standard accompanimental fashion, by full chordal
harmony. It can be said, in fact, that those measures—mm. 52–56—constitute the only normal phrase in the song. For the protagonist is experiencing an epiphany—an acceptance of his earlier self and a comprehension of the power of emotions long buried but still very much alive. It is
a recognition not unlike the one realized by the hero of "Am Meer"—
presumably the same man. Perhaps that is the reason for the recollection
of that song in the heart-stopping alteration of the fourth chord of the
ostinato in m. 59. Replacing C-sharp, C-natural is the root of a major
triad—the same one that began and ended "Am Meer"—that now leads
to a plagal cadence in B major. And here is another support for the traditional order. It produces a stark tonal contrast between "Am Meer" and
"Der Doppelgänger" that is briefly but vividly recalled by the intrusion
that leads to the final cadence of the latter.

Here, then, the traditional succession makes good sense poetically as
well as musically, in a narrative that binds the last three Heine songs together as the utterances of a single protagonist: two poems in which he
describes the present frame one in which he narrates the past. Thus the
hero, approaching (by water) the town of his youth, is reminded of a
fateful day by the sea long ago. That memory induces him to seek out
the house associated with his lost love. So in these three songs, at least, I
find ample justification for retaining the old order.

PART III

The Composer as Critic

ALTHOUGH THE IDEA that composers are at times "critics" of their own work, and occasionally those of others, is implicit in much of Cone's writing, the two articles in this section develop the notion in a uniquely concentrated manner.[1] Together they offer a profoundly original contribution to music analysis, and one that will no doubt encourage others to adopt similar perspectives.

"The Composer as Critic" was perhaps the most difficult essay to assemble. It existed in two related yet distinct draft versions, each consisting in part of commentary on works not mentioned in the other; and the present version is essentially an amalgamation of the two. Its principle argument is that in revising their own works and reworking those of others—indeed to an extent through the very act of composition itself—composers necessarily adopt the role of critic. Cone illustrates this by examining at length one work each by Brahms and Hindemith and two by Liszt. While three of these four compositions represent reworkings in the same medium of one of the composer's own previous compositions, the fourth, Liszt's *Don Juan Fantasy*, is a radical, yet strikingly skillful rethinking for piano alone of music drawn from an opera by Mozart.

In "Schubert Criticizes Schubert" Cone reinforces his point by examining a composer normally viewed as favoring a spontaneous, intuitive approach. Though it treats the same topic as the previous one, the essay takes its examples from a single composer, yet examines a considerably wider variety of compositional circumstances (though in all cases reworkings of Schubert's own music). Included is a new version of an earlier piano piece, the use of a previously composed orchestral theme as principal subject of a sonata-derived movement for string quartet, and the employment of melodies from existing songs as parts of extended instrumental compositions (in one case as the theme of a set of variations, in the two others within extended segments of multi-sectional works). Finally, the E-flat Piano Trio, Op. 100, the final movement of which was subsequently revised in a significantly cut version (mentioned briefly in the previous article), is analyzed as an instance of self-interpretation, and thus self-criticism, here involving the removal of a technique rarely found in Schubert: the simultaneous combination of one of its themes with another recalled from a previous movement.

---

[1] Cone's late published article "The Pianist as Critic," is a useful companion. In *The Practice of Performance: Studies in Musical Interpretation*, ed. John Rink (Cambridge: Cambridge University Press, 2000), pp. 241–53.

The Composer as Critic

"CRITICISM, I TAKE IT, is the formal discourse of an amateur."[1] When R. P. Blackmur, one of our most distinguished men of letters, wrote that he obviously did not mean to oppose "amateur" to "professional." As he expanded his definition he made it clear that he was invoking the root meaning of "amateur" and rejecting its unfortunate adventitious connotations of inexperience and lack of training: "When there is enough love and enough knowledge represented in the discourse it is a self-sufficient but by no means an isolated art."[2] Love and knowledge: neither is sufficient without the other. Love without knowledge produces superficial dilettantism; knowledge without love, sterile pedantry. Neither leads to what I assume to be the goal of criticism, which is not primarily judgment passed (although it may certainly include judgment) but rather appreciative understanding communicated and shared. As Leonard Meyer has put it, "In short, the critic does not come to praise masterpieces" (or, I might add, to denigrate lesser writing), "but to explicate and illuminate them."[3] A common aim of illumination unites historical, biographical, and psychoanalytic studies, stylistic and structural analyses, subjective appreciation and objective evaluations. The prospect of throwing light on the works of art that absorb his interest induces Blackmur's amateur to discipline his love and to organize his knowledge, making them available to the rest of us in the formal discourse that we call criticism. That, I think, is what Blackmur means when he says that criticism "names and arranges what it knows and loves, and searches endlessly with every fresh impulse or impression for better names and more orderly arrangements."[4]

Blackmur's emphasis on concepts of verbalization ("names" and "discourse") reminds us that his subject is literary criticism and that the literary critic is by definition a man of letters. His medium of expression and some of his techniques are those of the works he criticizes. (Poetry too, as Blackmur points out, "names and arranges.") But the man we typically

[1] [R. P. Blackmur, "A Critic's Job of Work," in *Language as Gesture* (New York: Harcourt Brace, 1952), p. 372.]

[2] [Ibid.]

[3] [Leonard B. Meyer, *Explaining Music* (Berkeley: University of California Press, 1973), pp. ix–x.]

[4] [Blackmur, "A Critic's Job of Work," p. 372.]

think of as a music critic is not necessarily a musician. Even if he is, his medium is not musical but verbal. This, I believe, is the primary source of the distrust most practicing musicians feel toward the professional critic: insofar as he depends on words, he is an outsider. Yet there is one music critic who does not depend on words. He is, and by definition must be, a musician. He is seldom recognized as a critic, perhaps because it is not his primary intention—or maybe not even his subsidiary intention—to be one; nevertheless, he disciplines his love and organizes his knowledge, making them available to us in a formalized setting that throws light on the music that interests him. I refer to the composer himself. Of course composers do, from time to time, produce verbal criticism that is often of great interest, but that is not what concerns me here. What I mean is the criticism produced by the composer when he composes—the criticism implicitly embodied by his own music.

In the most general sense, every artist, and therefore every composer, is at the same time necessarily a critic. Edgar Wind says that

> [the] age-old enmities between artist and critic, their historic quarrels and re-criminations, are perhaps but an outward reflex of a perennial dialogue within the mind of the artist himself. For however much his creative impulse may resent the critical acumen by which it is tempered, this discipline is part of the artist's own craft, and indispensable to the exercise of his genius. . . . [C]riticism can be a creative force in the very making of a work of art.[5]

Except for sheer improvisation, every act of composition necessarily involves constant critical attention to the work in hand. When we look at Beethoven's sketchbooks, we realize the extent to which composing consists of choosing among alternatives, and hence relies on a critical appreciation of the work as a whole, the critical scrutiny of a specific problem and the critical evaluation of its possible solutions. A more intuitive composer may relegate these tasks to his subconscious, but he cannot escape them. To write X at any point means that one has rejected Y and Z, whether consciously or not. Every compositional decision thus involves a process of critical selection.[6]

It may be argued that activity of this kind, in which the composer works with material not yet completely formed—material that achieves

---

[5] [Edgar Wind, "The Critical Nature of a Work of Art," in *Music and Criticism*, ed. Richard F. French (Cambridge: Harvard University Press, 1948), pp. 56–57.]

[6] David Lewin has argued that composers do not actually choose among alternatives: "[A] composer should never be thinking 'shall it be this *or* that'; he should only be thinking 'shall it be this?' If the answer is 'no,' he must work with the material . . . until the question once more presents itself: 'now, shall it be *this*?'" ["Behind the Beyond," *Perspectives of New Music* 7, no. 2 (Spring–Summer 1969): 66.] But the process of critical scrutiny followed by acceptance or rejection is no less essential here than in my own account.

its form only as a result of the activity itself—is so far removed from what we normally call criticism that another word should be applied to it. As a matter of fact, we usually do apply another word to it; we call it, simply, composition, and reserve the term criticism for a more narrowly defined operation. Yet I hope to show eventually that the line between the two is never so distinct as we imagine. Meanwhile, however, it must be pointed out that there are cases in which a composer does go to work on material to which he has already given presumably final and satisfactory shape—satisfactory at least to the point of performance or publication or both. I do not mean the kind of revision exemplified by the cutting and patching to which Schubert subjected the finale of his Piano Trio in E-flat in an attempt to make it more amenable to public performance.[7] The thoroughgoing revision or recomposition I have in mind involves the composer's creative and critical faculties in equal measure. Blackmur's love and knowledge are certainly relevant here. If "love" seems embarrassingly sentimental, call it concern or conviction. It is the interest that must inform the composer's regard for his own work, an interest deep enough to drive him to undertake a job that may prove even harder than the creation of something entirely new. If "knowledge" seems too broad, call it craft, that is, technique guided by insight. Years and experience, the composer hopes, have afforded him the insight to understand more fully his own structural and expressive intentions, and have enabled him to develop the technical equipment to realize those intentions more efficiently.

From this point of view one should understand Brahms's revision of his first Piano Trio, Op. 8, not merely as an improved version: it is too thoroughgoing a rewriting for that.[8] Rather it is a mature master's profound critique—demonstrated, not verbalized—of an affectionately regarded work of his youth. The Trio was composed in 1853–54; its revision was undertaken in 1889, thirty-five years later. Yet Brahms was able not only to appreciate its strong points but also to compose stylistically appropriate music to replace the many weak passages that he excised.

Most obviously, Brahms strengthened the Trio by imposing upon its garrulous exuberance the disciplined conciseness and concentration

---

[7] The publication of the complete version in Franz Schubert, *Neue Ausgabe sämtliche Werke*, ser. 6, vol. 7, ed. Arnold Feil (Kassel: Bärenreiter-Verlag, 1975), at last gives us the opportunity of deciding for ourselves whether the attempt was misguided or not. In my opinion the cuts deface the highly organized structure of the original and paradoxically produce a version that sounds longer. [For a more detailed discussion of this piece, see "Schubert Criticizes Schubert," the next article in this volume.]

[8] [Both the original and revised versions of the Trio are published in the Brahms *Gesamtausgabe*, vol. 9 (Leipzig: Breitkopf & Härtel, n.d.), republished as Johannes Brahms, *Complete Piano Trios* (New York: Dover Publications, 1988).]

characteristic of his mature style. Thus the first movement is reduced from 494 measures to 289, the third from 157 to 99, and the finale from 518 to 322. Only the Scherzo, which for the most part suffers only changes of detail, retains its full length. In fact, the new coda to that movement, the only major alteration, adds an extra measure; yet because of its concentration of effect it seems shorter than the one it replaces. The latter, taking its cue from the cadential progression that introduces it [original, mm. 423–30], inverts its rising chromatic figure [A–A-sharp–B] and uses it as the basis for a gradual *ritardando* governed by a descending chromatic scale. Brahms the critic realized that the progression effected by the rising figure, a dominant seventh on the lowered leading tone converted into a diminished seventh and then resolved to the tonic [original, mm. 429–31], not only was the most salient element in the whole passage but was also closely related to other crucial harmonic turns in the movement (the deceptive cadence that initiates the development [mm. 25–29, 2nd ending], the climactic appearance of the tonic major [mm. 69], and the transition to the reprise, mm. 85–120).[9] By basing the new coda entirely on an expansion of this single idea [revised version, mm. 423–60], Brahms replaced the slack running-down effect of the original with a striking comment on the harmonic unity of the whole movement.

An even more debilitating slackness infected the first version of the opening Allegro con moto; for, manifesting itself in the exposition, it influenced the course of the movement thereafter. Brahms rightly admired the lyrically expansive opening theme and realized that for its sake the movement must be recast, for he had earlier allowed its magnificent sweep to be dissipated into triviality. Thus he retained intact the grand spread of its first statement, some sixty measures, dispensing only with some irrelevant pseudo-polyphony. It was an act of appreciative insight, a tribute to the talented youth of twenty. But it was also an act of courage, for Brahms had long ago forsaken extended themes of this kind in sonata-allegro movements. Courage of a different kind was required for the ruthless dismemberment of the rest of the movement. For the slackness mentioned above overtook the splendid opening theme at its culmination, when a tonic cadence was suddenly cut off in favor of twenty measures of retreat, falling away from the climax in conventional sequences that prepared the dominant of the new key, the submediant G-sharp minor [original version, mm. 63–83].

The new theme that followed was ineloquent, and texturally bare [mm. 84–124]. Its only virtue was its derivation from the first—a deriva-

---

[9] It occurs prominently in the first movement as well, although transposed [E–E-sharp–F-sharp], mm. 54–60.

tion made painfully obvious by its preparation. The young composer must have thought that he needed to match the size of the opening as well as its material, for this second theme consisted of two gigantic balancing phrases, each of fifteen measures, and each overlapped by a further extension of six. The scherzando digression that followed was of no help, either; it statically reiterated the new submediant, E, for most of its twenty-four measures [mm. 124–47], only to sink back limply into G-sharp for fourteen measures of cadence [mm. 148–61]. All the momentum of the opening was thus lost—a fact immediately obvious to anyone trying to play the indicated repeat of the exposition.

The mature composer realized that only by denying his opening theme the satisfaction of a tonic close could he prevent a disastrous letdown—that, in fact, somehow the entire movement must be conceived as fulfilling the theme's demand for completion. And so the cadence of the climax is now deceptively bypassed as an unbroken progression pushes on to the new dominant. The revised transition replaces twenty-one measures by thirteen [revision, mm. 63–75], but its greater significance lies in its emergence as an extension of the first theme itself. As a consequence, the new second subject enters as a complement, or consequent, of the first, rather than as an independent section [revision, mm. 76–110]. At the same time its balanced phrases, concise and subtly textured, effect a strong expressive contrast. Its motivic origin in the falling thirds of the opening subject is intentionally veiled until the recapitulation; yet its connection with that theme is far more organic than was the case with its obviously derived predecessor.

It is unnecessary to contrast in detail the developments, recapitulations, and codas of the two versions, for they follow the principles suggested by their respective expositions. What is notable is the greater understanding of the opening theme—one might even say the greater sympathy for it—constantly revealed by the revision. For example, the original version predictably recapitulates that subject *in extenso* [m. 292ff.] (the third such statement if the exposition has been repeated). This occurs, however, between an episodic development and an equally episodic coda that subjects the theme to a number of uncharacteristic transformations [m. 410ff.]. In the revision, on the other hand, its noble lyricism is never violated, although in the interests of tighter organization its reprise emerges only gradually (from the submediant hitherto associated with the second subject) and is highly compressed [mm. 185–205]. Its final flowering is reserved for the coda [m. 255ff.]. Here the complementary relation between the two subjects is made even more explicit, and the final tonic arrives as the awaited resolution of both.

The same processes are at work in the remaining movements. In each case, as before, Brahms reshapes the form in order to clarify the significance of a remarkable opening subject, and to intensify its expressive effect. Thus his problem in the Adagio is to find contrast that will best set into relief the quiet dialogue of the beginning. This means substituting a grave submediant subject (G-sharp minor) [revised, m. 33ff.] for the sentimental subdominant one (E major) [original, m. 33ff.] serving as a second theme—a procedure that renders the return through that subdominant fresher and more convincing [m. 66ff.]. It also means suppressing the puzzling Allegro that interrupted the reprise [original, m. 82]. This passage, although based on a diminution of a motive from the original dialogue, was unclear as to formal function and too violent as contrast to be accepted as relevant.

In the finale, as in the first movement, the problem was lost momentum. The agitated first subject consistently avoided the tonic; nevertheless, here as before, it was brought to a cadence [original, m. 56], followed once again by a sequential transition and a relaxed second theme [m. 105ff.]. The revision demonstrates the composer's realization that the energy of the movement must not be allowed to dissipate. He applies much the same remedial treatment as before: a bypassed cadence [revised, m. 54], a compressed transition [mm. 54–63], and a complementary, appropriately vigorous second subject [m. 64ff.]. The rest of the movement now follows from these premises. Brahms's keen critical ear did not relax, however, and he recognized in the old coda the possibilities of a new one that would adequately discharge the forces pent up in his restless subject and allow its final resolution. The new coda [m. 246] is thus a reworking of the original to fit the revised content, a succinct and instructive Essay in Practical Criticism.

One may argue with some justice that the Trio, except for such passages as the coda of the finale and that of the scherzo, is not a real revision but a new composition—based, it is true, on the principal theme of each of the movements so treated. It implies a critique, but one that is less an appreciation than a rejection of the early work as a whole, mitigated by the approval of certain ideas worth salvaging. The new version suggests only occasionally how *that* composition could be improved, how *those* passages should be rewritten.

Such is not the case, however, with Liszt's *Vallée d'Obermann*. True, from one point of view the final version that appeared in the *Années de pèlerinage* of 1855 is, like the revised Brahms Trio, a completely "new" composition.[10] Yet it is closely derived from the 1835 version published in *Album d'un voyageur*. It is a revision that constantly struggles with

[10] The revision was apparently undertaken between 1848 and 1853. See Peter Raabe, *Franz Liszt* (Tutzing: Hans Schneider, 1968), vol. 2, p. 245.

the original thematic material, harmony, formal pattern—every element of musical structure. None remains unaffected; yet all are somehow accounted for.

The *Album* version begins with a typically Lisztian introduction, full of rhetorical recitative. It is based on a descending three-note germ-motif stated in isolation at the outset. Although the key of E minor is implied, it is not firmly established until the exposition of the sonata-allegro that follows [m. 23]. This is based on two subjects arising from the germ. The first, in the tonic minor (let us call it X), is to be played "avec un profound sentiment de tristesse" ["with a profound feeling of sadness"]; the second, in the relative major (Y), is played "dolcissimo con amore" [m. 43]. The development returns to the recitative of the introduction [m. 76ff.], which is gradually overwhelmed by what is apparently intended as the depiction of an Alpine storm [m. 86ff.]. When it has spent itself, the recapitulation ensues in the conventionally predictable keys of E minor and E major [m. 142ff.]; but this time the second subject [m. 159ff.] is expanded to produce a peroration that raises the dynamic level to *ffff con strepito*, and the *sostenuto* tempo of the exposition to *il più presto possible*.

A double realization—of the intrinsic value of his musical material and of the inadequacy of its original form—must have induced Liszt to undertake the complete reworking of the piece. He recognized in it an early attempt to derive from a single germ motif an entire tone poem, the contrasting tempi, textures, and moods of which would be unified by constant reference to the germ. It had failed because it was not bold enough. The formal pattern was standard. More crucially, its contrasts were insufficiently delineated. The first and second theme were obviously designed in accordance with an unwritten program to suggest deep melancholy followed by the hope of loving consolation: so much can be inferred from the directions to the performer quoted above, and from the composer's epigraphic citation of a passage from Senancourt's *Obermann* that speaks of "charme et tourment" ["charm and torment"], of "passion universelle, indifférence, sagesse avancée, voluptueux abandon" ["universal passion, apathy, foremost wisdom, voluptuous abandon"], of "besoins et d'ennuis profonds" ["wants and profound worries"]. Yet if the accompaniment of reiterated chords were not replaced by arpeggios, we should hardly realize the division between the two subjects. The first, although clearly in E minor, never cadences there. Its initial phrase moves to the relative major, G [m. 26]; its second, to the submediant, C major [m. 30]. So when the long dominant buildup that follows is resolved deceptively to the G major of the second subject, that harmony enters as an old friend. We hear the entire movement of the first subject as an expansion of its opening phrase, E minor to G major;

and we may even construe the whole passage as a huge upbeat to the second subject.

When the recitative of the development enters, we experience a different kind of *déjà vu*: it soon evolves into a reprise of the recitative heard at the outset. The storm ("vaste conscience d'une nature partout accablante" ["vast awareness of an overwhelming nature"]) seems to accomplish no clearing of the air. Despite its cadenza-like climax, followed by a suspenseful pause, we receive no revelation: the first subject reappears *come prima*, dutifully followed by the second, now in the proper key of E major. Even the *fortissimo-prestissimo* peroration, grand as it is, suffers because its chief pianistic device—the interpenetration of the melody by an accelerated version of the reiterated chords characteristic of the first subject—does not grow organically out of the preceding textures.

My verbal criticism has been an attempt to spell out what must have been Liszt's own strictures as we can infer them from his recomposition. Whether he based his judgment on purely musical or on quasi-programmatic grounds we cannot know; probably he relied on both. We can guess, however, from the revised version, the general outline of the implied programmatic design that *Vallée d'Obermann* was meant to embody—or perhaps, since his conception of the program might also have been subject to revision, the content that he had come to realize it ought to embody. For example, the piece can be thought of as referring to four stages in the spiritual life of a protagonist: dejection, hope of solace, violent outburst, and consolation and fulfillment. The revised version presents these successively, as scenes in a drama; its great merit is to contrive a convincing musical pattern that parallels and suggestively conveys the dramatic form. Scrapping the conventional sonata-allegro pattern, it nevertheless retains the principal thematic ideas of the original: the subjects dubbed X and Y, and the recitative of the storm. These are recombined in a structure that, although derived from the sonata-allegro pattern, so expands its components and heightens their contrast that they constitute four interconnected movements.

Dramatically, these correspond to the four stages enumerated above. Musically, they present X as a first subject, broadly expanded as a self-contained sonatina form—*Lento assai* in E minor; Y as a tentative and modulatory second subject—*un poco più di moto*, beginning in VI, C major [m. 75ff.]; the recitative as development—accelerating to *Presto*, with a *Lento* transition working around to the dominant [m. 119ff.]; and a new version of Y alone as a recapitulation—in the tonic major, still *Lento* but eventually *sempre animando sino al fine* [m. 168ff.]. By eliminating the introduction Liszt makes sure that the development will sound new. By extending and fully developing X in the opening section he obviates its anticlimactic return after the "storm." By giving the entrance of Y a unique pianistic color, by withholding its definitive form until the recapitulation, and by gradually transforming its lyrical cantilena, accompanied by undulating triplets, into a brilliant *martellato*, he guarantees the effective buildup of a grand peroration. So it is immaterial whether the recomposition implies a criticism primarily of the original dramatic conception or of its musical embodiment: Liszt's solution works on both levels, fusing the two into a single organism.

He carefully scrutinized his early harmonic palette and, finding it insufficiently varied for his broad canvas, proceeded to enrich it. A typical example of the result is offered by the third (formerly the second) measure of Y [m. 77], where the application of chromatic appoggiaturas [in all voices] to the bass of a bald, flat dominant seventh produces a characteristic detail of color that is not only vivid but also, through the half-step appoggiatura motif, integrally connected with the theme it modifies. But his masterstroke is his transformation of X, which moved too soon and too often toward the related major keys associated with Y. Influenced, no doubt, by the poignant diminished fourth (A-flat–E) of the original consequent cadence, in VI, the composer introduced that interval into the antecedent phrase [B–E-flat, mm. 2.4–3.1] in such a way as to turn it toward G minor. (Note also how the mawkishly chromatic A–A-sharp–B that brought the melody to a premature G major in the earlier version has been shifted to an earlier position in a subordinate voice [mm. 1–2], where it reinforces the somber color of the minor harmony.) The second phrase becomes an almost exact sequence of the first, thus ending up in B-flat minor, a tritone away from the tonic! The original "sentiment de tristesse" is, so to speak, explained: it is a result of homelessness, of wandering in a world where, according to another fragment of *Obermann* used as an epigraph, "Toute cause est invisible, toute fin trompeuse; toute forme change, toute durée s'épuise . . ." ["All cause is invisible, all result misleading; all form changes, all duration is exhausted . . ."]. Furthermore, Liszt daringly deprived his wandering theme of its harmonic bass, rendering its "cause" truly "invisible." Only the reprise of the opening phrases [m. 34ff.] supplies their proper bass, which turns out to be yet another manifestation of the chromatic motif [E–E-flat–D, mm. 34–36]. And since the E that initiates this bass is the first definitive appearance of the tonic, everything that precedes it—the entire exposition of the sonatina—becomes, as it were, a huge introductory upbeat—an upbeat that dissolves into an expansive dominant, extended still further by the interpolation of a startling chromatic sequence [mm. 26–31]. So the original introduction, which likewise embodied a search for the tonic, was not simply deleted; it was replaced by an extraordinary section that, simultaneously introductory and expository, emphasizes the restlessness of the theme as unappeasable. Like Senancourt's hero, it can well claim, "J'existe pour me consumer en désirs indomptables" ["I exist to be consumed in unconquerable desires"]. Liszt's love and knowledge—craft sympathetically applied—have coaxed from his early material a fulfillment of its potentialities.

So far the discussion has been restricted to self-criticism; and indeed, much, perhaps most, criticism that is effected through the medium of music, which we might call "compositional criticism," is of this kind. But normally we think of criticism as applied to the works of others, and here too we find compositional parallels—whenever, in fact, a composer appropriates the works of another to vary it, to develop it, to throw new light on it in any way. When Beethoven varied Diabelli's theme thirty-three times he was demonstrating the plasticity underlying a superficially trivial subject. When Liszt transcribed Schubert's *Wanderer* Fantasy as a concerted piece for piano and orchestra he was commenting on its form, its texture, and its expressive potentialities.

Liszt is, in fact, a prime source of this category of criticism, for much of his creative activity was inspired by the music of others. Probably the most extraordinary example of this phase of his work is the *Don Juan Fantasie* for piano, or *Réminiscences de Don Juan* (1841), which is by no means a potpourri but a composition carefully designed to present a personal view of Mozart's opera.

The opening page shows his method. He begins with the two pronouncements of the statue in the graveyard [toward the end of No. 21 of the opera], not separated by a transitional recitative as in the opera, but juxtaposed, so that their relationship as a modified sequence—D minor to its dominant, followed by C major to its dominant—is made apparent. Then follows an even more startling juxtaposition, for we are plunged into an arpeggio on the diminished seventh that announces the appearance of the statue at the banquet [from the Finale]. What is Liszt suggesting here? First of all, he is linking the two scenes involving the statue, an obvious dramatic connection. Musically, he is showing how the two passages of the graveyard scene, construed together, can be heard as pointing toward a tonality of D minor—a promise not fulfilled in that scene but held in abeyance until the Finale. And, by registrally linking the descending fourth motif common to all the passages [Liszt, mm. 1–4, 5–9, 10–13], he presents evidence that the connection between the two scenes was intentional on Mozart's part.

The rest of Liszt's introduction proceeds to develop this juxtaposition, calling on various aspects of the scene from the Finale—for example, combining the graveyard motif with an accompaniment figure from Don Giovanni's initial response to the entrance of the statue [m. 13.4ff.]. Particularly noteworthy is his expansion, on two occasions, of the dominant of B-flat. The first time he continues by means of a chromatic sequence extrapolated from the original [mm. 31–32, etc.], the second time by completing a previously begun modulation to A [mm. 52–68]. Both keys are directly derived from his source, but Liszt has another aim in view. The B-flat is to be saved for future explanation, but the A is to be expanded forthwith as the key of "La ci darem" [m. 69]. Even when Don Giovanni is at the point of damnation, he is still the ardent lover.

"La ci darem" is stated *in extenso*, followed by two variations [mm. 151ff. and 248ff.], the second of which is incomplete and merges with a return of the Commendatore's music [m. 285]. In addition to their pianistic brilliance, the variations are interesting in the way they demonstrate a basic unity beneath the contrasting ideas of the duet—the 2/4 dialogue and the 6/8 union with its animated close. The 2/4 of the first variation proceeds in sextuplet sixteenths, which are subtly transformed by cross-rhythms into a rocking sixteenth-note accompaniment for the 6/8 [m. 216]. The equation thus established between the two meters demonstrates their basic identity. But the 6/8 accompaniment suggests something more. Surely Liszt is reminding us here that other seductions in this opera have been similarly cast in 6/8, with accompanying sixteenths: the trio of Act 2, Don Giovanni's ensuing serenade, and even the resolution of "Batti, batti," which, to be sure, is also a kind of seduction.

The origin of the second variation is the dotted rhythmic motif that characterizes the end of the duet. This Liszt applies to the first theme, once again suggesting a basic identity beneath superficial dissimilarity. It is, moreover, the insistence of this motif that occasions the return of the sinister chromatics associated with the statue's appearance [m. 285]. The dramatic relevance of the ensuing transition is obvious and conventional: the kind of life suggested by the duet leads to the judgment represented by the statue. But the outcome is anything but obvious and conventional. Once more B-flat is introduced, and this time its meaning is made clear. It is the key of "Finch'han dal vino" [m. 377ff.], the most vivid expression of Don Giovanni's teeming energy. It is introduced, however, not in its initial major but in a typical Lisztian sequence (in major thirds) derived from the minor of that aria's "Ed io frattanto dal altro canto" [m. 343ff.]. In this passage Liszt found the link between the otherwise jubilant aria and the surprisingly similar B-flat minor by which, in the Finale, Don Giovanni scorns the statue's threats: "A torto di viltate! Tocciato mai sarò!" ["To wrong me as a coward! That will never touch me!"][11]

---

[11] In an alternate version of the *Fantasie*, Liszt underlines this connection by means of a greatly expanded transition that unites elements of the graveyard scene, the Finale, and the aria. See also the suggestive motivic combination at *più animato* in the coda. [For information about the history of this version, see Raabe, *Franz Liszt*, 2:228.]

From this refusal to be frightened, even by the imminence of damnation, rises the ebullient aria in ever more brilliant forms, translating sexual into pianistic virtuosity. Through Liszt's variations it absorbs and overcomes, as it were, the chromatics of Mozart's Finale, until at last it is able to triumph over the words of the statue in the graveyard—"Di rider finirai pria dell'aurora" ["You'll finish laughing before dawn breaks"]—forcing them into its own B-flat major at the close [10 measures before end]. For Liszt, it is obviously Don Giovanni who has the last laugh, for his vitality cannot be suppressed. And he has made his personal unromantic interpretation of the character as clear through his musical critique as, say, Kierkegaard made his own through prose.

The close relation between the kind of composition we have been examining and the verbal activity usually called criticism has been confirmed by at least one composer. When Hindemith published the 1948 revision of *Das Marienleben*, the song cycle he had written twenty-five years before, he prefaced it with a lengthy prose explanation of his reasons for producing a new version and of his general approach toward the recomposition. Believing the songs worth saving, he had nevertheless found them deficient in several crucial respects. Despite their expressive power they were vocally awkward, harmonically unclear, tonally vague, and insufficiently organized as a cyclic unity. These were the faults that he set out to correct in the new version. The preface explains not only his general method of approach in recomposing the cycle, but also, for each song, the specific goals of improvement. It makes clear, that is to say, how each new song—and the new cycle as a whole—constitutes a critique of its predecessor. Unfortunately, many listeners—perhaps most—find the revision more conventional and less intense than the original. Hindemith may have been too highly self-conscious, too articulate, in giving his aims such a precise verbal formulation. Perhaps, in Blackmur's terms, too much knowledge has been applied, balanced by insufficient love.

Hindemith defines the difference between the two versions in terms of instinct and calculation:

> The old version was actually a succession of songs, held together by the text and its narrative action, but beyond that following no general plan of composition. . . . Judicious distribution of forces, determination of the high and low points—these were unknown to the composer of the old version. Like all others he relied, knowing no better, on his musical instinct. . . . In our new version all these factors (and many others, as will be seen in the course of this introduction) have been taken into account.[12]

---

[12] [Paul Hindemith, *Das Marienleben* (New York: Associated Music, 1948), p. iv. Page references are to the untranslated German original. The English translations are apparently

But the issue is not calculation as such: it is calculation that is verbal or mathematical or abstract rather than musical. Throughout Hindemith's career there is always the suspicion that verbal formulation—of the need for Gebrauchsmusik, of reasons for simplifying his harmonic style—has preceded musical exemplification. Thus, for example, with reference to the elaborate system of tonal symbolism (from the E of Christ to the B-flat of human incredulity) he writes:

> Once a composer has set himself on the road of tonal symbolism described here, he is easily overcome by the fascination of the manifold possibilities of relationships between concept and key. At first he will perhaps only avoid writing tonal progressions that contradict the character or meaning of a textual phrase. Soon, however, he comes to the point of seeking and intentionally inserting elements that confirm and advance that meaning; and finally he writes down no single chord that does not share significantly in this tonal text-interpretation.[13]

He then adduces an explanation of the new key relationships resulting from the application of this system to the fourteenth song ("Vom Tode Maria II")—a prime example of revision motivated by verbal formulation.

A composer's aims should indeed be precise—but musically precise. And when he criticizes as a composer, his critique should be expressed in music, not words. Again, this is not meant to rule out calculation. Many of Liszt's effects in the second *Vallée d'Obermann* must have been carefully calculated, but musically calculated. For while it is true that the verbal approach to music can hardly be intuitive, it is not correspondingly true that the musical approach must be. One can think as rigorously in music as in words or as in mathematical symbols. But whether intuitive or calculated, free or rigorous, musical thought must be in musical terms if it is to yield convincing results. That is, I believe, why Brahms and Liszt could produce masterpieces of compositional criticism. What I have tried to verbalize, for them consisted of musical thought: musical thought applied to music. That is exactly what compositional criticism is.

So defined, the term obviously applies to more than the revisions of one's own music or variations of themes by others. It applies, at least, to revising others' music, and to writing variations on themes of one's own.

---

by Cone himself. A translation by Arthur Mendel of five sections of Hindemith's introductory remarks was published in the program booklet for the premiere performance, and is now located, along with a typed translation of the two missing sections by Luther Noss, in the Hindemith Collection at Beinecke Library of Yale University. But neither of these translations corresponds to Cone's.]

[13] [Ibid., p. ix.]

And why only variations? When we develop a theme, when we write a contrasting subject, whenever, in fact, we give a musical idea a context, we are commenting on that idea. We are, as it were, defining its significance. That is what I take composition to be—composition, that is, understood as more than a short burst of inspiration or mindless improvisation. Composing is defining the significance of one's musical ideas. But what is criticizing if not defining the significance of musical ideas? That is what I meant when I suggested that the line between composition and criticism is indistinct. Not every critic is a composer, but every composer is a critic.

Schubert Criticizes Schubert

SCHUBERT CRITICIZES SCHUBERT? That cannot be meant seriously! Surely of all the great composers Schubert must have been the most spontaneous, the least given to rethinking and rewriting? Even his good friend Josef von Spaun, who always tried to present him in the best light possible, admitted: "There is one fault with which Schubert can be reproached and it is that he never took his compositions in hand again and polished them."[1] Spaun was wrong, of course: his generalization was much too sweeping. The successive versions of some of the songs, the shortened finale of the Piano Trio in E-flat, Op. 100, the preliminary sketches for the *Unfinished* Symphony—all attest that sometimes, at least, Schubert did "take his compositions in hand again and polish them." Even so, Schubert's staunchest defenders must agree with Spaun that "tedious passages or inaccuracies occur here and there," and that, like Shakespeare, he might well have blotted out a few lines, if not a thousand.

What I mean by self-criticism, however, is not restricted to overt revision, nor does it necessarily involve a negative judgment of the passage or work criticized. The essential act of criticism is not judgment but appreciation. Primarily, the critic seeks to understand the work in question; insofar as he communicates with others, he tries to share that understanding.

Oddly enough, it is just the spontaneous composer—of the type that Schubert is often supposed to have been and probably to a great extent was—who perhaps can most clearly exemplify in his composition the critical appreciation of his own work. A composer like Beethoven, struggling with every detail, comes to a thorough understanding of his material even as he forms it. For him conception and criticism are typically as intertwined as statement and development in the musical result. With Schubert, on the other hand, the critical appreciation of a musical idea—the intellectual comprehension of its implications and possibilities—is often widely separated, sometimes by years, from the time of its conception. It was the apparent spontaneity of that conception that gave rise to the belief mentioned (though not shared) by Spaun, that Schubert was "only an excellent natural composer,"[2] a belief supported by contemporary accounts of

---

[1] [Otto Erich Deutsch, *Schubert: Memoirs by His Friends,* trans. Rosamond Ley and John Nowell (New York: Macmillan, 1958), p. 363.]

[2] [Ibid., p. 362.]

his trance-like behavior under the influence of obvious inspiration. But as Spaun realized, that side of the composer was balanced by another: "He possessed the most thorough musical knowledge and had studied the works of the great masters, both old and new, in the greatest detail. . . . With such knowledge one is no mere natural composer."[3] It was that knowledge, applied to the results of his inspired trances, that produced what I call Schubert's compositional criticism—passages that include some of the finest music that he ever wrote.

Schubert's inspiration was probably never so pure as it seemed to his enthralled companions; his states of rapture may well have been induced by extreme mental concentration involving precise, even if subconscious, cognitive processes. Conversely, for all we know, his most carefully calculated effects had their origins in flashes of insight. So when Schubert cast a critical eye—or ear—on earlier works, he may not have been doing so intentionally or even consciously; and it should not surprise us that the results not only sound as fresh as the originals, but often surpass them in their quality of musical invention.

Such is certainly the case with the rondo theme of the finale of the posthumous Piano Sonata in A major of 1828. Although its progenitor, from the E major Allegretto of the early A minor Sonata Op. 164 (1817), possesses a certain simple charm, it sounds like a preliminary sketch by comparison with its fulfillment in the late work. Although, in its role as the refrain of a rondo, it returns twice in varied form, the modifications are those of key and accompaniment figure; melody and harmony remain almost unchanged. The coda makes a brief attempt at development, but only through the reiteration of a single phrase derived from the cadence of the theme.

In the early sonata, then, there are no indications that Schubert was in any way dissatisfied with the theme as it then stood. Nor have we any evidence that he conceived the later subject as a "new, improved" edition of the original. Yet he unerringly corrected every questionable detail, and in so doing created an appropriate refrain for an extended rondo—a refrain both supple enough and sturdy enough to sustain the flowing descant, the modulatory extensions, the developments, and the retransitions, to which he subjected it.

The most immediately obvious superiority of the 1828 version lies in its greater rhythmic flexibility, as shown in such details as the transitions between phrases in m. 4 and m. 8. Even more subtle is the treatment of the very opening. In the original, a ponderously sustained melodic fifth degree (B) is followed by a rather bumpy syncopation—a motif typifying

[3] [Ibid., p. 363.]

the lumbering movement of the entire theme. The revision places the syncopation on the fifth itself (now E), preceding it by a marvelously ambiguous upbeat-like downbeat on the third (C-sharp). Already the composer is announcing one of his chief topics for future discussion, for the rhythmic motif of this first measure is to be amply developed. Indeed, the opening C-sharp alone, subtly notated as an eighth note followed by an eighth rest, might be considered as a rhythmic element "developed" by its recurrence in new contexts—in the next measure, and again in m. 10.

From a purely melodic point of view, the most interesting changes occur in the cadences of mm. 4 and 8. In the original, a conventional $\hat{3}$–$\hat{2}$ half cadence is answered, somewhat surprisingly, and uncomfortably, one step higher by a $\hat{4}$–$\hat{3}$ authentic cadence. The revision, realizing the implications of the 8–7 suspension in m. 2, returns to this motif to form the half cadence; this time the appearance of the full cadence—again one step higher, $\hat{2}$–$\hat{1}$—is completely satisfying, and indeed, necessary.

Despite a new accompaniment figure, the harmony remains substantially the same as before. There are, however, a few telling alterations of detail. The gratuitous deceptive cadence, V–VI, in mm. 2 and 6, is replaced by a V4/3–I6/3—a move effecting a more direct approach to the cadential dominant, and saving the submediant for a more important role later on in the movement. In mm. 10–13, the indecisive oscillation between the normal and the raised fourth degrees (A and A-sharp in the original) yields to a consistent chromatic descent from $\hat{5}$ to $\hat{3}$ (E down to C-sharp). And the arrival on $\hat{4}$ (D) is emphasized by a pure subdominant harmony—the unique occurrence in the theme of a chord strangely absent from the first version.

In pointing out the steps by which Schubert transformed his material one must not overemphasize the aspect of negative criticism. After all, the composer did recognize the potentialities of the early theme, whose basic shape remains untouched. He retained, too, the striking dotted rhythmic motif of the final cadence [mm. 15–16]. That passage, we remember, became the basis of a short coda; in its new setting it is developed so as to produce not only the transition to the second theme [mm. 32–45], but also, gradually truncated, the essential opening motif of that theme [mm. 47–48].

An entirely different attitude to old material is revealed by Schubert's adaptation of his familiar *Rosamunde* theme. Originally written for the entr'acte after Act 3 of Helmina von Chézy's play, it returns in the *Andante* of the A minor String Quartet [D. 804], virtually unchanged except for key, instrumentation, and details of voice leading. This time only a few months separate the two versions: the music for the play was written in the fall of 1823; the quartet, early the next year. The music was still fresh in his ears—actually so, for the play had been performed in December.

Schubert's concern in this case, then, was not the shaping of the theme: that was already complete, and its reuse in the quartet can be considered as a tribute to its perfection. But in the entr'acte it received no development: it was simply contrasted with two *minore* trios. The quartet movement, on the other hand, is cast in a form—one of Schubert's favorites—that ensured such treatment: a sonata-derived pattern in which a tonic recapitulation of the opening theme immediately follows the exposition, thus preceding a development section naturally based on the same theme. To be sure, developmental elaboration is not limited to the one section: the transition returning to the principal theme, the corresponding transition to the coda, the coda itself, even the varied recapitulation of the theme, all are pervaded by the opening motif and its rhythm. But what cries out for fuller explanation is not a motivic but a harmonic detail: the fermata on the major mediant (V of VI) of the original [m. 12] and its mysterious resolution. The quartet explores and clarifies the harmonic implications of this passage.

That is effected unexpectedly by returning to and dwelling on the augmented sixth that led to the cadential chord [in mm. 11.4–12]. In the original, the lines of melody and bass suggest its reinterpretation as a dominant seventh, and imply a modulation to flattened, minor-derived keys (IV♭7 = V7 of ♭VII). But no, the progression is short-circuited and leads surprisingly back to the tonic (IV♭7–VIIdim7–V4/3–I) [mm. 13–14]. The return is locally convincing but hardly permanent, as the entr'acte tries to pretend. In the quartet, Schubert insists on confirmation of the tonic before proceeding further [m. 17ff.]. And the entire development section can be heard as a fuller explanation, so to speak, of the strange thematic harmonies. The process begins with the recapitulation of the second half of the subject, now in minor and leading to a tonicized mediant (♭III) at the fermata (m. 69–72). Both here and a little later (m. 76), when the theme ends in the new key, the temporary V–I completes, as it were, the modulation left hanging by the original statement (IV♭7–♭VII6/5–♭III, or V7 of V–V7–I in ♭III).

The next phase of the development prolongs the flat mediant, expanding it in its turn as a dominant, V7 of ♭VI (mm. 80–84). Finally a deceptive cadence completes the circle: V of ♭VI resolves to ♭VI of ♭VI (m. 85). But that is enharmonically the same as the mediant (III♯) of the original fermata! Now, at last, without short circuit, the chord is led back to the tonic through a progression which, though subtle in detail, nevertheless unmistakably derives from the standard sequence of fifths: III–VI–II–V–I [mm. 89–93]. At this point the harmonic implications of the theme have been fully explored. It remains only for the tonic to be dutifully confirmed by the returning second subject (a theme which, it should be noted, on each occasion expands its key in minor as well as major), and for the original transition to introduce a coda [m. 110ff.] in which the principal theme, ready to be laid to rest, is reduced to its opening rhythm, now sounded beneath the same melody that extended the tonic once before (cf. mm. 118–22 and mm. 17–20).

If Schubert thought so highly of the *Rosamunde* melody, as I have insisted, why, then, did he alter it so drastically to provide a theme for his Impromptu in B-flat Major Op. 142 No. 3? One answer is that perhaps he did not. The Impromptu theme, composed in 1827, may have been conceived independently, and merely coincidentally related to the *Rosamunde* subject. Only three of its eighteen measures imitate those of its putative model, and one of these (m. 3) is given a different harmonic construction. But if Schubert did consider it as yet another version of the earlier melody, its total transformation might be taken as one more indication that he had come to realize that it was not independently viable in its original form. The variation theme, by contrast, eschews all ambiguous progressions: its major mediant, which occurs at the beginning of the second section, is merely the starting point for a normal (V of VI–VI–V of V–V) return (mm. 9–11). And the final measure of the theme is rounded off by two extra repetitions of the last measure. This suggests a belief that the strict variation form he had in mind would not have permitted explanatory developments.

Schubert did, of course, on occasion call upon previously written melodies, notably his songs, to provide themes for variation. It must be admitted, however, that the individual variations themselves seldom offered profound critical comment on their subjects. Delightful as they often are, they rarely offer more than elegant decorative elaboration. There is usually at least one in each set, however, that invests the theme with new meaning (e.g., in the B-flat Impromptu, the third and fourth, which move into the tonic minor and the flatted submediant, respectively). But the critical significance of Schubert's variations resides primarily in each set as a whole. Why was the theme chosen? How was it adapted? What light does the new context throw upon it? How do the variations form unified wholes? In cyclical works, how do the variations fit into their surroundings?

To cite briefly a few familiar examples: If it is true that the variations that have given the *Trout* Quintet its name were included at the request of Sylvester Paumgartner, the cellist who commissioned it, then the whole work may have been designed to furnish an appropriate setting for the song—much as if the poet's encounter with the fish were surrounded by a series of pleasant pastoral episodes. The variation movement itself may be taken as a little tone poem that expands and clarifies the dramatic structure of the original, emphasizing that the composer's final word is not the "rege Blüte" ["raging blood"] of the poet's protagonist. Rather, as suggested by the appearance of the song's original accompanimental figure in the final section, along with the return to major after the minor and ♭VI of the previous two variations, the mood is one of realistic acceptance.

In transforming "Der Tod und das Mädchen" into a theme for variations in the D minor String Quartet [D. 810], Schubert brought to light a concealed pattern in the song: omitting the Maiden's anguished appeal, he fashioned a binary construction by combining the piano introduction with a modified version of Death's reply. Except for the new key (G minor instead of D) and the instrumentation, the first section is virtually unchanged. The second section undergoes some modification. Originally succeeding the thematic and harmonic contrast of the Maiden's lines, which end on an extended half cadence, Death's first phrase returns to the opening tonic, which it confirms by a plagal progression before modulating to the relative major. In the quartet version, this latter section, following hard on the first period, requires more contrast: it opens on VI and supplies the missing half cadence before it too turns to the relative major [mm. 9–16]. From then on the quartet follows closely the accompaniment of the original. By choosing the piano melody as its own, the new theme clarifies the basic linear construction of the original, and by omission explains Death's vocal part as imperturbably static descant. By suppressing reference to the song's coda until the final variation, the movement emphasizes the symmetrical structure of the formerly latent binary form: eight measures on the tonic minor, then eight measures to the relative major plus eight measures returning to the tonic major.

If this is to be taken as a serious comment on the song, we must construe the latter neither as a three-part ABA [mm. 1–7, 9–21, 21–43] nor as a two-part vocal structure [mm. 9–21, 22–37] with an anticipatory introduction and coda. Rather, it is a freely rounded binary form interrupted by a contrasting interpolation [in mm. 9–21].

Despite its rejection of the Maiden's role, the variation movement as a whole manages to suggest some of the characteristic contrasts of the song. The theme itself sets up the basic opposition between tonic minor and major. Lacking the extension of a coda, the concluding turn to major cannot sound stable; it is the job of the variations to make it convincing. Thus the first two retain the contrast of mode; but the third remains in minor through its final cadence, only to be succeeded by a complete major version in the fourth. Moreover, taken as a unit, these last two variations reflect something of the Maiden's fear followed by Death's consolation. For although all the variations retain the original tempo, the third, with its reiterated accents and persistent double-diminution of the basic rhythmic motif, gives the effect of *agitato*, which, in its turn, is pacified by the smooth-flowing triplets of the ensuing major. Finally, the progress of the movement is summed up by the fifth and last variation. Beginning quietly, it rises to a climax of rhythmic and dynamic intensity, then subsides into a peaceful coda. The variation returns to the original layout of mode, but this time the coda effectively confirms the major.

Did Schubert mean for the subject of his song to refer in any way to, or to throw any light on, the emotional significance of the quartet as a whole? There can be no question about the passionate seriousness of the opening movement: even its relaxed second subject is transformed into a strenuous closing theme. And the Scherzo is certainly anything but light-hearted. But the mood of the final Presto is ambiguous, and in this case the proximity of the song theme may be an important clue to interpretation and performance. Like the theme and its variations, the Presto vacillates between tonic minor and major. If the variation movement is relevant, these alternations of mode should not sound capricious but rather highly expressive; its tempo should be not merely rapid but urgent. Only in the context of such an interpretation can the suspense of the coda and its final decision in favor of minor exert their effect. With Death in the background, this finale is no dance, but a race of the kind suggested by the old Eastern tale of the appointment in Samarra[4]—or if it is a dance, it must be based on one of the traditions associated with the tarantella, or with the Dance of Death.

More interesting than either of the foregoing is the transformation undergone by the song "Sei mir gegrüsst" in preparation for its appearance in the Andantino section of the Fantasy for Violin and Piano, Op. 159, of 1827 [D. 934].[5] The poem, by Friedrich Rückert, is characterized by a persistent refrain based on the words of the title, and the song faithfully reflects that device. The diagrammed proportions (table 9.1) show a rondo-like pattern (with x as refrain) governing a steady increase in complexity. From this highly irregular source Schubert has distilled a subtly balanced rounded binary form of 24 (repeated) measures (table 9.2).

The first ten measures are substantially the opening of the song. The final fourteen are derived from the b'-x of the fourth stanza [m. 61ff.], with three measures excised [mm. 62–64]. But cut and join do not show in the tightly constructed theme, which condenses and summarizes the

---

[4] [This tale deals with the inevitability of death, despite all efforts to avoid it. It was used as the title of a 1934 novel by John O'Hara.]

[5] [All score references are to the International Music Company edition of the Fantasy (New York, n.d.).]

TABLE 9.1
Schubert; "Sei mir gegrüsst": Relationship between Poetic and Musical Form

Stanza	1	2	3	4	5
Musical sections	a x a x	b x	a' + c x	b' x	a + d x
Length in measures	4 6 4 6 + 1	9 6	4 + 5 6 + 1	11 6	4 + 9 6 + 3

TABLE 9.2
Rounded Binary Form of "Sei mir gegrüsst"

Sections	‖: a x :‖: b x :‖
Length (mm.)	4 6 8 6

important points made by the original. Far from sounding like an abbreviation, the theme gives the effect of being a concentrated subject of which the song, by comparison, seems a somewhat rambling development.

The theme also makes an interesting comment on the original vocal line. The new melody, as stated alternately by piano and violin, is derived from the accompaniment of the song; only at the refrain does it take over the voice part. This suggests that the vocal line should not be construed as "the tune" of the song; rather it is an inner voice rising to full melodic status only at the refrains. An inner voice—could that not be taken as a musical pun on the *Innigkeit* of the poem and its setting?

The new melody moreover explains certain problematic elements of the song. It spells out the origin, as chromatic passing notes, of the unusual raised scale-degrees of the opening phrase, and it offers an almost Schenkerian analysis of the unresolved seventh in the refrain [cf. mm. 17–18 of the song and 7–8 of the Andantino].

The initial variations add little to what the theme has already told us. Their importance lies in the weight they give that theme in its new context. For real insight into the theme's role in the Fantasy one must turn to two incomplete variations—one that enters as the fourth of the set [rehearsal Aa] but dissolves into a transition leading into a reprise of the opening movement [Tempo I], and one [Allegretto] that appears in the wake of a deceptive cadence, interrupting the final peroration. The two have similar harmonic outcomes, modulating as both do from A-flat, the local tonic of the theme, to C, the tonic of the piece as a whole. Obviously this is a simple matter, involving one of Schubert's favorite progressions (already noted twice above). What makes these instances so telling is that each of them, in a different manner, utilizes the same striking detail of the melody, its juxtaposition of E and E-flat [compare mm. 14–15 of the song with mm. 6–7 of the fourth variation and mm. 8–9,

12–13, and 16–17 of the Allegretto]. In so doing, each in its own way re-minds us that the C major underlying that E, although temporarily a major III (or V of VI), is ultimately the underlying tonic of the piece.

Indeed, the first expansion of that tonic in the violin's opening can-tilena also plays with the same alternation of E and E-flat [e.g., mm. 1–2 and 5–6 of the opening]. But this is only one of several elements, com-mon to the variations and the opening rhapsody, which suggest a con-nection between the two that is made explicit when the one dissolves into the other. Together they seem to present a state of dreamlike ecstasy repeatedly forced to yield to the banalities of the active world, yet per-sisting in memory. Could the Fantasy be taken as a commentary on Rückert's apostrophe to an absent beloved: "O du Entriss'ne mir und m einem Kusse . . . Erreichbar nur meinem Sehnsuchtsgrusse" ["Oh you, torn from me and my kisses . . . reachable only by my longing greet-ings"]? Does it perhaps place words as well as music in a wider context?

The same question can be asked of Schubert's other great song-based fantasy, the *Wanderer* Fantasy for Piano, Op. 15 [D. 760], composed in 1822. The theme chosen for instrumental elaboration from the song of that name is associated with the second stanza of Schmidt von Lübeck's text, which emphasizes the wanderer's alienation: "Ich bin ein Fremdling überall" ["I am everywhere a foreigner," mm. 23–30]. It is easy to hear in the Adagio movement of the Fantasy devoted to this theme a musical symbolization of that mood: tempo, texture, color, key (the minor Nea-politan)—all suggest a world foreign to the extroverted virtuosity of the other three movements. Yet the design of the Fantasy is based on a sub-tler relation than mere contrast. Almost the whole work is based on two motifs derived from the song stanza. The first of these is one of Schu-bert's favorite rhythms, a simple dactyl. In duple or triple form, it perme-ates the three rapid movements [opening of the outer movements, m. 3 of the Presto].

Interestingly enough, in the earlier 1816 version of the song "Der Wanderer," that rhythm permeated the stanza in question as well, being persistently repeated in the accompaniment. At that stage, Schubert thought of the section as more active (it is marked *etwas geschwinder*)—as one step in the increasing excitement of the whole. By the time the song's definitive version appeared, in 1821, the verse had become the emotional pivot of the composition. It remained *sehr langsam*, and the dactyl of the accompaniment was restricted to one statement per mea-sure. Finally, in the Piano Fantasy, with the expansion of the section into a focal Adagio movement, the dactyl is restricted even further: it occurs only where it can be integrated naturally into the melodic line. Schubert evidently came to realize the true contemplative nature of his theme; it retains the active dactylic motif of the faster sections only as a memory. (True, the rhythm tries forcibly to intrude in mm. 18–27 of the Adagio, but it is soon subdued.)

The other pervasive motif is a melodic inflection found in the third measure of the theme [song, m. 25]. If the energy of the rapid movements penetrates the Adagio with the dactyl, this melodic detail suggests the influence of the Adagio—in prospect or in memory—on the other movements. It is used to shape the more lyrical moments of the opening Allegro [e.g., mm. 112–32] and the Scherzo [e.g., mm. 179–268], and some passionate development as well. Only from the finale, almost unrelenting in its onrush, is it excluded. And it is probably no accident that the keys in which it appears in its most characteristic form—E-flat, A-flat, D-flat—are more closely related to the C-sharp (equals D-flat) of the Adagio than to the prevailing C major of the outer movements.

As a variation movement the Adagio is extremely free. In fact, the eight-measure thematic statement is immediately followed by a lyrical expansion that raises expectations of a quite differed kind of design— perhaps an extended song form or a rondo. The passage, moreover, is of interest as a gloss on the song, for it reveals an unsuspected connection between the second-stanza melody and elements of the first stanza: the motif associated with the line from the first stanza "Ich wandle still," and the cadence that concludes it [cf. song, mm. 16–18 and 21–22, and Adagio, mm. 9–13]. But the expansive mood is not sustained: after two attempts the consolatory relative major gives way to the tonic minor, and the music rises in an angry outburst before settling down to two complete variations [mm. 27ff. and 39ff.]. Yet although these can be analyzed as such, their effect, as they move dreamily in and out of tonic minor, tonic major, and relative major, is rather that of a series of ruminations on the theme.

Like the song, the Adagio vacillates between C-sharp minor and its relative major, E. Like the song, it ends with a cadence in E major. But there is an important difference. In the Fantasy the E major is not allowed to hold: a D-natural is insinuated into the still restless accompaniment [m. 57].[6] The apparent dominant seventh thus formed is left hanging over a fermata; the ensuing Scherzo, in A-flat, resolves it as a German sixth.

The Fantasy, then, could use a device unavailable to the song—unavailable, that is, given the restrictions of style and history. Despite the unmistakable meaning of the final words, "Dort, wo du nicht bist, dort ist das Glück!" ["There, where you are not, there is happiness!"], the

---

[6]This crucial note did not find its way from the manuscript into the standard editions. [See Paul Badura-Skoda's note to his edition of the work, *Wiener Urtext Ausgabe*, 4th ed. (Vienna: Universal Edition, 1973), pp. vi–vii.]

song had to end on a tonic. The Fantasy's Adagio, under no such compulsion, can fade out as it fades in. Its dissolved cadence can suggest, more strongly than any passage in the song, that the roving hero never comes to rest—just as its free form, moving in and out of the variation pattern, can be taken as reflecting his perpetual dissatisfaction. Thus, on the one hand, the song suggests a specific interpretation of the content of its instrumental environment; on the other, it gains from that environment an opportunity of intensifying its own expressive powers.[7]

A final instance of self-interpretation should be mentioned, the thematic juxtaposition through contrapuntal combination of two apparently disparate subjects. A favorite of such nineteenth-century composers as Berlioz and Wagner, this device often has a programmatic motivation. Even when it does not, some unspoken comment of the composer may seem to linger in the air: "Now you can understand the real connection between those themes." Musical commentary here again approaches verbal criticism.

Schubert rarely employs the device, so its appearance in the finale of the E-flat Piano Trio, Op. 100 is worth attention. In the uncut version of this movement,[8] the principal subject of the Andante recurs three times, twice in the development [mm. 279ff., 477ff.] and once in the coda [m. 795ff.]. Of those statements the first and third are presented homophonically: the cello's cantilena is accompanied on the violin by a rhythmic figure familiar from the Andante and on the piano by a previously used chordal figuration [in the finale] that articulates the fundamental 6/8 of the movement—though disturbed by highly syncopated phrasing. These two recurrences are the only ones retained in the familiar cut version [at mm. 279 and 697 of that version], but even they present a critical point of view of some consequence.

The interpenetration of one movement by another newly illuminates both. The somber reference to the slow movement implies that the entire finale is more serious than it has hitherto seemed; and indeed, the ensuing developments and transformations applied to the finale's second thematic group suggest that its "cimbalom" theme (characterized by reiterated eighth notes) [m. 73ff.] and its associates are not so lighthearted as they may have sounded. But the influence works in the other direction as well. The assimilation of the Andante into the triumphant closing movement organically unites two phases of the slow movement (the melody

[7] [Cone also considers the Fantasy, but from a quite different perspective, in the next essay, "Schubert's Symphonic Poem."]

[8] Published for the first time in the *Neue Ausgabe sämtlicher Werke*, ser. 6, vol. 7, ed. Arnold Feil (Kassel: Bärenreiter-Verlag, 1975).

proper and its climactic development), which, during that movement, remained in opposition.

The composer authorized two cuts of some fifty measures each in the
development. The first excised section [50 measures], between mm. 357
and 358 of the revised edition, contains further expansion along familiar
lines. It is the second [51 measures], now replaced by three new measures, mm. 413–15 [revised edition], that concerns us, for here the cimbalom figure in the piano is intermittently counterpointed against the
Andante's cantilena in the cello. The new combination has the effect of a
revelation. The cimbalom idea, apparently so trivial at first, has assumed
more and more complex forms as the movement has progressed; its
mood has consequently gradually deepened and darkened. Now the goal
of that development has been attained: the cimbalom enhances the somber expressiveness of the song with its own mysterious, almost uncanny,
interjections.

Why did Schubert authorize and apparently insist on these excisions?[9]
No doubt because the work had been performed in concert and had
seemed too long. But if Schubert wished to shorten the movement, why
did he choose to cut out a passage unique not only in the Trio, but, so
far as I know, in his entire oeuvre?

One possible answer is that he felt uncomfortable with the completely
self-contained development section of the uncut version. That section
opens with the Andante theme in B minor; and it closes with the same
theme in the same key. Viewed superficially the entire development is
thus a huge ABA. Close inspection uncovers the startling outlines of a
sonata form, with the cantilena as first theme [m. 279ff.] (B minor), the
cymbalom melody as second theme [m. 321ff.] (D minor), a development of the latter, and the simultaneous recapitulation of the two in B
minor [m. 477ff.]. The original section as a whole was thus both thematically and tonally rounded. But the problem is not solved by the present
development. That is still tonally rounded, as it begins with a sudden
modulation to B minor [m. 231, revised version] and ends with a return
to that key [mm. 410–22], punctuated by several emphatic cadences, before its transition back to the E-flat tonic. Moreover, it lacks the thematic
reprise to justify its apparently willful closure on B minor.

Perhaps, then, there is an additional reason. The very uniqueness of
the passage may have counted against it. Possibly Schubert found it foreign to his style, depending as it does on a self-conscious device. It is true

---

[9] In a letter to Heinrich Albert Probst, his publisher, Schubert stipulates: "The cuts indicated in the first movement are to be most scrupulously observed." [Quoted in Otto Erich
Deutsch, ed., *The Schubert Reader: A Life of Franz Schubert in Letters and Documents*,
trans. Eric Blom (New York: W. W. Norton, 1947), p. 774.]

that to an unfriendly ear the passage may sound adventitious and even forced. On the other hand, it provides a point of focus for this hugely swollen movement. As a result, a careful listener may find that a performance of the complete score sounds shorter than one using the standard version. But whether Schubert's experiment was successful or not, he was trying to set the two musical ideas against each other in such a way as to illuminate the significance of each. In a word, he was using each to criticize the other—writing music to criticize music.

One can argue, of course, that in all the cases I have adduced, the true compositional process consists in the creation of new values rather than in the discovery of those already inherent in the material under musical discussion. Although the composer may have thought that he was revealing the hitherto-hidden import of a musical idea, he was wrong: there never was any such hidden import, and all additional meaning has been injected, not uncovered, by the composer. But one could say the same about any critical interpretation of a work of art: that the significance that the critic claims to find there has in fact been introduced by him. My answer is the same in both cases. If the critic, or the composer, can persuade us of the relevance of his interpretation, then it is valid. And that is what Schubert does. When he reworks a musical idea, he convinces us he is letting us hear what was there all the time, only we were too deaf to discover it for ourselves.

PART IV

Analysis

ALL FIVE OF THE primarily analytical essays deal with works by a single composer: one each for Schubert and Debussy and three for Stravinsky. Combined with the other two in this volume, however, the Schubert essay also makes three on that composer. Entitled "Schubert's Symphonic Poem," it deals with the Piano Fantasy and was apparently written to introduce a performance of that work. While it is among the more informal of these essays, it is especially valuable as a complement to the preceding one on Schubert as self-critic, which also looked briefly at that piece. But whereas there Cone related the Fantasy to the song "Der Wanderer," from which it was partly derived, here he treats the composition's overall nature and form. The connection with the song is taken up again at its end, however, leading to some fascinating and partly skeptical closing speculation on what Cone terms the "genetic fallacy": the belief that knowledge of a piece's creative chronology takes precedence over its internal, musical chronology.

"Debussy's Art of Suggestion" is a welcome rarity, treating a composer about whom Cone had previously said relatively little. Its central point is that most aspects of Debussy's style—his melody, phrase structure, form, quotation, and program music—depend as much on implicit suggestion as overt statement. Like some of the others, this essay seems to have been conceived to provide commentary for extended musical passages performed at the piano. Its insight into Debussy's path-breaking manner is nonetheless impressive.

The three Stravinsky essays, on the other hand, are concerned with a composer Cone often wrote about. Here, however, he examines the work from three essentially new perspectives. "Stravinsky at the Tomb of Rimsky-Korsakov" looks at the composer's orchestration, arguing that his way of handling instruments contradicts the notoriously negative position regarding musical meaning asserted in his *Autobiography*. "Stravinsky's Version of Pastoral" confines itself to a single work, the *Duo Concertant*, asking what it is that makes us hear it as "lyrical" and "pastoral." The result is one of Cone's signature analyses: brilliantly conceived, yet from an unexpected angle. Finally, "Stravinsky's Sense of Form" is the most analytically complex of all these essays. It revisits a topic—musical form—that occupied the author extensively and about which he wrote at length; yet its focus is on a recurring feature in Stravinsky's formal organization that Cone had previously left largely unexplored: symmetrical balance.

Schubert's Symphonic Poem

Schubert's Piano Fantasy in C major was written in 1822 and published by Cappi & Diabelli as Op. 15, early in the following year. Two contemporary comments are of particular interest:

> The fantasy has always been recognized as that kind of musical piece in which the composer's art, freed from the shackles of form, may most clearly unfold itself and wholly prove its worth. Herr Schubert has certified his master-hand in this latest work, in which he has shown that he not only possesses the gift of invention, but understands how to develop his felicitous themes according to all the exigencies of art. The present Fantasy stands worthily side by side with similar works by the foremost masters and therefore merits in every way the attention of all artists and lovers of art.[1]
>
> A fantasy is . . . a piece of music where an abundance of musical inventiveness is not subject to any . . . constraint of form and may, as it were, meander through the most delightful fields of musical art like a stream running in all directions and in any ramifications, freed of all obstructions. Such a piece of music may for that reason be best suited to a faithful reception and reproduction of the feelings which inspired the composer at the time of its creation; it may properly be regarded as a mirror of his soul. Seeing that a composer like Herr Schubert, who had already betrayed such profound sentiments in his generally esteemed songs, presents us with a soul-image of this kind, the musical world can only rejoice.[2]

The Fantasy was Schubert's only really virtuoso piano solo. For this reason pianists have always been attracted to it, perhaps more than to the sonatas, which have only become popular comparatively recently. One of the first was Liszt, who even made a piano concerto out of it in 1850 or 1851.[3] But there was another reason Liszt was attracted to it—the reason

---

[1] Quoted from an advertisement that appeared in the *Wiener Zeitung*, February 24, 1823.

[2] From a review in the *Allgemeine musikalische Zeitung*, April 30, 1823. I read both of these comments by way of evidence against the myth of the unknown, unloved Schubert. On this, see also Otto Biba, "Schubert's Position in Viennese Musical Life," *19th-Century Music* 3 (1979): 106–13.

[3] The concerto was first performed, though not by Liszt, on December 14, 1851. [See *New Grove Dictionary of Music and Musicians*, ed. Stanley Sadie (London: Macmillan, 2001), vol. 14, p. 836.]

that made this piece, much more than other greater pieces by Schubert, a forward-looking work: it is, as Tovey called it, "the earliest and best of all symphonic poems. . . . Schubert had not the slightest idea that he was writing a symphonic poem; but in that piece he achieved everything that Liszt attempted, even to the metamorphosis of whole sections."[4]

What does he mean? A symphonic poem, as developed by Liszt and later by Strauss, is an orchestral piece in one movement, based on some kind of literary or other extramusical program. Schubert's is for piano, it is in four movements, and it has, so far as we know, no program—except that suggested by the title by which it is known, a matter we shall address later.

The point is this: the essence of the symphonic poem, as developed by Liszt, was neither in its orchestration nor in its program. It was in its attempt to unite within a single movement all the various moods and tempi of a symphony, and to do so through the use of a single set of motifs and themes, transformed in various ways to produce the material of the various sections. Moreover, in some of Liszt's symphonic poems, as in some of his works not so called, like the piano sonata and some other piano pieces, there is an attempt to create a kind of double form (at least double): a form for each formal member, and an all-embracing form for the whole. For example, in the four movements of a symphony: the first movement is the exposition of Theme I; the slow movement is Theme II; the scherzo is the development; and the finale is the recapitulation. Thus the whole is a kind of sonata form encompassing the characters of the four symphonic movements.

Now that kind of treatment—unification of all movements, the use of a single set of motifs, a double form—is what we find in the Schubert Fantasy. In this respect it is unlike any other work of the period I can think of, except that extraordinary and unique movement, the finale of Beethoven's Ninth Symphony, first performed in 1824.

How does the Fantasy work in formal terms? The four movements, corresponding to the movements of a sonata, are: Allegro con fuoco ma non troppo, Adagio, Presto, and Allegro. But none of them, except the last, is complete; each, except for the last, ends on either a dominant of the key of the next movement (the first and third) or a dissonance (also the first and the second). Thus there is a grand cadential progression: I (C) to V6/5 of D-flat (first movement), ♭II (D-flat) to augmented sixth of A-flat (second), ♭VI (A-flat) to V of C (third), I (C) (fourth).

Formally, each movement suggests, but never quite completes, a standard pattern: sonata form, variations, scherzo, and fugue. And what is

[4] [Donald Francis Tovey, *Musical Articles from the Encyclopedia Britannica* (London: Oxford University Press, 1944), p. 236.]

more, all the themes of all the movements can be derived from a common source: the opening of the first. The work's first three measures are almost sufficient. One can distinguish in this motif three components: the rhythmic opening, the rising arpeggio, and the rising third with its chromatic interpolation. Later the theme adds one more important element: C–E–D [m. 28].

The first theme of the Allegro is clearly developed at the opening and proceeds as if in normal sonata form. But as we go further in the movement, we are constantly offered new ways of looking at it and confronted with several questions: where is the real second theme, the real development, the real recapitulation? More and more the movement resembles a stream-of-consciousness, each episode calling forth the next without reference to a predetermined pattern. (This too makes it a forward-looking work, suggesting another reason why Liszt should be interested.)

In particular, the first movement suggests that we take longer and longer formal perspectives, as suggested in table 10.1. In each of the three perspectives there are questions regarding the second half. In the first, are the returns of the first and second themes simply repetitions, and thus form a recapitulation without development; or are they a development of the first half? Similarly, in the second and third, are Theme II and the Adagio actually developments, and should a transition be indicated?

The Adagio is a free theme and variations. The theme has four sections: I–I [mm. 1–4], I–III [5–8], III–V [9–13], and III–I [14–18]. It is

TABLE 10.1
Schubert, Piano Fantasy, Movement 1: Three Increasingly Larger Formal Perspectives (the Last Including Movement 2)

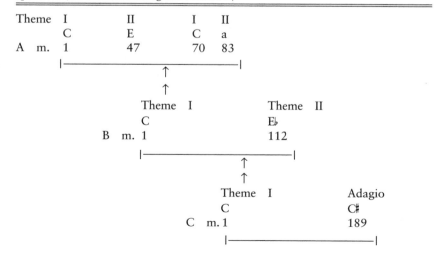

followed by a short development and then the variations, which concern only the first two periods of the theme. There are two of these [mm. 27ff., 39ff.], but because of changes of texture and treatment they sound like four. The second again leads to a development, after which there is a coda [m. 49ff.]. Note the pianistic writing here, which surpasses even Beethoven in its impressionist treatment and, in the coda, textural cloudiness. Again, Liszt would have loved it.

If the Adagio is a development in terms of the whole, then the Scherzo is a recapitulation; or if the Adagio is a second theme, the Scherzo is a development. But actually, the Scherzo can be seen as either! Thematically it is a recapitulation, as the first movement's first theme recurs in the Scherzo and the second (the E-flat major one) recurs in the Trio [m. 179ff.].[5] But in key the Scherzo is not a recapitulation: it is in A-flat, and the Trio in D-flat. So if it is a recapitulation, it is a false one. And instead of a complete reprise after the Trio, the return [m. 268ff.] moves into another development or transition, returning to the original C major.

So now we get the real finale. It is a fugue at first, but it becomes a free virtuoso movement. As a very free transformation of the original theme, it can be said to recapitulate all of its versions, so that whatever we want to take as the exposition—whether part of the first movement, the whole first movement, or the first movement plus the Adagio—the finale is a free recapitulation of it!

Because of the tempo and the fugue subject, it sounds closest to the first movement, lending some favor to this design:

Allegro	Adagio	Scherzo	Finale
Exposition	Development	False Recapitulation	Recapitulation

So perhaps that is how the piece was composed: a constantly varying development from a single theme presented at the opening. But no, that is not how the piece was composed. And here we must turn to the question of the work's present title: the *Wanderer* Fantasy. In 1816 Schubert had composed a song to a poem of that name by Schmidt von Lübeck; and it was published in 1821 in a revised version as Op. 4 No. 1 (D. 493a), becoming very popular. The second stanza of that version is the source of the theme of the Fantasy's second movement; and the first stanza is used for part of the second half of the theme.[6] Historically, then, this is the

---

[5] There is also a new theme in the Scherzo, the latter's own second theme [m. 79ff.]. (Interestingly, this theme, which is the furthest of any from the material of the first movement, is said to quote a borrowed popular waltz by Wenzel Müller.)

[6] [A more detailed discussion of the Adagio's derivation from the song appears in the previous essay, "Schubert Criticizes Schubert."]

source theme; and the first movement was developed from it, not vice versa. But we must be careful. In the first place, we don't really know that this is the case. Maybe Schubert started composing the fantasy as we suggested originally—with the first movement, and the stream of consciousness we referred to led him, perhaps unconsciously, to the theme he had used before in the "Wanderer."[7]

But let us assume that Schubert did indeed intentionally use his song as a basis for the composition: that he composed the Allegro using the material of the song, and not vice versa. Should that alter the way we hear the piece? No. The piece as it stands is as I have described it: a fantasy developed from its opening measures. That is the way it unfolds in time, and that is the way the composer meant us to hear it.

There is today a great deal of what we might call genetic criticism. There is a lot of interest in sketches, preliminary versions, revisions, etcetera. Sometimes we forget that the real locus of aesthetic interest is the finished work, that the composer did not mean for us to see his sketches, that all the information he intended for us to have is right there in the final version. To use our knowledge of the origin of the Fantasy, then, as a means of criticizing the work—i.e., as a way of getting inside it and understanding it—is wrong. In fact, if anything it works the other way: we can use the Fantasy as a way of understanding the song. It is, to a certain extent, a comment on the song.

That is the way I originally intended to end this essay. But I was vaguely dissatisfied with this so to speak anti-historical presentation, one I once expressed in an essay on musical form: "Viewing the entire [Fantasy] as an object, one could see the Adagio as a center from which the three surrounding movements are derived. Historically [from the point of view of its creation], that would be correct. But temporally [from the point of view of the listener] . . . we hear the Adagio and the two subsequent movements as derived from the first."[8] But suppose we hear both the song and the fantasy together? Then, as I suggested in a later study of thematic derivation, "One who is familiar with the song and is aware of the chronology of the two compositions might possibly wish to consider them together and thus to hear the Adagio as a spectacular case of rederivation—after a period of years!"[9] But recently I came up with yet another suggestion: "Perhaps . . . there are really two Fantasies. One is

[7] Schubert himself didn't give the work the title "Wanderer"; and the song is not mentioned in either of the contemporary write-ups quoted at the opening of this essay.

[8] ["Music and Form," in *What Is Music?*, ed. Philip Alperson (University Park: Pennsylvania State University Press, 1994), p. 140.]

[9] ["On Derivation: Syntax and Rhetoric," *Music Analysis* 6, no. 3 (1987): 250–51.]

the Fantasy alone, in which the derivations occur as the piece unfolds in time. The other is the Song-plus-Fantasy, in which the remembered song is gradually disclosed by rederivation. The latter is the richer of the two versions. . . ."[10]

---

[10] ["Responses," written in reply to essays by a group of music scholars participating in a panel on *The Composer's Voice*, published in *College Music Symposium* 29 (1989): 76.]

Debussy's Art of Suggestion

ORIGINALLY, I INTENDED to call this essay "Debussy's Art of Implication." Then I realized that implication has two distinct meanings: one referring to something without specifically mentioning it; the other, leading to a logically justified conclusion. And since I did not wish to get involved in the question of musical logic, which I consider at best a rather crude metaphor, I chose to use the term "suggestion"—although I shall occasionally refer to implication in its suggestive sense. But although I shall be dealing with an art of suggestion, I want to try to deal with it as clearly and unsuggestively as possible. The trouble with a lot of writing about Debussy is that the writers seem to think that to talk about ambiguity one must be ambiguous, to talk about vagueness one must be vague.

SYMBOLISM AND IMPRESSIONISM

In the interest of this proposed clarity, then, the first thing I wish to do is to get out of the way, so far as possible, the question of Debussy the Impressionist and Debussy the Symbolist. I find myself on the whole sympathetic with the point of view of the Polish musicologist Stefan Jarocinski. In his book on Debussy, he begins by showing the inadequacy, and indeed the inapplicability, of the "Impressionist" label. He finds Debussy closer to Symbolist poetry in his ideals and his methods; but he ends by admitting that to substitute symbolism for impressionism as a characterization of Debussy would be "to replace a greater by a lesser evil, without emerging from the labyrinth of erroneous generalizations."[1]

One understands, nevertheless, what these generalizations were getting at. Impressionism in painting, as we know, was a form of extreme realism; the painters were trying to paint the effects of light as accurately as possible. But in their emphasis on pure color they had to suggest shapes by blurred outlines. The board of the *Academie des Beaux-Arts*

---

[1] [Stefan Jarocinski, *Debussy, Impressionism and Symbolism*, trans. from French by Rollo Myers (London: Eulenburg Books, 1976), p. 159. The book was originally published in Polish in 1966 and translated into French by Thèrése Douchy, in 1976 (Paris: Seuil). Page references are to the English version; Cone's translations, however, are evidently his own, made from the French edition.]

must have felt something of the same thing going on in Debussy's *Printemps*, a work he sent back during his Roman fellowship in 1887: "One recognizes here a feeling for musical color, the exaggeration of which makes it easy for him to forget the importance of line and form. It would be very desirable for him to guard against this vague 'impressionism,' which is one of the most dangerous enemies of truth in works of art."[2] No wonder that Debussy disliked the term as applied to his music.

He found himself much more sympathetic with Mallarmé and the symbolists around him. He took part in their *mardis*—Tuesday salons hosted by Mallarmé—and he set their poetry. No doubt he read or heard these famous words by Mallarmé with complete approval:

> To *name* an object is to suppress three quarters of the poetic enjoyment, which comes from finding out, little by little; to *suggest* it: therein lies the dream. It's the perfect use of this mystery that constitutes the symbolic.[3]

One can of course make a connection between this kind of poetic evocation and the programmatic aspects of Debussy's music. And indeed Debussy himself has encouraged us to think of him as a tone poet or tone painter:

> Music is precisely the art that is closest to nature, the one that spreads the subtlest net . . . only the musicians have the privilege of capturing all the poetry of night and day, of earth and sky, of reconstructing its atmosphere and of rhythmicizing its immense throbbing.[4]

But it does him an injustice to think of him solely, or even mainly, in such terms. Jarocinski may exaggerate, but he is surely on the right track when he calls Debussy the "purest musician" since Mozart. It will be primarily from this point of view—to regard him as first of all an absolute musician—that I wish to approach the music. I will try to be as systematic as possible, and hence not chronological.

PHRASE CONNECTIONS

I will start with a familiar work, the *Reflets dans l'eau* from the first set of *Images* (1905), because that is where I really got my start on this investigation—many years ago when I was in high school and my piano

---

[2] [Cited in Jarocinski, *Debussy, Impressionism and Symbolism*, p. 11.]

[3] [Cited in Jarocinski, *Debussy, Impressionism and Symbolism*, p. 32, quoted from Stéphane Mallarmé, *Oeuvres Complètes* (Paris: La Pléiade, 1945), p. 897.]

[4] [Cited in Jarocinski, *Debussy, Impressionism and Symbolism*, p. 96. See also *Debussy on Music*, ed. François Lesure and trans. Richard Langham Smith (New York: Alfred A. Knopf, 1977), p. 295.]

teacher used to play it. Whenever I *heard* the opening theme, I thought I heard a balanced melody: a phrase consisting of a single motif of three slow notes, requiring a resolution that came in an answering phrase [mm. 1–4]. But when I *saw* the music, I looked in vain for the resolution: it was even difficult to find that the chord of the first phrase had been resolved, and as for melody—there was none. I looked at the two reprises [m. 36ff., m. 72ff.]: the same thing again. Was I wrong, then, in hearing the answer that I thought I heard? Not if Debussy intended the piece's conclusion as relevant. For here, spelled out—although rather lazily and unwillingly—was an answer to the first phrase, very much like the one I had thought I had heard.

What I like to think Debussy was doing here—intentionally or not—was offering an explanation of his suggestive mode of presenting a melody—by stating the first half and then leaving the completion up to the listener. What he has done is to leave space for us to supply the melody, by continuing the accompaniment, its harmony, texture, and rhythm. (Another subtler point is the missing leading tone just before the first reprise [m. 35], which I also thought I heard.) We can find variations of this technique, more complex, but basically similar.

Cloches à travers les feuilles, from the second book of *Images* (1907), begins with a whole-tone motif that is already more suggestive, in the sense that its harmonic possibilities are so much more open, or vaguer. The first double statement [mm. 3–4] is followed merely by a continuation of the same whole-tone harmony [m. 5]. The second statement [mm. 6–8] offers two different possible directions [mm. 9–10, 11–12]. But only in the reprise does the continuation suggest a real tonal resolution, to F [mm. 40–43]. One can even imagine a tonal form of the motif as an answer here—although it is defeated by the final chord [mm. 44–49].

In *The Little Shepherd*, from *Children's Corner* (1908), we find a more irregular situation. A little phrase of two measures [mm. 5–6] is repeated and extended to three measures, ending on V7 [mm. 7–9]. But now, instead of any answering melody, we have simply a V–I cadence [mm. 9–11]—a truncation, as it were, of the space needed for the answering group. And in *Minstrels*, from Preludes I (1910), even that space is missing: the opening phrase, twice stated, I–V [mm. 1–4; 5–8], is followed, not by its own answer, but by an entirely new theme. The same thing happens in the reprise [m. 78ff.], only this time interrupted after a single statement by the drum figure [m. 62ff.]—which doesn't really give us space to imagine an answer, since it only prolongs the V, with a new rhythm.

In *Et la lune descend sur le temple qui fut* (from *Images* II), there is a peculiar combination of techniques. The folk-like theme is first presented over a pentatonic motif in counterpoint [mm. 12–15], as an isolated interruption in key and material of the opening section. But when it returns, it suggests a balance: the folk theme appears first [mm. 25–26], with two balancing measures standing in for an unspoken consequent [mm. 27–28]; then the pentatonic motif, replacing the folk theme for two measures of a hypothetical—but *not* balanced—repetition [mm, 29–30], continues as if there had merely been another but lengthier interruption. But then the answering two measures come again later, as yet another interruption of the opening material [mm. 41–42]. The last appearance of the folk and pentatonic pair is in the same order—folk, then pentatonic— but no longer beginning as an interruption of the opening material, but *over* it, and now providing conclusion [m. 51–57].

SUGGESTION

So far we have considered Debussy's very personal treatment of the classical periodic form of balancing phrases. I do not mean to imply that Debussy does not use complete balancing phrases—only that they are rare, and often in the spirit of naiveté, or to represent popular music. But very often Debussy avoids all reference to periodic structure, stated or implied, by reducing his melody to a single isolated motif. Whereas we might call the incomplete period "implicative," since an answer is implied but not stated, these other motifs are purely suggestive—they are usually open both melodically and harmonically, and they could lead almost anywhere. This usage appears very early in Debussy. In *Nuages* (ca. 1895–99), the first of the *Nocturnes*, the English horn motif [mm. 5–8] is never developed: it is stated first in isolation, then against a moving background, sometimes with tiny variations [mm. 21–24, 25–28], and then extended (after a fashion) by horns [mm. 43–47, 50–51] and low strings. The opening statement gives us all the material this motif needs: it never changes, except for these slight variations; only its background is altered.

This piece perhaps presents the Debussyian motif in its purest form. To drive the point home, let me contrast Wagner's leitmotif technique, with which Debussy's technique has often been compared. I don't deny a close relation—much of Debussy comes right out of Wagner, especially from *Parsifal*, a work Debussy continued to revere even when he turned against Wagner in general. But consider a typical Wagnerian motif, say "Walhalla." One can think of it in isolation, but it does violence to do so. When we first hear it, it is immediately developed; and only after that long development does it reappear—and only occasionally—in isolation. When, rarely, a motif is *announced* in isolation, it is merely an adumbration of what is to come. The "Sword," which seems to come out of the blue when it first appears at the end of *Rheingold*, returns the next night to be subjected to a lengthy development.

One can justly say of the English horn motif in *Nuages* that, despite the possibilities it suggests, nothing ever really happens to it: it never really gets anywhere. That is certainly not always the case. *Feux d'artifice*, from Preludes II, is just as dependent on a single motif as *Nuages*; but here the motif is allowed to move in many directions. Yet even here there is no true development but only *suggestions* of development, hints of the various forms it might take. But none of these is completed. Even its last development [20 measures from the end] simply explodes and fizzles, perhaps symbolic of Debussy's low opinion of conventional development.

At the other extreme is *Les Sons et les parfums tournent dans l'air du soir* (Preludes I). Here the motif sets up a stream of consciousness. On the one hand, this stream may latch on to a fragment of the motif, as at the beginning [mm. 3–8, where its closing falling interval is developed], and let it suggest its own melody; on the other, it may move rapidly from one motif to another in a kaleidoscopic play of images [m. 34ff.]—a sort of free association, in which many possibilities are suggested but none followed through.[5]

Debussy, as we know, wished to avoid strict repetition, and hence strict recapitulation: "Do you think that in a composition the same emotion can be expressed twice?" "I should like to achieve a music truly free of motifs, or formed from a single continuous motif, which nothing interrupts and which never returns on itself."[6] Of course he never did achieve this, but still it is not surprising to find reprises merely hinted at rather than stated (as in *La Fille aux cheveux de lin*, where the real reprise is completely disguised). In *Poissons d'or*, from *Images* II, for example, the opening theme promises some periodicity: a six-measure phrase (extended to seven), I–V [mm. 3–9]. There then follows an answering four-measure phrase, elaborating V [mm. 10–13], which is repeated, leading to a chord that turns out to be an altered VI [m. 18], extended for four measures. But when the opening theme is then immediately repeated, it dissolves on the fifth measure [m. 21–26]. And when it is recapitulated, the first phrase begins away from I and, extended to eight measures, moves to V [mm. 86–93]. And instead of an answer, there is a cadenza that closes the piece in the tonic [m. 94ff.], thus suggesting a kind of concealed consequent.

---

[5] The result, I confess, is not always successful: I'm not really happy about this piece.

[6] [Cited in Jarocinski, *Debussy, Impressionism and Symbolism*, p. 98 and p. 106. Jarocinski quotes both from André Fontainas, *Mes souvenirs du symbolisme* (Paris: La Nouvelle Revue Critique, 1928), pp. 92–93.]

FORM

Here we merge with another and more far-reaching technique: the suggestion of a musical form without completing it. Debussy investigates this as early as the song *Beau soir* (1891), where the postlude has to stand in for the entire reprise. The form is: introduction, mm. 1–4; section A, mm. 5–19 (to V of V); section B, mm. 20–34 (to V), postlude, mm. 35–41 (I). But the postlude not only brings back the piano introduction complete but suggests a return of the A section, aided by the return of the voice for its final phrase, which mimics the opening of its first.

The drum imitation in *Minstrels*, mentioned previously, obviously introduces an important division of the form, and the music-hall parody that follows could well stand in for a sort of trio [m. 63ff.]. But we are given only the suggestion of the typical ballad form—the end of its first phrase [mm. 63–67] and then a phrase that would perhaps come in the trio's reprise [mm. 67–71]. There are only twelve measures in all, followed by a retransition to the reprise. And the reprise is cut down to a minimum, the drumbeats returning to introduce the brief coda. So the form of the whole, a larger ternary, and that of the ballad, a small ternary, are *both* truncated.

In the Sonata for Violin and Piano the title naturally leads us to expect a certain form, particularly in the first movement. And the beginning seems auspicious: a piano introduction, followed by a tentative thematic statement [m. 5], with a melodic and harmonic extension that leads to a firm downbeat cadence on the tonic [R1 (rehearsal 1)]. What now ensues therefore sounds like a definitive statement of some kind—the confirmation of the first theme and its key before modulating to the second theme. That is indeed what seems to happen; but this statement never recurs: the vigorous piano theme [2 after R1], with its distinctive violin countersubject, is heard once only. In addition, the modulation to the second theme is aborted: instead of the expected F, adumbrated from the very first two chords, we have a distant E; and instead of a sonata-like second subject we have a new section in a slower tempo (even with a new meter) and a new texture—a dreamy violin meditation over a piano ostinato [*Meno mosso*, 21 after R2]. This section goes its own way, converting the apparent sonata form into something more like a huge song form and trio. But when the original idea is recapitulated [R4], it is combined with motifs from the middle section—both simultaneously and successively. So three kinds of form are suggested, and blended: sonata, ternary, and "synthesis."

In the finale, after an introduction recalling the first movement, a theme is introduced that might well be the refrain of a rondo [m. 29: 9/16 meter]—and so it seems for a while. Then the movement reaches an important turning point with a modulation and retard. Apparently the "big" contrasting section has arrived {*Le double plus lent*], and four measures of introduction prepare us even further. But what we get is a theme consisting of only one phrase, sounding as if it is improvised by the violin, and filled out by a return to the four measures of introduction. So an entire contrasting middle section has been condensed into fifteen measures. This is, incidentally, one of several such passages in the finale, which thus seems a much longer movement than it really is.

HARMONY

Accounts of Debussy's harmony are, in my opinion, often oversimplified. They are based, in the main, on a contrast between functional and coloristic uses of harmony. This is certainly a useful distinction: functional harmony is the use of chordal progressions to define a key according to the standard usages of tonality; whereas coloristic harmony is the use of chords for their own sake, for their sheer sound, for either the sound of the chord itself (V9, whole-tone, etc.) or its contrast with its neighbors. But this distinction is too gross, especially for a composer like Debussy, whose use of harmony is subtle in the extreme. So we must look for gradations of distinction between the two extremes.

Let me start by distinguishing between two possibilities of functional harmony: chords whose functional implications are immediately fulfilled (the normal case) and those in which those implications are postponed (as in the Prelude to *Tristan*).[7] But now suppose that a resolution, strongly implied as before, is not merely postponed, but simply omitted, as is the case with the previously mention expected F in the first movement of the Violin Sonata before the second theme. Here we can speak of a harmony—indeed of a key—that is present by implication, but only by implication. Though F is never directly stated, however, one cannot understand the harmonic processes of the movement without taking it into account. One may argue whether Debussy wanted us to hear this implication. May he not have wanted us merely to hear the chords as pure sonorities? But for an answer, look at the cadence on G in the first theme [R1]. Here we have at least three quasi-dominants, to F, B, and G [5, 3, and 1 measure before R1] (and perhaps D as well), and the V of G is satisfied. And that satisfaction tells us, surely, that we are supposed to hear a V7 as an actual dominant. So we must take all three dominants seriously and hear three keys as implied, of which only the last is explicitly stated. (Even in the half cadences of the middle theme of the second

---

[7][See Cone's comments on the *Tristan* Prelude in section 3 of "The Silent Partner," included in this volume.]

movement, where none of the dominants is satisfied, the last one does lead to a V–I in C [m. 53].)

What often takes the place of harmonic resolution is what we might call contrapuntal resolution: the individual notes of the chord resolve stepwise, as polyphonic voices, ignoring the possible harmonic implications. At the end of the second movement of the Violin Sonata, for example, the dominant of G-flat [9 measures before end] resolves to C instead of G-flat, so that the voice leading is completely stepwise. But let us go one step further. Suppose we juxtapose these implicative chords directly in a parallel fashion, whether literally or simply parallel in function, thus avoiding the laws of tonal voice leading. If it is done like Wagner, leaving out the intervening steps (as in the *Verklärung* from *Tristan*), we get a kind of transfer of implication from one chord to the next similar one. And this is one reason why classical harmony forbids such parallelism, since each chord *suggests* a new key, with no transitional connection; and that is one reason why Debussy delighted in it.

Sometimes Debussy uses such harmonic parallelism but keeps the implications in mind. In *La Fille aux cheveux de lin* (Preludes I) there is a passage, stated twice, that simultaneously combines components suggesting two different keys, followed by a single-chord resolution that suggests a combination of both resolutions [mm. 8–11]. This double harmony, with one chord suggested over another, returns in varied form for the prelude's final cadence [mm. 28–32].[8]

Sometimes Debussy uses such parallelism so quickly that we cannot hear the individual implications, as in the *Sarabande* from *Pour le piano* (1896–1901). This is one possible meaning of coloristic harmony: harmony in which the implications move so fast that we cannot take them in (and dissonances are not necessary for this effect). Some chords and progressions, on the other hand, are so open to a number of possible resolutions or continuations that we can hardly speak of implication but must fall back on suggestion. Debussy loved harmony of this kind; hence his predilection for the whole-tone scale, which often forms a chord such as an altered dominant ninth, combining two augmented chords. (Consider the two different resolutions of the whole-tone chord—discussed previously—at the beginning and end of *Cloches à travers les feuilles*.) The nearest to a pure whole-tone composition is of course *Voiles*. Here, in the central section, an E-flat chord is presented as one resolution of

[8][The harmony of the repeated passage at m. 8 suggests functional resolution to C-flat, while the melodic material suggests G-flat (to which the passage ultimately resolves at m. 11). When the passage returns at m. 29, the G-flat melodic material actually does sound over a C-flat major chord; but it again resolves to G-flat at m. 32, this time through E-flat minor (cf. m. 6).]

the whole-tone material; but note that the key is there only by implication, as a tonic 6/4 chord. And the end of the piece is very vague—not necessarily pointing to the same E-flat resolution or to any other. Indeed, here one might raise the question: does the whole-tone need a resolution? Is not the sense of the piece perhaps the opposite of what I have seemed to suggest, namely that the whole-tone is the "key" and the E-flat the "dissonance" needing resolution back into the whole-tone? (Tempting as this may be, however, I think the rhetoric of the piece works against that solution.)

I have mentioned the suggestion of one chord simultaneously over another. Sometimes this becomes one key over another, as at the end of *Feux d'artifice*, where both C and D-flat are suggested [last nine measures]. The same contrast is at work more extensively in *Brouillards* (also Preludes II). Here C is strongly implied by the left-hand chords at the beginning (which are not strictly parallel), though the harmony is also not entirely functional. But against these chords there is a cloud of sound suggesting G-flat and D-flat [later spelled F-sharp and C-sharp]. The motif turns V of C into V of C-sharp (= D-flat), which resolves [at m. 18ff.]. Near the end, the cadence is diverted back to C [mm. 38–43ff.]; but note that the end remains ambiguous, with neither key resolved.

More subtle is the use of certain modal scales to suggest more than one key. One of Debussy's favorites is the dorian: G dorian, for example, can also represent C mixolydian, or F major. At the opening of the Violin Sonata, the first two chords could suggest any one of those three keys. But the new chord at m. 8—E-flat minor—fits none of them. In fact, it contradicts each of the preceding ones; so if the first two are suggestive, this one is counter-suggestive. Here then is yet another kind of coloristic harmony—one that clashes with *any* suggested key. But the following dominant chord strongly implies G (major, not minor); and when G minor follows, it does not cadence but moves again to C major! The stage is set for what follows. We have seen that F is hinted at, but the main course of the movement (and of the whole sonata) depends on the relation between G and C. At the end of each movement there is a strong C followed by G. Indeed, I believe that the only real authentic V–I cadence in the piece is the one (with minor V) we noticed previously [mm. 12–14]. As a result, one feels that it is almost a matter of chance whether we end on C or G. This then is not functional tonality, either stated or implied, but what we might call "suggestive tonality": a system that sets up not one key but a family of suggested keys, relying not on harmonic necessity but on subtleties of rhythm, dynamics, voice leading, and texture to determine a satisfactory impression of a tonic.[9]

---

[9] [Debussy's harmony is also discussed in "The Silent Partner," printed above.]

QUOTATION

We can now return to the question we touched on at the outset—the poetic or pictorial symbolism that many find embodied in Debussy's works. Despite the literary and pictorial interest of his titles, and despite the interest in musical landscape painting revealed by his words, Debussy is rarely an out-and-out composer of program music. (*Feux d'artifice* is in this respect one of the few exceptions.) Usually his programmatic ideas are expressed in the form of motivic fragments, which tend to be more isolated than is usual. They often evoke instrumental sounds: the *sonneries de Cors* at the end of *Les Sons et parfums*; the panpipe in *La Flûte de Pan* [m. 1], the first of the *Trois chansons de Bilitis*; the distant dance in *Soirée dans Granade* [m. 61ff.] (*Estampes*); the "Marseillaise" at the end of *Feux d'artifice* [seven measures before the final bar]. And as we see, these are often afterthoughts—new rhythms introduced toward the end of a work by way of colorful contrast—and suggestive of another spatial dimension by virtue of the implied distance.

The "Marseillaise" in *Feux d'artifice* also illustrates Debussy's use of quotation. It is rarely complete, including only enough, as here, to remind us of the source. Its treatment is more heavy-handed in *Hommage à S. Pickwick Esq. P.P.M.P.C.* [m. 1] (Preludes II) and *En blanc et noir* [II, 27 measures after R1], though in neither of these works is the quotation actually complete. The same is true of the *Nous n'irons plus au bois* quote in *Jardins sous la pluie (Estampes)*, a well-known example [m. 75ff.].[10] More successfully humorous, on the other hand, is the reference to *Tristan* in *Golliwogg's Cakewalk* (from *Children's Corner*) [m. 61]— just enough to suggest an entire parody.

SYMBOLISM AND PÉLLEAS ET MÉLISANDE

To consider the symbolic aspect more seriously, we might recall Debussy's words about the *Pastoral* Symphony. With regard to the bird imitations in Beethoven's "Scene at the Brook," he wrote:

> It is unnecessarily imitative and the interpretation is entirely arbitrary. How much more profound an interpretation of the beauty of a landscape do we find in other passages in the great Master, because, instead of an exact imitation, there is an emotional interpretation of what is invisible in Nature. Can

---

[10] [The entire piece alternates between material derived from two French children's songs. The one Cone does not mention, *Dodo, l'enfant do, l'enfant dormira bientôt*, appears in m. 1.]

the mystery of a forest be expressed by measuring the height of the trees? Is it not rather its fathomless depths that stir the imagination?[11]

If Debussy did indulge at times in tone painting, he thus preferred to suggest rather than depict objects, just as he preferred to suggest his musical objects. Perhaps one might say that for him the musical suggestion was symbolic of the pictorial or poetic suggestion.

Certainly he matched musical and poetic suggestion in *Pélleas et Mélisande*. Recall the opening of the Prelude of Act 1. Here, in three striking musical motifs, three dramatic motifs are adumbrated. One is a somber background, consisting of a circularly repetitious melody and a harmonic progression that is tonally relatively explicit. The other two are melodic figures which suggest protagonists, as it were [mm. 5–6/12–13, and mm. 14–17]. Both contrast with the background in being tonally very unclear and projected over a static pedal. Yet the two are also sharply differentiated from one another, one being primarily rhythmic and the other primarily melodic. They are first given in isolation, then in uneasy counterpoint to each other [mm. 18–19], linked by a common chord. If we momentarily forget Debussy's distrust of the leitmotif—his denial that a given succession of chords can represent a given feeling or a given phrase a certain person—we can name the three the "Forest," "Golaud," and "Mélisande." But can we find any specific descriptive elements to link the motifs with these names? Later, for example, because of dramatic context, orchestration, harmonization, we may find Golaud's motif threatening, but not here. No specific action, not even any specific character, is portrayed. What we can say is that here the motif is, like Mélisande herself, rootless (as is literally true of all but the first motif).

It is thus better not to look for literal programmatic meanings. Rather, we should just note that in two short pages Debussy has suggested a dramatic idea: two protagonists, both lost, coming together in an uneasy alliance against their surroundings; and that this has been done by suggesting a musical procedure—the statement of three themes in succession and then in combination—that it took Wagner the whole of the *Meistersinger* Overture to work out in overt statement.

---

[11] [Claude Debussy, *Monsieur Croche the Dilettante Hater* (London: Noel Douglas, 1927), p. 88. Also in Lesure, *Debussy on Music*, pp. 117–18.]

Stravinsky at the Tomb of Rimsky-Korsakov

AS INTRODUCTION, I SHOULD like to take a text from my own book, *The Composer's Voice*. In the chapter called "A Lesson from Berlioz" I wrote:

> So far as I know, Berlioz never tried to expound a general dramatistic theory of instrumentation, but his treatise on the subject attests on almost every page to his faith in the power and the duty of each instrument to individualize and bring to life the musical ideas assigned to it.

> Here are just a few examples culled from his pages devoted to the woodwinds: "The feelings of being abandoned, forgotten, and mournfully isolated that this forsaken melody [at the end of the third movement of the *Fantastic Symphony*] arouses in the hearts of some of its hearers would not have one quarter of their effect if it were assigned to any instrument but the English horn." "The lower register [of the clarinet] is well suited, especially in sustained tones, to those *coldly threatening* effects, those dark accents of *motionless rage*, whose discovery is due to Weber's ingenuity." "[The middle and higher registers of the flute] can be used for various kinds of melodies and accents, without however being able to match either the naïve cheerfulness of the oboe or the noble tenderness of the clarinet."

> It is little wonder that Berlioz's absorbing concern for this expressive character *of* the instruments should lead him to the concept of instrument *as* character—and that is exactly what happened. Here, for instance, is what he has to say about the use of the clarinet in its middle register: "Its voice is that of heroic love; and if the united brasses in grand military symphonies arouse us to thoughts of a troop of warriors clad in glittering armor, marching to glory or death, the sound of numerous clarinets in unison, heard in the same context, seems to represent their women: their beloved wives, their proud-eyed, deeply passionate lovers, who are inspired by the sound of arms, who sing in the midst of battle, who crown the victors or die with the vanquished."

> Today we are inclined to laugh at such instrumental personification as a typical excess of ingenuous Romanticism. It may therefore come as a surprise to find Stravinsky adopting a not dissimilar point of view, and in the very book that claims that "music is, by its very nature, essentially powerless to *express* anything at all." And in describing a lost *Chant funèbre* [of 1908] that he had written to the memory of Rimsky-Korsakov, he states that "all the solo instruments of the orchestra filed past the tomb of the master in succession, each

laying down its own melody as its wreath against a deep background of trem-olo murmurings simulating the vibrations of bass voices singing in chorus."[1]

Nor is this the only Stravinsky remark of this kind. There is the fa-mous passage describing the genesis of *Petroushka*:

I wanted to refresh myself by composing an orchestral piece in which the piano would play the most important part . . . I had in my mind a distinct pic-ture of a puppet, suddenly endowed with life, exasperating the patience of the orchestra with diabolical cascades of arpeggios. The orchestra in turn retali-ates with menacing trumpet blasts. The outcome is a terrific noise which reaches its climax and ends in the sorrowful and querulous collapse of the poor puppet." Or his description of the *Symphonies of Wind Instruments*: "It is an austere ritual which is unfolded in terms of short litanies between differ-ent groups of homogeneous instruments"; and his mention of "the *cantilène* of clarinets and flutes, frequently taking up again their liturgical dialogue and softly chanting it."[2]

Stravinsky was certainly familiar with Berlioz's music; it was much played in Russia, and he states that he heard a good deal of it. He ad-mired his "perfect imagination of each new instrument he used, as well as the knowledge of its technique. But the music he had to instrumentate was often poorly constructed harmonically."[3] And he goes on to criticize his basses and his voice leading. So I do not mean to claim any direct con-nection here. Still, before going on to look at Stravinsky's music from this point of view, which we might call an instrumental-dramatistic one, it might be interesting to speculate as to whether there might not be a con-nection with Berlioz through Stravinsky's teacher Rimsky-Korsakov—for whom, you will remember, the *Chant funèbre* with the parading instru-ments was composed.

Rimsky-Korsakov tells us in his autobiography of teaching himself or-chestration from Berlioz's treatise, since his teacher, Balakirev, seemed to be deficient in this knowledge. In fact, Rimsky-Korsakov writes of using natural brasses in Balakirev's circle as late as 1866, for they were still following the *Traité*: "And yet all that would have been necessary was a talk and consultation with some practical musician. However, that was

---

[1] [Edward T. Cone, *The Composer's Voice* (Berkeley: University of California Press, 1974), pp. 81–83. The three Berlioz quotations are from the *Grand traité d'instrumentation et d'orchestration modernes* (Paris: Schonenberger [1843]), pp. 124, 137, and 154. The Stravinsky quotes are from *Stravinsky: An Autobiography* (New York: W. W. Norton, 1962 [1936]), pp. 53 and 24.]

[2] [Stravinsky, *An Autobiography*, pp. 31 and 95.]

[3] [Igor Stravinsky and Robert Craft, *Conversations with Igor Stravinsky* (New York: Doubleday, 1959), p. 28.]

too humiliating for us. We followed Berlioz rather than some talentless orchestra leader."[4]

I think Rimsky's study may have had some effect in the direction of our interest. For example, he says: "In general, I had always been inclined to more or less individualization of separate instruments. In this sense, *Snegurochka* [*The Snow Maiden*] abounds in all manner of instrumental solos, for both wind and string instruments. . . . Solos for violin, cello, flute, oboe and clarinet occur very frequently in it, especially solos for the clarinet. . . ." And he describes the solo violin that characterizes *Scheherezade* as "delineating Scheherezade herself as telling her wondrous tales to the stern sultan."[5]

In his *Principles of Orchestration* we find Rimsky-Korsakov, in a much more pedantic manner than Berlioz, characterizing the instruments, as he puts it, "from a psychological point of view." Flute: "cold in quality." Oboe: "artless and gay in the major, pathetic and sad in the minor." Clarinet: "pliable and expressive." Bassoon: "in the major, an atmosphere of senile mockery; a sad ailing quality in the minor." In low registers, the oboe becomes "wild," the clarinet "ringing, threatening," the bassoon "sinister."[6] And so on. And when we realize that Rimsky-Korsakov taught Stravinsky orchestration from 1903 to 1906, we should expect something of this attitude to rub off.

Be that as it may, it is clear that Stravinsky did develop his own vivid sense of instruments, not only as *characteristic*, but as *characters*. Here are some other interesting examples, taken this time from his various books of conversations. On the *Epitaphium*: "I conceive[d] the idea of a series of funeral responses between bass and treble instruments."[7] On *L'Histoire du soldat*: "[T]he characteristic sounds of *Histoire* are the scrape of the violin and the punctuation of the drums. The violin is the soldier's soul, and the drums are the diablerie."[8] The mention of *Histoire* brings us to an interesting point, which Stravinsky had discussed in his remarks about *Histoire* and *Les Noces* in the *Autobiography*: his insistence on the importance of the visibility of the instrumentalists. Regarding *Histoire*, he discusses its genesis from the idea of a traveling theater during the war, hence the necessity of a small chamber group instead of an orchestra. And he adds:

[4] [Nikolay Andreyevich Rimsky-Korsakoff, *My Musical Life*, trans. Judah A. Joffe (New York: Alfred A. Knopf, 1923), p. 66.]

[5] [Ibid., pp. 205 and 247.]

[6] [Nicolay Rimsky-Korsakoff, *Principles of Orchestration*, ed. Maximilian Steinberg, trans. Edward Agate (Berlin: Edition russe de musique, 1912?), p. 19.]

[7] [Igor Stravinsky and Robert Craft, *Memories and Commentaries* (Berkeley: University of California Press, 1960), pp. 105–6.]

[8] [Igor Stravinsky, *Expositions and Developments* (London: Faber and Faber, 1962), p. 92.]

"Another consideration which made this idea particularly attractive to me was the interest afforded to the spectator by being able to see these instrumentalists each playing his own part in the ensemble."[9] And on *Les Noces*: "I wanted all my instrumental apparatus to be visible side by side with the actors or dancers, making it, so to speak, a participant in the whole theatrical action. For this reason, I wished to place the orchestra on the stage itself."[10] Why? He provides an explanation:

> I have always had a horror of listening to music with my eyes shut, with nothing for them to do. The sight of the gestures and movements of the various parts of the body producing the music is fundamentally necessary if it is to be grasped in all its fullness. All music created or composed demands some exteriorization for the perception of the listener. In other words, it must have an intermediary, an executant. That being an essential condition, without which music cannot wholly reach us, why wish to ignore it, or try to do so—why shut the eyes to this fact which is inherent in the very nature of musical art? Obviously one frequently prefers to turn away one's eyes, or even close them, when the superfluity of the player's gesticulations prevents the concentration of one's faculties of hearing. But if the player's movements are evoked solely by the exigencies of the music, and do not tend to make an impression on the listener by extramusical devices, why not follow with the eye such movements as those of the drummer, the violinist, or the trombonist, which facilitate one's auditory perceptions? As a matter of fact, those who maintain that they only enjoy music to the full with their eyes shut do not hear better than when they have them open, but the absence of visual distractions enables them to abandon themselves to the reveries induced by the lullaby of its sounds, and that is really what they prefer to the music itself.[11]

In other words, the orchestral instruments are not just characters, they are dancers. The play of the instruments is itself a ballet. But we must never forget that it is still primarily a ballet for the ear, not the eye, by which I mean that the purpose of *seeing* the instruments is to *hear* them better—as Stravinsky says, to "facilitate one's auditory perceptions."

One can understand from the foregoing why Stravinsky's developed orchestration comes more and more to depend on elements that can be soloistically treated rather than on massed strings: "I am in sympathy with Milton Babbitt when he says that he is 'depressed by the sight of duplicative'—Mr. Babbitt has his own vocabulary—'musicians.'"[12] And

---

[9] [*An Autobiography*, p. 72.]
[10] [Ibid., p. 106.]
[11] [Ibid., pp. 72–73.]
[12] [Stravinsky and Craft, *Memories and Commentaries*, pp. 120–21.]

so in *Symphony of Psalms* we find a restricted string section, without violins and violas, and in the Concerto for Piano no strings at all.

It is also easy to see why the concerto genre, with its built-in role playing, should be especially congenial to Stravinsky. When he first performed his Concerto for Two Pianos, on November 21, 1935, in Paris, he prefaced it with a little talk, which is very interesting in this respect:

> In the etymological meaning of the word, a concerto is a musical composition of a certain magnitude and in several movements, assuming the architectural form of a sonata or a symphony, with the difference that, in this instrumental ensemble, one or more instruments (e.g., in the *concerto grosso*) play a role called *concertant*. This last expression is derived from the Italian word *concertare*, which means "to compete," to participate in a contest or a match. Consequently the concerto logically depends on a rivalry between several so-called *concertant* instruments, or between a single instrument and an ensemble opposed to it.
>
> Now, this conception of the concerto is no longer put into practice in the works bearing that name, nor has it been for a long time. The concerto has become a work for a solo instrument without a rival, the role of the orchestra usually being reduced to that of accompaniment.
>
> In the four concertos I have composed—the Concerto for Piano, the Capriccio, the Concerto for Violin, and finally, the last, the Concerto for Two Solo Pianos—I stick to the old formula. To the principal *concertant* instrument I have opposed, in my orchestral ensemble, other *concertant* instruments, either as several individuals or as entire groups. Thus I have safeguarded the principle of competition.[13]

So even here, at the height of his so-called neo-classic period, Stravinsky is so to speak personifying his instruments, now in terms of contestants in a match of some kind. Indeed, the same principle applies to a great extent to the orchestration of his three mature symphonies—the Symphony of Psalms, the Symphony in C, and the Symphony in Three Movements. These contain so many *concertant* elements that extensive sections of them, at least, sound like concertos. (The *Symphonies pour instruments à vent* doesn't really come into question here, for it is a chamber piece, but the *concertant* principle pervades it too.) From the true symphonies, I have in mind, for example, the second movement of the Symphony in C, with its persistent solo oboe, alternating with and counterpointing against other wind and string solos—a movement that as a whole sounds like a concertino movement for a small group of soloistic

---

[13] [This talk is included in French as appendix 6 of Eric Walter White, *Stravinsky: The Composer and His Works* (Berkeley: University of California Press, 1966), pp. 581–85. The translation of the quoted passage, from p. 584, is presumably Cone's own.]

instruments between the tuttis of the other movements. And the same is true of the Andante of the Symphony in Three Movements. In this work especially I find the *concertant* principle pervading all movements. In the first, instead of a true development, there is a series of concertino-like episodes assigned to varying groups of instruments [R38ff.]. The entire finale is built on a frank alternation of tutti and concertino passages—the most obvious occurring when the peculiar bassoon duet succeeds the first theme, and when a fugato replaces that passage in the recapitulation [R148ff. and R170ff.]. In the *Symphony of Psalms*, the so-called double fugue of the second movement is really built on the opposition of two ideas, presented in fugal exposition, one by the orchestra and one by the voices.

Stravinsky goes on to say in his lecture: "Just as an accompaniment is most naturally conceived as harmonic in texture, so the rivalry of the concerto, by its very nature, requires contrapuntal texture."[14] Just so, and this contrapuntalizing of texture is a progressive theme in Stravinsky's music as we move from the massed blocks of sound of *Sacre*, through the much sparer and more transparent orchestration of the neoclassic and other middle period works, to the final twelve-tone compositions. *Movements for Piano and Orchestra* is Stravinsky's last essay in concerto form—but the look of the score is much more that of a chamber work. Doubling is now practically nonexistent: every instrument is fully individualized. "Duplicative" strings appear in only 68 of its 193 measures—and not at all in two of the movements (the second and third); and in a third they are confined mainly to pizzicato punctuations (the fifth). In their most sustained appearance, moreover, they are restricted to a very special effect: long-held chord harmonics (the fourth). In fact, one suspects that a prime motivation in Stravinsky's conversion to his special form of twelve-tone writing was its adaptability to just such orchestration.

What particularly interests me, though, is the less obvious ways the composer individualizes his instruments, particularly during the middle period, when he was dealing with a more conventional kind of orchestra, with less thoroughgoing polyphony. In the Piano Concerto, for instance, even where the orchestra is essentially doubling the solo instrument, individuality is preserved by a number of characteristic devices. Consider the use of selective doubling in the presentation of the principal theme of the first movement [R27]. First of all, the orchestra creates its own rhythmic pattern by punctuating, rather than continuously doubling. Second, the bass (contrabass and trombones) creates its own line by selecting notes from the piano's bass (A–C), then its soprano (G-sharp–A), and connect-

[14] [Ibid.]

ing these (with E). Finally, a new countermelody appears in the trumpet, created by picking out notes from the piano's bass and inner parts; or by registral individualization in the tutti presentation of the first theme of the Largo [R48], where both trumpet and piano play the melody but the trumpet confines it to a single octave while the piano utilizes octave displacement to range widely.

Such practices can lead to full-fledged heterophony. In the second theme of the *Ebony Concerto*, for example, the clarinet and trombone simultaneously state different versions of the same melody [R10]; and the same occurs between the saxophone and trumpet in the recapitulation [R10a].

Stravinsky's emphasis on instrumental characterization in the passage about Rimsky-Korsakov's memorial contains another revealing point: the mention of the simulation of a bass chorus. For simulation, in one form or another, has always been a feature of Stravinsky's instrumentation. Occasionally it is of nonmusical sounds, like the barking dogs of *Petroushka*, but more often it is of *musical* sounds—one instrument or group of instruments imitating another, like the accordion imitation in *Petroushka* [R103]. In the *Duo Concertant*, the violin imitates a hurdy-gurdy in one movement; and in another, the piano imitates a cimbalom.[15] But there are more subtle forms. There is a passage in the Violin Concerto finale [R116 to R122] in which the solo violin is joined for a while by another solo from the first violins. Since this occurs on the heels of a passage in which the solo is playing double-stops—one violin simulating two—the effect is that the solo has now divided itself into two, its two polyphonic voices having become fully independent: two violins imitate one violin imitating two violins! And when the second violin then returns to be a member of the section, the illusion is that it has merged with the soloist. As I previously wrote, "An understanding of the way this role emerges, as if graduating from the imagination of the protagonist to achieve independent existence, is essential to its intelligent performance."[16]

A more problematic passage, but one that I hear as related, is the opening statement of the fugato theme of the finale of the Symphony in Three Movements [R170]. Here the piano, of all things, spins off from the trombone solo, to create a line of its own, becoming independent of the trombone line. It is as if the trombone were audibly engendering the piano line—which in turn re-engenders the trombone as a new spin-off. The opposite effect, that of two instruments simulating one composite, seems to me the object of the strange passage for two bassoons (already

---

[15] [A more detailed discussion of the Duo is found in the next essay, "Stravinsky's Version of Pastoral."]

[16] [*The Composer's Voice*, p. 103.]

mentioned) in the same movement [R148]. Here the two seem to blend into a single anomalous woodwind capable of playing "double-stops."

In a sense, we might think of simulation as one of the bases for Stravinsky's entire neo-classic or neo-baroque phase: the simulation of a style which, like *trompe-l'oeil*, must never succeed completely as an imitation. We must always realize that the music is really by a twentieth-century composer. Thus Stravinsky's compositions are far from being the kind of pastiche written, say, by Kreisler, which really did aim at, and succeeded, in passing itself off as an older work.

And this brings us to our last example of characterization through simulation—a work which I want to consider in somewhat more detail. This is the Serenade in A, an example of simulation par excellence: of a style (the divertimento of the eighteenth century), of an instrument (among others, the harpsichord), and of a texture (the tutti-concertino of the concerto). Indeed, as we shall see, it is an imitation of an imitation: the piano is imitating a harpsichord that in turn is imitating a concerted group. Stravinsky implies as much in what he says about the "program" of the Serenade:

> The four movements constituting the piece are united under the title "*Sérénade*," in imitation of the *Nachtmusik* of the 18th century, which was usually commissioned by patron princes for various festive occasions, and included, as did the suites, an indeterminate number of pieces. Whereas these compositions were written for ensembles of instruments of greater or less importance, I wanted to condense mine into a small number of movements for one polyphonic instrument. In these pieces I represented some of the most typical moments of this kind of musical fete. I began with a solemn entry, a sort of hymn; this I followed by a solo of ceremonial homage paid by the artist to the guests; the third part, rhythmical and sustained, took the place of the various kinds of dance music intercalated in accordance with the manner of the serenades and suites of the period; and I ended with a sort of epilogue which was tantamount to an ornate signature with numerous carefully inscribed flourishes.[17]

The opening movement seems to me clearly imitative of a tutti and concertino alternation, as in Bach's Italian Concerto. At the outset, this differentiation is supported by forte and piano alternation, by melodic register (higher for the tutti), by harmony and implied tonality (the tutti stays mainly within F major–A minor, while the concertino moves away toward A major), and by persistent octave doubling in the tutti. On this basis, I hear three sections: one of alternation, closing with a striking tutti cadence [mm. 1–29]; a second, predominantly concertino section

---

[17][*An Autobiography*, p. 124.]

(though it does include a countermelody in the tutti range), brought to an end by the same tutti cadence [mm. 30–51]; and a final, very soloistic section, which is probably a combination of the tutti and concertino: tutti octaves (now piano) in the right hand and arpeggios in the left (mm. 52–81). The harmony is mainly F major–A minor, except for some interpolations and merging at the end—as if the concertino is now influencing the usual tutti cadence. At any rate, the final A is ambiguous—and neither major nor minor.

Is the long final section a further imitation? The piano was imitating a harpsichord, which in turn was imitating a chamber group; but at the end, is the chamber group now imitating a choral hymn, as suggested by the title?

The modal cadence of the first movement, made from D–G–B, foreshadows the "program" of the *Romanza*, in which the keyboard now imitates a smaller group of instruments—maybe one or two melodic ones like violins, with lute or guitar accompaniment. Certainly there is some preliminary tuning up or finger warming by the accompanimental lute or guitar in the little cadenza that follows the solo opening melody [m. 4]. But note that this instrument is trying to move away from the opening A to a new key, G [see especially mm. 7–8]. Possibly it is one of the instruments contributing to the final cadence of the *Hymne*. Be that as it may, *another* lute or guitar then seizes the chance to jump in and pull the music back to A [mm. 5–6]—to no avail; the G instrument returns and prevails [mm. 7–8]. So the key of the main melodic section [mm. 9–75] is predominantly G, moving to C—although with numerous ambiguities: do these represent "A" instruments trying to be heard, or simply the influence of that key on the ensemble as a whole? (Most likely both.) At the end, a pause after an ambiguous half cadence gives the A its big chance, and the earlier cadence in that key returns [mm. 76–77]. Once more the G–C guitar tries to turn the tonality its way, this time to C [m. 78]; but once more the A guitar brings it back to A, this time for a final cadence [mm. 79–80], though the G chord gets the final word.

The *Rondoletto* is the clearest example of pure harpsichord simulation, and Stravinsky's note suggests that he had keyboard dance suites in mind. Even here, though, there is still a suggestion of the old key-rivalry. There are persistent interpolations of G-natural into the predominant A major, and the subsidiary sections are in some kind of E minor–G major and G major-minor respectively [mm. 28ff., 89ff.]. So perhaps the *Rondoletto* is seeking some kind of modus vivendi between the opposing keys of the *Romanza*. Another amusing opposition exists between the two hands in the main theme: the left hand has *no* A—which is like writing a novel without using the letter E. What the left hand alone suggests is perhaps a Phrygian mode on C-sharp.

The final cadence of the *Rondoletto*, like that of the other two movements, contains the G major chord—with a franker collision between G-natural and G-sharp, the "correct" leading tone for A major, than before. This is probably a hint that the opposition has not yet been entirely worked out.

What does Stravinsky mean by describing the last movement as a signature? A signature of the soloist? Or, as I suspect, of the composer? This movement is more characteristic of Stravinsky than any of the others; it is certainly the most pianistic in modern terms. That is, it sounds like real piano music and not an imitation of anything else. I think he may be saying that, under all this eighteenth-century make-believe, there is a real composer writing real music—another level of impersonation if you will; for now the piano, after representing a harpsichord imitating a chamber ensemble of the eighteenth century, backs away from all this and speaks directly as the persona of the composer himself. I like to think, too, that Stravinsky gives us here his final word on the G–A conflict: at last, he says, I am showing you how that opposition can be resolved: the note G appears as a dissonance within a complex chord of A, and the triad on G appears as a neighbor to the triad on A [e.g., mm. 3–4, 5–6]. In the final cadence, both G and G-sharp again disappear into the final pure A—but G now is related through C [last two measures].

One final point. Most of Stravinsky's piano music was written for a specific performer—and in most cases that was himself, the performer he obviously knew best of all. But if we look through the catalogue of all his works, we find that very few of them are *not* written with a specific performer or group in mind. Abstract composition, in the sense of composition divorced from specific instrumental sound, and even specific performance, was always foreign to him. This is why he insisted on composing at the piano—to make sure he had the actual sound in his head as he composed; he was unwilling to rely on his imagination. As he wrote: "I think it is a thousand times better to compose in direct contact with the physical medium of sound than to work in the abstract medium produced by one's imagination."[18] And so I think we can understand why he thought of his instruments, his music-producers, in such personal terms. In one sense, in writing for specific instruments he was writing also for specific people whom he knew—he was not only creating a role, but often a role for a specific actor. But there is a still more personal element involved. Here is his account of the origin of the Octet:

[18] [Ibid., p. 5.]

The *Octuor* began with a dream in which I saw myself in a small room surrounded by a small group of instrumentalists playing some very attractive music. I did not recognize the music, though I strained to hear it, and I could not recall any feature of it the next day, but I do remember my curiosity—in the dream—to know how many the musicians were. I remember too that after I had counted them to the number eight, I looked again and saw that they were playing bassoons, trombones, trumpets, a flute, and a clarinet. I awoke from this little concert in a state of great delight and anticipation and the next morning began to compose the *Octuor*.[19]

Interestingly and oddly, this contradicts his earlier account in the *Autobiography*: "I began to write this music without knowing what its sound medium would be—that is to say, what instrumental form it would take. I only decided that point after finishing the first part."[20] Eric White suggests that "it seems reasonable to assume that after drafting the first movement in short score and casting about in his mind for the ideal instrumental ensemble, he embraced with alacrity the wind octet cue offered by his dream."[21] But if he made up the dream it is even more important to him. After all, music in a dream seemed to be a recurring feature of his creative life. And what better way could he tell us than by this dream, or parable, or what you will, that all the instruments are extensions of a single personality—the composer's own?

[19] [Igor Stravinsky and Robert Craft, *Dialogues and a Diary* (London: Faber and Faber, 1968), p. 39.]
[20] [*An Autobiography*, p. 103.]
[21] [Eric Walter White, *Stravinsky: The Composer and His Works*, p. 309.]

Stravinsky's Version of Pastoral

We have several sources of first-hand (or almost first-hand) information from Stravinsky on the *Duo Concertant*. Among them are the sketch manuscript, in the collection left by the composer, the account of its composition in a note appended to the published score, later confirmed in the autobiography, and the violinist Joseph Szigeti's reminiscences of his rehearsals with the composer.[1] Let us begin with the version in his *Autobiography*. Stravinsky had written his Violin Concerto for (and with) Samuel Dushkin in 1931, and it was first performed in October 1931. He then says of the Duo:

> Far from having exhausted my interest in the violin, my Concerto, on the contrary, impelled me to write yet another important work for that instrument. I had formerly had no great liking for a combination of piano and strings, but a deeper knowledge of the violin and close collaboration with a technician like Dushkin had revealed possibilities I longed to explore. Besides, it seemed desirable to open up a wider field for my music by means of chamber concerts, which are so much easier to arrange, as they do not require large orchestras of high quality, which are so costly and so rarely to be found except in big cities. This gave me the idea of writing a sort of sonata for violin and piano that I called *Duo Concertant* and which, together with transcriptions of a few of my other works, was to form the program of recitals that I proposed to give with Dushkin in Europe and America.
>
> I began the *Duo Concertant* at the end of 1931 and finished it on the July 15 following. Its composition is closely connected in my mind with a book which had just appeared and which had greatly delighted me. It was the remarkable *Petrarch* of Charles Albert Cingria,[2] an author of rare sagacity and deep originality. Our work had a great deal in common. The same subjects occupied our thoughts, and, although we were now living far apart and seldom saw each other, the close agreement between our views, our tastes, and our ideas, which I had noticed when we first met twenty years before, not only still existed, but seemed even to have grown with the passing of the years.
>
> "Lyricism cannot exist without rules, and it is essential that they should be strict. Otherwise there is only a faculty for lyricism, and that exists everywhere.

---

[1] [Joseph Szigeti, *With Strings Attached: Reminiscences and Reflections* (New York: Alfred A. Knopf, 1967 [1947]), pp. 124–28.]

[2] [Cingria, a French-Swiss poet, was a friend of Stravinsky.]

What does not exist everywhere is lyrical expression and composition. To achieve that, apprenticeship to a trade is necessary." These words of Cingria seemed to apply with the utmost appropriateness to the work I had in hand. My object was to create a lyrical composition, a work of musical versification, and I was more than ever experiencing the advantage of a rigorous discipline which gives a taste for the craft and the satisfaction of being able to apply it—and more particularly in a work of a lyrical character. It would be appropriate to quote in this connection the words of one who is regarded above all as a lyrical composer. This is what Tchaikovsky says in one of his letters: "Since I began to compose I have made it my object to be, in my craft, what the most illustrious masters were in theirs; that is to say, I wanted to be, like them, an artisan, just as a shoemaker is. . . . (They) composed their immortal works exactly as a shoemaker makes shoes; that is to say, day in, day out, and for the most part to order." How true that is! Did not Bach, Handel, Haydn, Mozart, Beethoven, to cite the best-known names, and even leaving the early Italians out of consideration, compose their works in that way?

The spirit and form of my *Duo Concertant* were determined by my love of the pastoral poets of antiquity and their scholarly art and technique. The theme that I had chosen developed through all the five movements of the piece which forms an integral whole, and, as it were, offers a musical parallel to the old pastoral poetry.[3]

The insistence on craft, on discipline, is of course a well-known leitmotif in Stravinsky's thought about composition. What is special here is the notion of "musical versification" and the reference to the pastoral poetry of antiquity. I don't think we will get very far by trying to find musical versification that parallels the hexameters of Theocritus or Vergil. But I do believe that Stravinsky did want to invest his music with a pastoral spirit. This may indeed be the theme to which he refers, "developed through all the five movements"—although, on the other hand, that might refer to a musical theme, which we'll discuss later.

What does pastoral mean as applied to music? There are two traditional uses of the word. One refers to the musical setting of a pastoral dialogue or play—an early form of opera. That of course does not apply here. The other refers to the imitation of bucolic music: shepherds piping and dancing. That form was conventionally associated with some sort of ostinato or drone, imitating a bagpipe or similar instrument; and also with a 6/8 meter, probably through association with the *siciliano* dance. Think of the *Pastorale Symphony* from Handel's *Messiah*, the *Sinfonia* opening the second part of Bach's Christmas Oratorio, the *Pastorale* movement from Corelli's Christmas Concerto, and even Beethoven's *Pas-*

[3] [Igor Stravinsky, *An Autobiography* (New York: Simon and Schuster, 1936), pp. 170–71.]

toral Symphony, which has a rustic peasant dance in the scherzo and a typical pastoral air at the beginning of the finale. And later, there is the slow movement of Berlioz's *Fantastic Symphony.* Stravinsky himself had written pastorals. I don't mean in the Empsonian sense, which would make one of the *Sacre du printemps*—but then Empson makes a pastoral of *Alice in Wonderland!*[4] I mean pieces like his Op. 2, a little cantata written in 1906 on Pushkin's *The Faun and the Shepherdess,* in which a few passages can be found suggesting the conventional pastoral; and more especially, the *Pastorale* in Scene 2 of *Soldier's Tale,* which is a duet for clarinet and bassoon against a drone in the strings (mostly violin, on a C–B seventh). But particularly relevant is the *Pastorale* for soprano (wordless) and piano of 1907, because this was one of the compositions Stravinsky rearranged to play with Dushkin. I think it can be shown that Stravinsky had this one in mind by a look at the manuscript of the *Duo Concertant*'s *Dithyrambe,* whose lovely opening violin quintole, as now written, was originally an ordinary turn in 64ths.[5] My suspicion is that the change was inspired by the thought of the melody of the *Pastorale.* In fact, in a funny way the whole *Dithyrambe* might be considered as a rewriting of the 1907 *Pastorale* in a much more advanced style, and a much loftier manner. It must have been interesting to hear them on the same program.

What are the specific pastoral references in the Duo? To begin with, of course, there are the titles of the movements. *Cantilène* doesn't tell us much, but it is followed by two *Eglogues* and then a *Gigue*—not a *Siciliano,* but in 6/16. Finally a *Dithyrambe*—not precisely pastoral, but a hymn to Dionysus, which one of the early pastoral poets might well have written.

Much more important, of course, is the musical content. It is in the second movement, the first *Eglogue,* that we hear the most obvious reference to rustic instruments. Here is an imitation of the bagpipe or the hurdy-gurdy in the violin—a continuous drone with a simple chant reiterated above it, in this case also appearing in imitation in the piano. But Stravinsky's ostinato is not just the droned A of the violin: the chant itself is an ostinato [bottom system, p. 7].[6] The piano accompanies it with two others—one stationary but pulsating, around G, in the left hand, and one in the right hand in constant motion yet clearly implying, by its constant scalewise movement, an ostinato on C. There is yet another ostinato, an

---

[4] [Cone is referring to William Empson and his influential book *Some Versions of Pastorale* (London: Chatto & Windus, 1935).]

[5] [See Vera Stravinsky and Robert Craft, *Stravinsky in Pictures and Documents* (New York: Simon and Schuster, 1978), pp. 308–9, which includes a sketch of the earlier version.]

[6] [References are to the Edition Russe de Musique/Boosey and Hawkes score.]

intermittent one in the violin [seventh quarter, top of p. 8], consisting of seven sixteenths (vs. the steady quarters of the piano). And it spells out the fifths C–D–G plus A—hence C, G, D, and their fifths! These fifths— C, G, D (see also the descent of scale into the piano's bass [before the first 3/4 measure on p. 9])—form the same kind of relation presented by Beethoven at the beginning of the finale of the *Pastoral* Symphony (F–C– G). There the lower one proved to be the tonic; while here the middle one wins out, for the second section of the piece is on another kind of moving ostinato in the piano, based on G [p. 9, m. 2ff.]. And here the piano probably imitates some kind of rustic strings-percussion combination, while the violin imitates—if I may say so—a rustic fiddle. Much of Stravinsky's music involves musical imitations of one kind or another— styles, forms, instruments—and in this case a violin imitates a violin. According to Szigeti, Stravinsky called this a *kazachok*—a rustic Cossack kicking dance.[7]

There are imitations in the Gigue as well. Both trios, I believe, are stylistic imitations, and one of them, the first [m. 92ff.], is again attested by Szigeti's memoir. Stravinsky, when rehearsing this section, began singing a waltz from the Finale of Act 1 of *Die Fledermaus*: "Glücklich ist / wer vergisst / was doch nicht / zu ändern ist."[8] And here again the violin is imitating a violin—this time a Viennese one. And although the trio is written in 2/4, there is a waltz concealed here. In actuality the piano keeps up the steady 16ths, in which the gigue rhythm tries to assert itself. The second trio [m. 159ff.] is less precise, but I hear an evocation of a music-hall tune. This time it is in the piano, while the violin keeps up an ostinato in gigue rhythm. For both these modern dance-songs are framed by yet another stylistic imitation—the baroque gigue. Indeed, an imitation of an imitation, for the baroque gigue was a conventionalized imitation of a jig. What do these imitations have to do with pastoral? I'll suggest an answer later.

One important instrumental imitation we have not yet mentioned occurs at the very beginning. We know that Stravinsky was intrigued by the cimbalom (a kind of zither played with hammers), which, according to Craft's *Explorations and Developments*, he used for *Renard* (another Empsonian pastoral?) instead of the *guzla*, a kind of balalaika that he found impractical:

> One day near the end of 1914 I heard a cimbalom for the first time, in a Geneva restaurant, and decided it could be used as a substitute for the *guzla*. . . . I learned to play the cimbalom, and to love it, and I composed *Renard* "on" it (as

[7][With Strings Attached, p. 127.]
[8][Ibid.]

I normally compose "on" a piano), with two sticks in my hand, writing down as I composed. I used the cimbalom in my *Ragtime* for eleven instruments, also, as well as in incompleted versions of the *Chant dissident* and *Les Noces*.[9]

So I believe I have good reason to hear an imitation cimbalom at the beginning of the Duo, which sounds like some passages in *Renard*. What succeeds the cimbalom [in m. 1] I don't know—perhaps a string (the piano imitating the violins "warm-up"), or perhaps a balalaika of some kind. Perhaps though it is just a different kind of writing for the cimbalom, for the cimbalom repetitions return within it; and then the whole introduction returns as a coda [m. 55ff.]. And again, in the second section of the work [m. 26ff.], there is a moving ostinato, or combination thereof, in the piano: D-flat alternating with C minor in the bass, and C–B-flat–G alternating with C major in the right hand. (These in turn get out of sync [m. 35ff.], as the right hand moves away from the left while the left continues with the D-flat–C alternations.)

I have mentioned the ostinato of fifths C–G–D that opens the first *Eglogue*. This is in fact a kind of leitmotif that occurs in some form in every movement. The first sonority heard is A–B-flat–E (resolved to A minor). The chord that supports the beginning of the true cantilena, the first goal of musical motion, is a ninth on E-flat [m. 15], which can be heard as filled-in fifths (note the F–B-flat in the violin with the piano's E-flat bass). An inversion of the same chord (now with D–G–A) opens the first *Eglogue*, resolving to D–E–A [m. 3] as a sort of dominant preparation for the triple ostinato to follow. The movement ends on the same chord with which it began. When the opening motif of *Eglogue I* (from which the chant was derived) returns in *Eglogue II*, it brings along a very similar chord. And in *Eglogue II* there is a succession of statement—cadences, punctuated by that opening motif or something very close to it, on G, D, and A, then F and C.

The fifths return in the Gigue as fourths—suggested incompletely by the opening sonority (C–F–E-flat) and then soon spelled out in many ways by the Gigue itself. Indeed, almost the only material in the Gigue proper seems to be the scale, the arpeggio, and the fourths. Finally, the *Dithyrambe* begins with a new version of the opening of the *Cantilène*—and ends with yet another version of the same. So perhaps *this* is the "theme" that Stravinsky mentions as being developed throughout the movements—although I shall return again to this question later on.

There is at least one more motivic return that must be discussed, the most striking of all. This centers on the highly dissonant series of chords

---

[9] [Igor Stravinsky and Robert Craft, Expositions and Developments (London: Faber and Faber, 1962), p. 120.]

that is used to develop the E-flat ninth at the entrance of the *Cantilène* proper [m. 15]. They climax on a form of the *Petroushka* chord: two major triads a tritone apart [m. 20], or—as it becomes—a diminished seventh chord plus two extra notes [m. 22]. Reference is made to these two versions of the chord—especially the last—in all the movements at striking points: the end of *Eglogue I*, the similar end of *Eglogue II*, the modulation to C minor after the second Trio in the Gigue. But above all, the climax of the *Dithyrambe* [m. 9] recapitulates the entire progression that introduced the *Cantilène* (and tonally, at the same time, traces the D-flat–C relationship prominent in that movement). It is an extraordinary moment—almost unique in the music of one who said, "I relate only from an angle to the German stem (Bach-Haydn-Mozart-Beethoven-Schubert-Brahms-Wagner-Mahler-Schoenberg), which evaluates largely in terms of where a thing comes from and where it is going."[10] That is a typical exaggeration, but one can see what he means. Yet here is a movement that consists largely of the steady rise of a melody, pushing to a climax—a climax that makes complete sense only by reference to where it came from, its origin in the first movement.

What did Stravinsky mean by "my object was to create a lyrical composition, a work of musical versification"? Lyrical has, of course, two connotations: poetry that is sung (to the accompaniment of a lyre, originally), and poetry expressing personal mood or emotion. We can coalesce the two in this case, so as to avoid any conflict with Stravinsky on the subject of emotion, as meaning the representation (by instrumental means) of a very personal, individual kind of song. But it is equally clear that Stravinsky has given us a work not only of song but also of dance—sometimes contrasted with song, sometimes combined with it.

Versification, on the other hand, I take to mean the various kinds of phrase-rhythms (analogous to, but by no means identical with, metrical lines) by which these various movements are characterized. Let me try to identify the main ones:

> *Cantilène*. As we have said, a kind of tuning-up introduction (which returns as a coda) with a central song. The tuning up is phrased by the expansion and contraction of a single rhythmic motif. The song, by contrast, is broad and expansive—but again made broad by expansion and contraction, although now on a much larger scale. Against it there is the pulsation of the ostinato, perhaps as an imitation of primitive additive meters as opposed to the divisive meter of the song. The two finally synchronize at the climax and then dissolve into the coda.

[10] [Igor Stravinsky and Robert Craft, *Dialogues and a Diary* (London: Faber and Faber, 1968), p. 14.]

Eglogue I. This movement I take to be, by contrast, a purely "instrumental" one. First, over an almost undifferentiated continuous accompaniment, there is the single phrase of the folk-like melody, reiterated in both instruments in always different imitative patterns. In contrast to this single phrase there is in the second half the *kazachok*, which is made up of combinations of small motifs, at first fragmented but gradually coalescing into longer phrases—yet still based on the original tiny motifs.

Eglogue II. Here the material from the introduction of the first *Eglogue* returns to create a frame for the most conventionally "lyrical" movement of all. After tentative phrases, separated by the introductory motif, the song emerges in two long, almost exactly balanced phrases [mm. 12–19, 19–26], in which both instruments intertwine.[11] This dissolves again into a coda that returns to the introductory material.

Gigue. The most lyrical movement is now followed by another "instrumental" one. Here the phrasing is derived from long lines and elided phrases of late baroque counterpoint—one thinks especially of a Bach gigue, or Bach's gigue-like D major Toccata. Even Eric Walter White finds this "a long garrulous movement."[12] But actually it is beautifully put together if one hears it as a parody of a gigue attempting to come to a conclusion but being interrupted twice—once by the Strauss parody and once by the music-hall song—and having to get back on track again each time and finally being able to complete itself. Thus, in contrast to the apparently endless flow of constantly elided phrases of the gigue imitation proper, we have two other parodies: the Strauss, with its concealed waltz phrasing; and the popular song, which begins with strict four-by-four phrasing but gradually breaks away—first by diminution, then by the gradual takeover of the gigue rhythms.

Dithyrambe. The closing movement is defined as a Bacchic hymn of wild, irregular, and passionate character, which Stravinsky has interpreted in his own individual way. Once again there is an introduction, a central melody, and a coda that returns to the introduction. This time the main tune is metrically free—unbarred—until the return at the climax of the phrase from the first movement. The rise to that climax is, I think, meant to be heard not just in the violin but in the piano, in several contrapuntal lines—a choric hymn, as it were, possibly with one solo voice represented by the violin. This is, if you will, the goal toward which the cantilena of the first movement was pushing and which is now achieved by rising to a climax in one huge line: a single rising phrase, this time not encumbered (or aided) by a rhythmic ostinato, but pervading all musical voices.

---

[11] Compare the two Arias in the Violin Concerto, which have the same long lines, widely extended melodies, and irregular but balanced phrases.

[12] [Eric Walter White, *Stravinsky: The Composer and His Works* (Berkeley: University of California Press, 1966), p. 373.]

So Stravinsky's exercise in versification is very thorough: each section is characterized by its own kind of phraseology—some song-like, some dance-like, and some a combination of both. They range from the tiny motifs of the first *Eglogue*'s *kazachok*, the reiterated phrase of that movement's bagpipe imitation, the balanced phrases of the second *Eglogue*, the progressive phrases of the *Cantilène*, the endless elisions of the *Gigue*, to the single continuous line of the *Dithyrambe*. It is almost as if all of the earlier stages contribute to that final revelation, as if all of them enforce, in various ways, the "rigorous discipline" of which Stravinsky wrote; perhaps it would not even be too fanciful to see them as symbolizing various phases of the "apprenticeship to a trade," which Cingria called necessary.

However that may be, I am convinced that the various types of versification are artfully arranged to develop a pastoral theme—and this theme, rather than a purely musical one, is what I believe Stravinsky meant when he wrote of the theme "developed through all the five movements of the piece which forms an integral whole, and, as it were, offers a musical parallel to the old pastoral poetry." The pastoral convention implies two kinds of contrast: first, the highly sensitive, sophisticated lyricism against the rural setting; and second, the more natural values of the country against the artificiality of city life. Is that not what we find here? The first contrast is symbolized initially in the *Cantilène*, by the rhapsodic outpouring of the melody against the cimbalom and the other rustic instruments of the accompaniment, with their earthy and rather *Sacre*-like rhythms. This simultaneous conflict becomes separated into the two *Eglogues*—the first completely rustic in character and the second entirely lyric, though framed by memories of the harmonies developed in the first. With the *Gigue* and its two trios, comes the second contrast: the artificial and conventional as opposed to the natural and spontaneous.

Are the *Gigue*'s fourths, an interval that White says is "not one of Stravinsky's favourite[s],"[13] to be understood as an inversion, a set of anti-fifths? This would indeed symbolize the two poles between which the lyricist is moving! And there may be an intention in this movement to present entertainment music of three centuries: the eighteenth-century suite, the nineteenth-century operetta, and the twentieth-century music-hall. Be that as it may, it stands in contrast to all the rest of the work, particularly to the finale which follows, the *Dithyrambe*, which is the one pure lyric of the entire work—as if the poet, purified by his contact with the rustic realities of the earlier movements, is now ready to throw off the influences represented by the *Gigue* and make his offering to Dionysus, completely free and untrammeled. Only, of course, beneath this

---

[13] [Ibid., pp. 373–74.]

apparent freedom it is as rigorously composed as everything else Stravinsky wrote.

Let me return to Cingria: "Lyricism cannot exist without rules, and it is essential that they should be strict. Otherwise there is only a faculty for lyricism, and that exists everywhere. What does not exist everywhere is lyrical expression and composition. To achieve that, apprenticeship to a trade is necessary." If I may attempt a paraphrase, based on the *Dithyrambe*, what he seems to be saying is: It takes enormous discipline and control to enable one to give the effect of freedom of expression. Not freedom, but the opposite, is the result of insufficient control. Or, as Stravinsky himself put it in his *Poetics of Music*: "What is important for the lucid ordering of the work—for its crystallization—is that all the Dionysian elements which set the imagination of the artist in motion and make the life-sap rise must be properly subjugated before they intoxicate us, and must finally be made to submit to the law: Apollo demands it."[14]

[14] [Igor Stravinsky, *Poetics of Music*, trans. Arthur Knodel and Ingolf Dahl (Cambridge, MA: Harvard University Press, 1947), pp. 80–81.]

Stravinsky's Sense of Form

George Boas once wrote: "Whether a book have a beginning and a middle is not so important as that it have an end."[1] The same, I take it, is true of a musical composition. Probably the single most valuable instinct a composer can have (or acquirement, if indeed it can be acquired) is what we might call a feeling for punctuality: of getting to the right place at just the right time, neither early nor late, and above all of getting to the end at the right time. Mozart had this instinct to a preeminent degree: almost every one of his works is exactly as long as it should be. Dvořák, for all his merits, lacked it: many of even his best compositions go on long after they should be over. That is why I considered entitling this essay, or subtitling it, "On Knowing When to Stop." For what I shall really be trying to show is that Stravinsky, like Mozart and unlike Dvořák, knows when to stop.

Now, if you will think about this for a moment, you will realize that this knowledge includes a great deal more than the mere ability to end a whole work convincingly. It means that the composer knows exactly how long each phrase, each theme, each section should be, for these determine the shape of the whole work. In other words, the composer has a sense of proportion, and this in turn is an important aspect of a sense of rhythm. Form is simply the rhythm of the entire work. I think it can be shown that this sense of form as rhythm and proportion has characterized Stravinsky's work from the very beginning—certainly from *Firebird* on—in spite of Constant Lambert's judgment that "Stravinsky's ballets . . . can hardly be considered as possessing any formal qualities that are not dictated by their dramatic interest";[2] or in spite of Alfred J. Swan's dictum: "we are disappointed . . . by the frequent collapse of his thought in the middle of a composition, to cover up which he invariably resorts to endless repetition."[3]

By now most of us realize that Stravinsky's ballets, far from being dependent on dramatic interest, are composed primarily as pure music, and that his repetitions, far from being endless, are precisely designed to give

---

[1] [George Boas, *A Primer for Critics* (Baltimore: Johns Hopkins Press, 1937), p. 149.]

[2] [Constant Lambert, *Music Ho! A Study of Music in Decline*, 3rd ed. (London: Penguin, 1948), p. 33.]

[3] [In David Ewen, *The Book of Modern Composers* (New York: Alfred A. Knopf, 1950), p. 81.]

each section exactly the length appropriate to it. But it would be foolish to deny that there is a problem here: how, in a style characterized by the persistent use of repetitive motives, and ostinato harmonies, does the composer achieve a satisfying form? Why, in fact, don't the repetitions go on forever? That is what we shall try to find out; so we shall concentrate on passages of just this kind.

We must realize, of course, that the problem is not unique to Stravinsky. No doubt when a passage such as the one in the first movement of Beethoven's *Eroica* Symphony was first heard [m. 631 to the end], critics spoke of "endless repetition." But we can hear a perfectly clear form there: a phrase that is stated in pairs, four measures on I plus four on V, is presented four times, preserving again the bilateral balance: four measures by four measures, eight measures by eight measures, and sixteen measures by sixteen measures. Each successive statement keeps only these two harmonies, but changes—and increases—the orchestration, until the final tutti, with the theme in the trumpets and woodwinds. After this passage, which is no longer than it should be for the culmination of a long and complex movement, the expansion of the phrase length to ten measures [mm. 663–72] heralds the close of the movement.

THE FIREBIRD

Now let us turn to a well-known passage, the finale of what, I fear, is still Stravinsky's most popular work: *The Firebird*. Now, admittedly, Stravinsky's problem is not Beethoven's. Beethoven was using a theme that he had developed throughout a long work, and his repetitions came as a kind of earned enjoyment of a long-sought goal. Stravinsky's theme is introduced only here, by way of contrast with all that has preceded it; and it creates an entire section or movement. Yet there are similarities. Stravinsky's harmonic scheme is almost as simple as Beethoven's alternation of V and I, and in spite of its elaborations reduces to just that. Let us see how he builds up an entire movement out of a single idea.

There are six statements, *Lento maestoso*, of a four-measure theme in two parts, a and b, in 3/2 and in the key of B major; but the repetitions are by no means monotonous. The first two are stated by horn over a V pedal, but the harmonies above are different each time; the next two are stated by violins, over a I pedal, but with ever-growing orchestration, and the second of these is extended by a repetition of b (the last two measures, positioned in the center of this section); then two more over V, growing to full orchestra. The first phase, essentially extending V, is now completed. Then a four-measure crescendo on I, acting as both cadence and transition, leads to a new phase, *Allegro non troppo*, now with the originally differentiated rhythm of the theme characteristically equalized and placed in a contrasting 7/4 meter. It begins with two statements on I (the real downbeat tonic for which everything before has been a long upbeat); but this time instead of swinging directly back to V, we go by an indirect route. Using the theme's two-part division, we get, over a G pedal (Neapolitan 6/4), the grouping aaabb, and then, over E (Neapolitan 6), a single a (thus aaabba in all, all building up over the Neapolitan). After this, now twice as slow, *Maestoso*, we return to V, alternating with I in the bass in ever-faster divisions of the 7: V for 7 beats; I for 4, and V for 3 (4 + 3 = 7); I for 3, and V for 4; I for 4, and V for 3; I for 3, V for 2, and I for 2; and finally V and I alternating at one beat each for seven beats. This time the melodic pattern is ababbb—the increase in b's due to the fact that the section makes a stronger V effect (but note that overall the number of a's and b's are equal in the second half [from the *Allegro*]); and since it does not begin with a rest, it gives a more breathless effect of climax, even as the tempo slows down to the final tonic (*Molto pesante*) with its startling foreign chords above it. Schematically, this can be shown as in table 14.1.

The constant variety of Stravinsky's treatment of this theme is not just variety for variety's sake: it is obviously building to the triumphal climactic conclusion. We can see how skillfully it is done: just when we catch on to the rhythmic swing of V and I, he changes tempo and meter; just when we are in danger of tiring of the V–I pedals, he shifts to the Neapolitan; just when the complete repetition of the theme would become monotonous, he breaks it up into component parts; and just when the 7/4 would become monotonous, he reduces it into shorter and shorter divisions.[4]

Sacre du Printemps

If we separate the *Firebird* passage into three elements, (1) cumulation, (2) melodic repetition, (3) harmonic repetition–ostinato, it is the first and last of these that most clearly characterize *Le Sacre du printemps*. There is melodic repetition, to be sure, as well, but that is never so persistently unvarying as in the passage just considered. What does persist in *Sacre* is the harmonic repetition, now as an out-and-out ostinato—a repeated rhythmic figure constantly on the same notes or chord—and the effect of cumulation, now present as the piling up of successive orchestral strata, rather than as a steady crescendo.

---

[4] By contrast, consider another, later composer, also Russian (for this kind of treatment may indeed be a Russian characteristic). A famous, or notorious, example of the same device—but how different—appears in the first movement of Shostakovitch's Seventh Symphony [R19 to 45], where the same theme of twenty-two measures appears twelve times. Again there is ever-increasing orchestration, but otherwise the theme remains essentially the same; and it soon becomes unbearable.

TABLE 14.1
Stravinsky, *Firebird*: Formal Layout of Finale

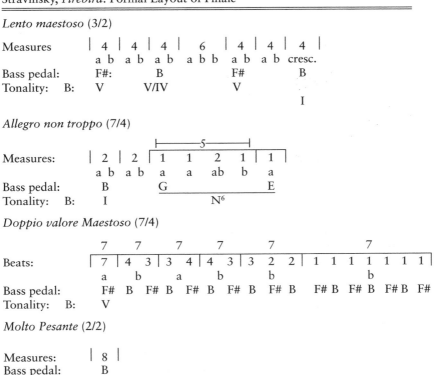

Lento maestoso (3/2)

Measures		4	4	4	6	4	4	4	
		a b	a b	a b	a b b	a b	a b cresc.		
Bass pedal:		F#:		B		F#		B	
Tonality:	B:	V		V/IV		V			
								I	

Allegro non troppo (7/4)

| 5 |

Measures:		2	2	1	1	2	1	1	
		a b	a b	a	a	a b	b	a	
Bass pedal:		B		G				E	
Tonality:	B:	I				N^6			

Doppio valore Maestoso (7/4)

| 7 | | 7 | | 7 | | 7 | | 7 | | | | | | 7 | | |

Beats:		7	4	3	3	4	4	3	3	2	2	1	1	1	1	1	1	1
		a	b		a		b			b				b				
Bass pedal:		F#	B	F#	B	F#	B	F#	B	F#	B	F# B	F# B	F# B	F#
Tonality:	B:	V																

Molto Pesante (2/2)

Measures:		8	
Bass pedal:		B	
Tonality:	B:	I	

Both of these appear in the first dance, *Les Augures printaniers* and *Danses des adolescentes*—the ostinato being the four-note figure with its implied chord [3 after R12, R13]. Here we have a perfect example of what Roger Sessions called "textural" form. We can easily divide the dance up into sections, depending on the specific melody, the orchestration, and the way the ostinato is used: the heavy chords, alternating with lighter passages, and the return of the heavy chords with an added theme, ending with a marked pause [2 before R22]; then the ostinato figure against a trill [2 after R22], with a new melody [R25], to which eventually another melody is added [4 after R28]; and finally, leaving the ostinato, a transition passage [R31] harmonically leading to the next dance [R37]. But is this all we can say? Can we find no principle by which Stravinsky determines how long each section is to last? Note that normal criteria are not relevant here: harmonic motion, melodic resolution, periodic phrase-structure. What then is there?

One thing is immediately clear—the persistence of the beat. Except for two 3/4 measures, the whole dance is 2/4 (in spite of the many cross-accents). And except for two measures with pauses, there is an attack on every eighth note throughout 178 measures; these beats are so clear that they invite us to count them. In other words, the music itself suggests that its proportions should be measured in time. And if we do so, what do we find? First of all, there are two main articulations: the pause of two measures and the farewell to the ostinato as we enter the transition (table 14.2).

TABLE 14.2
Stravinsky, *Le Sacre du printemps, Les Augures printaniers* and *Danses des adolescentes*: Formal Balances (in Measures)

Ostinatos		Pause		Ostinatos		Transition
69	+	2	+	69	+	32

Before the pause there are 69 measures, and after it there are 69 more; and the transition has 32 measures (8 × 4). This is almost too neat—and it is, because the second half is really 70, since it has the two 3/4 measures. But it is clear that the balance is exact enough, especially if we include the first of the pause measures as part of section A and the second as part of B, in which case we have 70:70:32, with the pause between the equal sections.

But there is another way of dividing this. If we look within the sections we can construct the plan shown in table 14.3. Can this be accidental? First 22:12; then 12:22, separated by one extra measure: so 2 × 34 (+ 1); then following the pause, 44:24 *enclosing* a third group of 34 measures. So the whole gives us:

$$34 + 34 (+1) \quad + \quad 2 \times 34 (44 + 24 = 68)$$

the second group enclosing 34. And note the further subdivisions, which make it easy to hear the balance.[5]

But why doesn't Stravinsky make it perfect? Why the extra measure in the second main section? Because there is still another form at work

[5] [Cone also identifies (in pencil) the following subdivisions of the 44-measure group in the second half: 11 (introduction), 22 (*col legno*), 11 (with clarinet ostinato). His counting of 11 measures (rather than 10) for the final subgroup (immediately preceding R28) reflects the final two measures being in 3/4 rather than 2/4. (Note, however, that in previously identifying the 69 + 69 measure balance, and also in indicating the proportions in the analytical table following this one, he counts these measures as normal.) Cone also indicates that the two eight-measure subgroups within the next major articulation (R30 and R31) are connected by the presence in both of ostinato rhythmic motifs.]

TABLE 14.3
Stravinsky, *Le Sacre du printemps*, *Les Augures printaniers* and *Danses des adolescentes*: Alternate Formal Balances (in Measures)

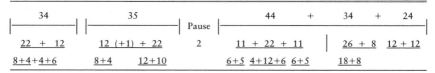

34		35	Pause	44	+	34	+	24
22 + 12		12 (+1) + 22	2	11 + 22 + 11		26 + 8	12 + 12	
8+4+4+6		8+4 12+10		6+5 4+12+6 6+5		18+8		

TABLE 14.4
Stravinsky, *Le Sacre du printemps*, *Les Augures printaniers* and *Danses des adolescentes*: Correspondences among Lengths of Ostinati

Double chord [R13–15, R18–21]	22 + 35, or 57: 3×19
E-flat fifths [R16–17, R28–30]	12 + 26, or 38: 2×19
C violin trill [2 after R22, 2 before R24, R24–27]	4 + 1 + 33, or 38: 2×19
Everything else [R22, R23, 1 before R24, R31] (two-measure pause omitted)	2 + 3 + 1 + 32, or 38: 2×19

here, also carefully measured. Simultaneously with the simple form of successive parts there is an interpenetrating and much subtler one. It is a simple version of what became the later Stravinsky's favorite technique of interruption. We can see how the passages using the ostinato chords form one group that is twice interrupted [at R14 and R16]. But the first interruption, retaining in another form the "double" harmony of the first section, is really part of the first section; while the second, which moves to E-flat in the bass, is the first appearance of a second ostinato [the E-flat bass fifths], which, combined with the first, appears at length again later on. A third ostinato is the violin trill on C, which we hear for a short time twice [two measures after R22 and two before R24], then as the root of an entire section [R24].

Now if we take the entire dance and add up these various ostinati separately, we get table 14.4. And here everything is accounted for! So the form is—at least—a double one, and the two aspects are simultaneous—one results from the proportions among successive sections, the other from the proportions among the sections bound together by a common ostinato harmony.

THREE PIECES FOR STRING QUARTET, NO. 1

In Stravinsky, from *Firebird* on, we find passages that, like the one in Beethoven's *Eroica*, combine melodic repetition with harmonic ostinato.

But unlike Beethoven, these do not have the justification of appearing at the end of a long development. They often are self-contained forms—even complete movements—and as such cannot draw on the impetus of an entire movement behind them to carry them forward. What makes them work?

Let us look at one of the purest examples, the first of the Three Pieces for String Quartet, written in 1914 (and orchestrated much later as the third of the Four Studies). We find a combination of ostinato with melodic repetition. But unlike in the *Firebird* and *Sacre*, now there is no cumulation. Stravinsky had perhaps come to feel that cumulation without harmonic and melodic change was somehow unjustified—that one couldn't simply repeat over and over and arrive at a climax simply by increasing the volume and instrumentation.

The movement is based on a basic 3 + 2 + 2 or 7/4 rhythm, which is clearly articulated by the ostinato in the cello and by the repeated D in the viola (which also sustains a D throughout). There are fourteen of these groups, plus the beginning and ending 7/4's, which have no rhythmic motion.

Against this there is a low melody in violin I of 23 beats, which is given four times and grouped into two parts of 11 and 12 beats each (*a* and *b*). It appears four times without pause, which doesn't come out even (seven would be necessary); so a short coda is added to round it off. Why four times? Well, the first time through we have no idea how long the whole pattern is, especially since it is so restricted in pitch and motif. The second time, then, we are still off guard. But the third time we try to catch it, and the fourth time we probably succeed.

But there is a third ostinato, much more irregular than the other two: the four notes in violin II. It alternates single (*x*) and double (*y*) statements; and together, each single plus double statement covers three of the 7/4 groups. There are four of these complete statements, plus one extra single statement in the coda. The double statement always begins on the second beat of the first 2/4 measure of the 7/4 group; but although all five of the single statements occur within the 3/4 measure, they do so at different points: second, third, first, first, and second beats respectively. Now all four of the complete single-plus-double combinations fit within one statement of the violin I melody, but at different points within it. Why, though, are there two successive appearances of the single statement on first beats? One would think that Stravinsky would be aiming at the greatest possible variety here in relating his out-of-phase parts. Indeed if we compare this part with the *melody*, as opposed to the 7/4 group, we find this is so. On each successive statement, *x* (single) + *y* (double) occurs at an earlier point (table 14.5).

But there is another reason. Here again Stravinsky wishes to build another proportion, one that echoes the 7/4 on a higher level. Thus the two

TABLE 14.5
Stravinsky, Three Pieces for String Quartet, No. 1: Violin I Melody in Relation
to the Third Ostinato

23-beat violin I melody	1		2		3		4		(5)
2 phrases of melody (11 + 12 eighths)	a	b	a	b	a	b	a	b	a
Beat where x (single statement) begins	9		8		4		2		1
Beat where y (double statement) begins		8		6		4		2	

appearances of the single (x) on the first beat of the 3/4 measure, which
is after all the first beat of the 7/4, give us the following grouping of the
fourteen bass ostinati:

$$(7 \times 7) + ([3 \times 7] + [4 \times 7])$$

This equals $(7 \times 7) \times 2$. [The beginnings of the last two groups, the
eighth and eleventh statement of the ostinato, are thus articulated by the
single (x) downbeats.] Now we see that the 14 statements were no accident—they were twice 7!

One further point about the violin melody: there is never any division
between its repetitions; the divisions come within it. The last beat (the
pitch A) could serve as an elision, becoming the first beat of the succeeding statement. In this case, beginning with its second statement, the melody has 24 beats, clearly divided 12 + 6 + 6. (This is suggested by the
beginning the melody's second subphrase, which then becomes a diminution of the first; indeed the whole second half of the phrase becomes a
compressed and repeated diminution of the first.) Furthermore, if we
think then of the last note of the melody as being also the first of the restatement, and hence of peculiar importance, then the end comes when
this tone coincides with the first beat of the 7/4 ostinato [six measures
from the end], and we get one 7/4 measure of melody plus a cadence to
finish it off. So once more we have a piece that on the surface seems
quite arbitrary as to form—it could go on that way indefinitely. But un-
derneath, we find a careful decision on every point, and the result is peculiarly satisfying.

SYMPHONY OF PSALMS

Evidence, if not proof, that Stravinsky came to feel that a crescendo must
be supported harmonically and melodically, and not just by increase in
orchestral texture, is offered, in a positive and in a negative fashion, by
the *Symphony of Psalms*. On the positive side, there are two crescendos
in the first movement: one leads to the big return of E minor (R10 to

R12); the other leads at the end of the movement to the final cadence on G, as V of the next movement. They are crescendos first in orchestration, but in each case Stravinsky marks "crescendo" at the end. Both are passages of harmonic and melodic progression—in fact, the only two such in the movement. There is no crescendo passage in the second movement; and in the last movement, the crescendos are again restricted to points of progression.

The striking place in this last movement—the negative evidence—is the one we wish to look at: the extraordinary long ostinato episode before the final return of the Alleluia [R22 to R29]. This is just the kind of passage—with both an ostinato bass and a reiterative melody—that might suggest the methods of either the *Firebird* or the *Sacre*, or both; but no. There is a crescendo here (R21), *before* the ostinato passage, marking the modulation from the harmonic area around D–G–C to the new one around E-flat. The long, impressive, static passage that follows is marked *p subito*. The one short crescendo (*ma non troppo*) in the latter [R25] marks a rising vocal line after eight measures reiterating B-flat; but then the *p subito* again takes over and continues.[6] As I say, I find the negative evidence in the essentially static nature of the passage—Stravinsky now evidently finds such passages as contraindicating crescendo or cumulation. But then, what determines its limits? What keeps it from going on forever?

Again, it is the counterpoint of various metrical and rhythmical patterns. The passage is 42 measures long. What divisions do we find? Here are four: (a) the beat, in half notes; (b) the measure, in three half notes; (c) the ostinato, in four half notes; (d) and the ostinato together with the measure, which, since the two coincide every fourth measure, gives twelve half notes.

In addition, there is the tune, consisting of two basic phrases (four *a*'s and one *b*), which is primarily in groups of six measures (18 whole notes):

$$(a) \quad (a) \quad (b) \quad (b) \quad (a) \quad (\text{coda without melody})$$
$$6 \;+\; 6 \;+\; 12 \;+\; 6 \;+\; 6 \;+\; 6$$
$$(8 + 4)$$

But since the ostinato coincides with the measure only every fourth measure, it coincides with the *a* phrase only once every twelve measures. What

---

[6]This indicates that Stravinsky was more restrained than is suggested by a description of one commentator: "An even slower tempo is soon established with a solemn bell-like *ostinato* in the orchestra against which the chorus builds a long crescendo of irresistible power. The cumulative effect of this sustained section is tremendous: its sheer weight, together with the dissonant chords in the wind instruments, makes it most impressive. The climax subsides with the repetition of the modal cadence figures on the words "*Alleluia, laudate Dominum.*" [William E. Brandt, *The Way of Music* (Boston: Allyn & Bacon, 1963), pp. 526–27.]

we really get, therefore, is two different forms of phrase *a* in relation to the four-measure ostinato. What is more, if we hear *a* as consisting of four repeating measures plus a two-measure tag, then we hear each of its four repeating measures against a different phase of the four-beat ostinato! (Note that just when E-flat in the theme would come out again against the E-flat of the bass in the fourth measure after R22, a change is made in the melody so that it is no longer E-flat but D.)

The two statements of *a*, then, in spite of the great internal repetition, are not wholly repetitions. But since the next statement would be if they continued, *b* enters with a new melody at R24. And here we also get new rhythms: 8 (4 + 4) + 4, now with irregular subdivisions, for the first time crossing the bar producing syncopations. (The woodwinds now have a new two-measure figure, repeated four times, plus four measures of a rising melody accompanying the previously mentioned voice crescendo.) Thus we have had twelve regular measures [R22] followed by twelve irregular [R24], then a return to the twelve regular ones [R26]. The final coda-like orchestral passage of six measures [R28] refers briefly to the cross-rhythm of the middle section, with a figure of three whole notes plus a dotted whole, which now breaks up the six measures into 3 + 3 for the first time. But notice that these final six measures do not give the bass time to complete its ostinato; poised on V, it leads now into the concluding Alleluia.

Why did Stravinsky, in the original 1930 version, keep the passage from R22 through R28 at half note equals 48 (thus leading from the preceding and into the closing passage, both also measured at 48), yet in the revision (1948), insist that the passage must be *Molto meno mosso*, with the quarter at 72 (half note = 36)?

The answer, I think, is that he does indeed wish to emphasize the complete calm and stasis of the section, and to prevent any hint of pressing on to a goal (just the opposite of Puccini's operatic climax—see note 8). Here is what he says about this change in *Dialogues and a Diary*:

> I was much concerned, in setting the Psalm verses, with problems of tempo. To me, the relation of tempo and meaning is a primary question of musical order, and until I am certain that I have found the right tempo, I cannot compose. Superficially, the texts suggested a variety of speeds, but this variety was without shape. At first, and until I understood that God must not be praised in fast, forte music, no matter how often the text specifies "loud," I thought of the final hymn in a too-rapid pulsation. . . . The final hymn of praise must be thought of as issuing from the skies, and agitation is followed by "the calm of praise"—but such statements embarrass me.[7]

---

[7] [Igor Stravinsky and Robert Craft, *Dialogues and a Diary* (London: Faber and Faber, 1968), pp. 44–45; 46.]

Apparently, he was not satisfied that previously he had achieved enough of the "calm of praise," and that is why he decided upon the new tempo.[8]

Yet not even now does his sense of proportion, of metrical unification, desert him. The old scheme had two fundamental alternating tempos for the movement: 48 and 80. Now we have three, 48, 80, and 72; and instead of one tempo uniting three diverse sections at the end, we have two tempos [48 and 72] creating an ABA of beat relationships reflecting the contrast between the C areas [at R20 and R29] (the D major [at R20] is over a G pedal and moves at the end to C again) and the E-flat areas [at R22], a contrast characteristic of the tonal scheme of this piece from the beginning. How, then, can there be a unification of meter here—the unity Stravinsky would seem to desire instead of a superficial variety of speeds? The clue, I think, is that it is not just *molto meno mosso* [at R22] but quarter = 72 *rigorosamente*. In the slower tempo, each *measure* of the ostinato passage is now equal to each *measure* of the opening tempo of the conclusion [six beats of quarter = 72 at R22, equaling four beats of quarter = 48 at R20].

So far, so good—but there is yet another stage to consider. The most recent Stravinsky recordings again unify the tempos of the last movement—of the opening Alleluia, the florid section, and the long ostinato—but at the new tempo [quarter = 72]! The calm of praise has now enveloped the whole of the last movement. Stravinsky is never satisfied: each performance requires a rethinking of the composition, and that is one reason why so many versions, orchestrations, revisions, and so forth exist of the pieces he most often performed. If he is, as he says, embarrassed by explanations of these revisions that depend on expressive reasons, then he can always call up reasons of another kind: technical and formal. But here, as in all the best music, form and content, or technique and expression, are one—they are merely two ways of looking at the same object, two different points of view.

THE FLOOD

One would expect that this kind of repetitive pattern would be characteristic of Stravinsky's Russian period, since it seems related to the reiter-

---

[8] A very different way of handling a similar situation helps clarify and even partly explain Stravinsky's intent. At the end of the first act of a work hardly associated with the *Symphony of Psalms*, Puccini's *Tosca*, there is an interesting contrast with Stravinsky's heavenly calm. The closing Te Deum is built on the same kind of swinging ostinato, and is even in the same key, E-flat, and on a bass moving between B-flat and F; but it is employed in the service of a theatrical crescendo.

ative pattern of primitive East-European folk song. And indeed, the *Sacre* and *Les Noces*, among others, are full of such passages. But although they become less obvious in the neo-classic period, we can still find them—as we have just seen—at the end of the *Symphony of Psalms* or in the syncopated theme in the first movement of the Symphony in Three Movements.

Where we would definitely *not* expect to find them, however, is in the twelve-tone works; but the leopard does not change his spots. Even here we can find them, and I have chosen one of the most obvious: the instrumental flood music from *The Flood* [mm. 399–456]. Here there is clearly harmonic stasis. Except for the introductory music and its three returns [mm. 399–400, 417–19, 435–37, 454–56], the entire harmonic underpinning is a seven-note chord derived from tones that have been stated serially in the woodwind interludes and held over into the string-piano-harp chords of what I call the ostinato sections (the contrabass clarinet is common to both instrumental groups). Melodically, the latter's material consists of two important strands: the 16ths in the flute and violins, and the slower-moving line in the brasses, neither of which is exactly repetitive (unlike the accompanying chord), though both *sound* repetitive. (For orientation, see table 14.6.)

This is true of the high line more than the other, for it is not so strictly twelve-tone. It moves not by whole rows so much as by hexachords, which are rotated and combined freely, so that a few notes in a restricted range get emphasized. The other line moves mostly by entire rows; but by the repetition of the same intervals and the avoidance of any clear motivic division, it too contributes to the overall static effect. How then do we feel any sense of form here?

First of all, the piece has a built-in design: a palindrome that is almost exact (table 14.6). This in itself would hardly be sufficient, though it is made crystal-clear by the punctuation of the longer ostinato sections by the short interlude measures, and by occasional longer sections derived from the introduction. The proportions in sixteenths are given in table 14.6.

TABLE 14.6
Stravinsky, *The Flood*, Instrumental Flood Music: Retrograde Balances (in Sixteenths)

Lightning	2											2
Introductory	20				28			28				20
Interludes		14	14	6	5	5	8	7	7	7	14	14
Ostinato		11	24	31	30	57	57		30	31	24	11
			135			134			138			

It is clear that the palindrome is inexact only in the lengths of the chordal interludes. The interesting point is that a very clear proportion among the introductory and interlude sections emerges if we look at the latter half alone: it consists almost purely of multiples of 7: 1×7, 4×7, 1×7, 1×7, 2×7, 2×7, and 3×7. Isn't it likely that the palindrome was the basic plan, but that, in order to give greater urgency to the buildup of the storm, the interludes become progressively shorter? After the climax [mm. 421–26] they appear in more relaxed form; and their woodwind chords are now followed, as well as preceded, by complete rests, so that they are not connected to the next phrase.

But what about the proportions of the ostinato sections? They appear to increase gradually, but in no regular way. At this point we must look at two internal factors: the progress of the individual measures and the repetitions of the accompanying chord (both measured in sixteenths). The measure-lengths of the ostinato, each containing a continuous group of sixteenths (whose number changes with almost every measure), show a clear pattern, at least on paper:

mm. in 16ths: 5-6, 7-8-9, 10-11-10, 9-8-7-6, 7-8-9-10-11-12

And this is followed by a complete retrograde. Note how, with the reversal, this supports the tripartite division, for we now get three sets of increase and decrease in the length of measures, the first and last being similar but reversed, and the middle one going to and returning from the longest measure (12 sixteenths) [see figure 14.1]. But are these groupings hearable? Stravinsky certainly wanted us to hear them. He shows carefully just how the sixteenths are to be articulated in every case. And in no case do the articulations cross the measure. In addition, in the long buildup from 7 to 12 the pitch series in the flute and violin helps make it clear by adding a new note each time—emphasized by adding the second flute. And note here that the achievement for the first time of a complete twelve-tone row by the high voice marks the climax and the arrival at the midpoint [m. 426]: the row is being used in a rhythmically functional way to create the sense of form.

FIGURE 14.1

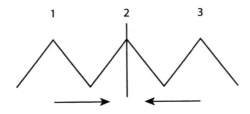

As for the ostinato's repeated chords, the lengths of their repetitions do not coincide by any means with the pattern of measures, but make the following pattern:

16ths: 11, 12-12, 11-10-10, 10-10-10, 10-9-9-8-8-7-6

followed by its reversal. In other words, except for the first element (which couldn't be longer than 11, because that is the length of the phrase), these show a steady acceleration to the climax, and hence a steady deceleration afterward.

Note how the three elements of the ostinato sections contrast with one another. First, the high flute-violin voice points up the tripartite pattern, because it gives overall a tripartite pattern of increasing and decreasing metric groups. The second element, the string-piano-harp chord repetitions, emphasizes the overall duple division of the palindrome, since it progresses to and away from the climax. And the third, the brass melody, is almost independent of the others, since it is the steadiest: it moves mainly in eighths and dotted eighths, with a slightly perceptible tendency toward the longer values as the phrases lengthen (it even has one quarter note in the longest phrase [m. 424]). But its relative steadiness is in clear contrast with the other two. Perhaps this triple contrast is meant to create a sense of flood-like confusion, yet confusion nevertheless under the iron control of the Deity—or of the composer.

MOVEMENTS FOR PIANO AND ORCHESTRA (1959)

A final, very subtle example is movement IV from the Movements for Piano and Orchestra. Here we have a very obvious ostinato in the form of a sustained chord. There are two different chords, stated three times in an ABA arrangement [mm. 96–104, 110–17, and 123–32], each composed of two fifths derived from some form of the row. The movement is accordingly very clear in form: three sections, each based on one of the chords, and each similar in three-part layout: (1) an introduction, consisting of flute figures introducing the held chord, which is then sustained with high string harmonics, and an answering figure in lower instruments; (2) a continuation, consisting of a piano solo [with the chord still sustaining]; (3) a conclusion [after the chord stops], consisting of a passage for low strings, followed by a passage for piano solo.

The most obvious correspondence among the three sections is that, once complete, each of the chords is almost exactly the same length: 20,

TABLE 14.7
Stravinsky, Movements for Piano and Orchestra,
Movement 4, Section A: Formal Balances (in Eighths)

		Section A		
Introduction		Continuation		Conclusion
14	+	14	+	14
7 + 7		7 + 7	+	9 + 5

19, and 20 (in eighths).[9] In addition, the third section is very similar to
the first, and is often isorhythmic with it, suggesting an ABA' form.

The first section shows a further careful division, reflecting both the
instrumentation and the use of the row. The introduction consists of 14
eighths, 7 in the flutes plus 7 in the cello, and one complete row. The
continuation also has 14 eighths (or 13½), divided almost exactly into
14 + 14 sixteenths by two complete forms of the row. (I say "almost exactly" here, and elsewhere, because there is occasional overlapping,
making it impossible to place the division completely accurately.) Finally,
the conclusion has 14 eighths and one complete row, divided into 9
(strings) + 5 (piano). This gives us table 14.7. There is an overlap here,
but I begin the section when the piano stops, as a clear-cut division.

So far, then, there is almost an exact division into three groups of 14.
But the last one has also suggested a new grouping based on nine. This is
taken up in the middle section, which is more complex, with much more
obvious overlapping. The introduction of that section is 10 eighths, while
the conclusion is 18 eighths (9 in cello and 9 in piano). This is not only almost exactly 9's, but also exactly 28—the same as the introduction plus
conclusion of the first section! But now, within the Introduction, there are
only 8 active eighths [mm. 110–12], which are divided into 7 plus 9 sixteenths by instrument [flutes + clarinets], and also by row (although the
row structure is irregular here). And the piano, by overlapping the Conclusion, achieves 18 eighths, or twice 18 sixteenths [mm. 113–19]. And
even within this, there are signs of breaking down to smaller groupings by
9 (table 14.8; overlaps have been omitted in tables 14.8 and 14.9).

The third section, though very similar to the first, still incorporates
some of the more complex techniques of the second. Although it begins
with 14 eighths, this overlaps with the piano entry. But again taking
only *active* beats, there are 7 sixteenths (flute) followed by 7 eighths
(trombone, bass clarinet). And the division between the continuation's

[9] The instrumental entries that build to the complete chords add respectively 4½, 1½,
and 2 eighths to these durations.

TABLE 14.8
Stravinsky, Movements for Piano and Orchestra, Movement 4, Section B: Formal Balances (in Eighths and Sixteenths)

	Section B				
			28		
	Introduction		Continuation		Conclusion
8ths	10	+	18	+	18
16ths	rests 16		18 + 18		9 + 9
	7 + 8		9 + 9 9 + 9		

TABLE 14.9
Stravinsky, Movements for Piano and Orchestra, Movement 4, Section A': Formal Balances (in Eighths)

	Section A'				
	Introduction	+	Continuation	+	Conclusion
8ths	14		14		14
	rests + 7/16 + rests + 7/8		7 + 7		9 + 5

piano solo and the conclusion is again somewhat obscured by the piano being held over. Nevertheless, the following seems to emerge quite clearly (table 14.9).

Although Stravinsky disclaims any sort of rhythmic structuralization of his row, it is obvious that he is acutely conscious of the elapsed time taken by a statement of a row, and he is careful to bring these into exact and subtle correlation. That is what he has always done in his music.

Published Works of Edward T. Cone

BOOKS

Musical Form and Musical Performance. New York, 1968.
The Composer's Voice. Berkeley, 1974.
Music: A View from Delft. Selected Essays, edited by Robert P. Morgan. Chicago, 1989.

As Editor

Perspectives on Schoenberg and Stravinsky, with Benjamin Boretz. Princeton, 1968. Revised 2nd ed., New York, 1972.
Berlioz: "Fantastic Symphony." New York, 1971. Includes three original articles: "The Composer and the Symphony," 3–17; "The Symphony and the Program," 18–25; "Schumann Amplified: An Analysis," 249–77.
Perspectives on American Composers, with Benjamin Boretz. New York, 1971.
Perspectives on Contemporary Music Theory, with Benjamin Boretz. New York, 1972.
Perspectives on Notation and Performance, with Benjamin Boretz. New York, 1976.
Roger Sessions on Music: Collected Essays. Princeton, 1979.
The Legacy of R. P. Blackmur, with Joseph Frank and Edmund Keeley. New York, 1987.

ARTICLES

"Roger Sessions' String Quartet." *Modern Music* 18, no. 3 (1941): 159–63.
"The Creative Artist in the University." *American Scholar* 16, no. 2 (1947): 192–200.
"The Old Man's Toys: Verdi's Last Operas." *Perspectives USA* 6 (1954): 114–33. Reprinted in Cone, *Music: A View from Delft*, 159–75.
"Words into Music: The Composer's Approach to the Text." In *Sound and Poetry*, edited by Northrop Frye, 3–15. English Institute Essays, 1956; New York, 1957. Reprinted in Cone, *Music: A View from Delft*, 115–23.
"Musical Theory as a Humanistic Discipline." *Juilliard Review* 5, no. 2 (1957–58): 3–12. Reprinted in Cone, *Music: A View from Delft*, 29–37.
"Analysis Today." *Musical Quarterly* 46, no. 2 (1960): 172–88. Reprinted in *Problems of Modern Music*, edited by Paul Henry Lang, 34–40. New York, 1960. Also reprinted in Cone, *Music: A View from Delft*, 39–54.
"Music: A View from Delft." *Musical Quarterly* 47, no. 4 (1961): 439–53. Reprinted in *Perspectives on Contemporary Music Theory*, edited by Benjamin

Boretz and Edward T. Cone, 57–71. New York, 1972. Also reprinted in Cone, *Music: A View from Delft*, 13–27.

"The Not-So-Happy Medium." *The American Scholar* 30, no. 2 (1961): 254–67. Reprinted in *Essays Today*, vol. 5, edited by Richard Ludwig, 87–96. New York, 1962.

"Stravinsky: The Progress of a Method." *Perspectives of New Music* 1, no. 1 (1962): 18–26. Reprinted in *Perspectives on Schoenberg and Stravinsky*, edited by Benjamin Boretz and Edward T. Cone, 155–64. New York, 1972. Also reprinted in Cone, *Music: A View from Delft*, 293–301.

"The Uses of Convention: Stravinsky and His Models." *Musical Quarterly* 48, no. 3 (1962): 287–99. Reprinted in *Stravinsky: A New Appraisal of His Work*, edited by Paul Henry Lang, 21–33. New York, 1963. Also reprinted in Cone, *Music: A View from Delft*, 281–92.

"From Sensuous Image to Musical Form." *American Scholar* 33, no. 3 (1964): 448–62.

"A Budding Grove." *Perspectives of New Music* 3, no. 2 (1965): 38–46.

"On the Structure of 'Ich folge dir.'" *College Music Symposium* 5 (1965): 77–85.

"Toward the Understanding of Musical Literature." *Perspectives of New Music* 4, no. 1 (1965): 141–51.

"Conversations with Roger Sessions." *Perspectives of New Music* 4, no. 2 (1966): 29–46. Reprinted in *Perspectives on American Composers*, edited by Benjamin Boretz and Edward T. Cone, 90–107. New York, 1971.

"The Power of *The Power of Sound*." Introductory essay in Edmund Gurney, *The Power of Sound*, i–xvi. New York, 1966.

"Beyond Analysis." *Perspectives of New Music* 6, no. 1 (1967): 33–51. Reprinted in *Perspectives on Contemporary Music Theory*, edited by Benjamin Boretz and Edward T. Cone, 72–90. New York, 1972. Also reprinted in *Music: A View from Delft*, 55–75.

"Webern's Apprenticeship." *Musical Quarterly* 53, no. 1 (1967): 39–52. Reprinted in *Music: A View from Delft*, 267–80.

"What is a Composition?" *Current Musicology* 5 (1967): 101–7.

"Conversation with Aaron Copland." *Perspectives of New Music* 6, no. 2 (1968): 57–72. Reprinted in *Perspectives on American Composers*, edited by Benjamin Boretz and Edward T. Cone, 131–46. New York, 1971.

"Beethoven New-Born." *American Scholar* 38, no. 3 (1969): 389–400.

"Schubert's Beethoven." *Musical Quarterly* 56, No. 4 (1970): 779–93.

"Radical Traditionalism." *Listener* 2229 (1971): 849.

"Inside the Saint's Head: The Music of Berlioz." *Musical Newsletter* 1, no. 3 (July 1971): 3–12; 1, no. 4 (October 1971): 16–20; 2, no. 1 (January 1972): 19–22. Reprinted in *Music: A View from Delft*, 217–48.

"In Honor of Roger Sessions." *Perspectives of New Music* 10, no. 2 (1972): 130–41.

"Editorial Responsibility and Schoenberg's Troublesome 'Misprints.'" *Perspectives of New Music* 11, no. 1 (1972): 65–75.

"The Miss Etta Cones, the Steins, and M'sieu Matisse." *The American Scholar* 42, no. 3 (1973): 441–60.

"Bach's Unfinished Fugue in C minor." In *Studies in Renaissance and Baroque Music in Honor of Arthur Mendel*, edited by Robert L. Marshall, 149–55. London, 1974.

"Sound and Syntax: An Introduction to Schoenberg's Harmony." *Perspectives of New Music* 13, no. 1 (1974): 21–40. Reprinted in *Music: A View from Delft*, 249–66.

"In Defense of Song: The Contribution of Roger Sessions." *Critical Inquiry* 2, No. 1 (1975): 93–112. Reprinted in *Music: A View from Delft*, 303–22.

"Sessions' Concertino." *Tempo* 115 (1975): 2–10.

"Yet Once More, O Ye Laurels." *Perspectives of New Music* 14, no. 2; 15, no. 1 (1976): 294–306.

"Béatrice et Bénédict." Boston Symphony *Program* (October 1977): 9–15.

"Beethoven's Experiments in Composition: The Late Bagatelles." In *Beethoven Studies*, vol. 2, edited by Alan Tyson, 84–105. London, 1977. Reprinted in *Music: A View from Delft*, 179–200.

"One Hundred Metronomes." *The American Scholar* 46, no. 4 (1977): 443–59.

"Three Ways of Reading a Detective Story—Or a Brahms Intermezzo." *Georgia Review* 31, no. 3 (1977): 554–74. Reprinted in Cone, *Music: A View from Delft*, 77–93.

"Aunt Claribel's 'Blue Nude' Wasn't Easy to Like." *Art News* 79, no. 7 (1980): 162–63.

"Berlioz's Divine Comedy: The *Grande messe des morts*." *19th-Century Music* 4, no. 1 (1980): 3–16. Reprinted in Cone, *Music: A View from Delft*, 139–57.

"The Authority of Music Criticism." *Journal of the American Musicological Society* 34, no. 1 (1981): 1–18. Reprinted in Cone, *Music: A View from Delft*, 95–112.

"On the Road to *Otello*: Tonality and Structure in *Simon Bocanegra*." *Studi Verdiana* 1 (1982): 72–98.

"Roger Sessions: Symphony No. 6." San Francisco Symphony *Stagebill* (May 1982): v–ix.

"Schubert's Promissory Note: An Exercise in Musical Hermeneutics." *19th-Century Music* 5, no. 3 (1982): 233–41. Revised version reprinted in *Schubert: Critical and Analytical Studies*, edited by Walter Frisch, 13–30. Lincoln, 1986.

"The Years at Princeton." *The Piano Quarterly* 119 (Robert Casadesus issue, 1982): 27–29.

"A Cadenza for Op. 15." In *Beethoven Essays: Studies in Honor of Elliot Forbes*, edited by Lewis Lockwood and Phyllis Benjamin, 99–107. Cambridge, 1984.

"Schubert's Unfinished Business." *19th-Century Music* 7, no. 3 (1984): 222–32. Reprinted in Cone, *Music: A View from Delft*, 201–16.

"*Musical Form and Musical Performance* Reconsidered." *Music Theory Spectrum* 7 (1985): 149–58.

"A Tribute to Roger Sessions." *Kent Quarterly* 5, no. 2 (1986): 29–31.

"Twelfth Night." *Musiktheorie* 1 (1986): 41–59. Reprinted in original English version in *Journal of Musicological Research* 7, nos. 2–3 (1987): 131–56.

"Brahms: Songs with Words and Songs without Words." *Intégral* 1 (1987): 31–56.

"Dashes of Insight: Blackmur as Music Critic." In *The Legacy of R. P. Blackmur*, edited by Edward T. Cone, Joseph Frank, and Edmund Keeley, 10–12. New York: Ecco Press, 1987.

"Music and Form." In *What Is Music? An Introduction to the Philosophy of Music*, edited by Philip Alperson, 131–46. University Park: Pennsylvania State University Press, 1994 (1987).

"On Derivation: Syntax and Rhetoric." *Music Analysis* 6, no. 3 (1987): 237–56.

"The World of Opera and Its Inhabitants." In Cone, *Music: A View from Delft*, 125–38.

"Responses" (to "*The Composer's Voice*: Elaborations and Departures"). *College Music Symposium* 29 (1989): 75–80.

"Harmonic Congruence in Brahms." In *Brahms Studies*, edited by George S. Bozarth, 165–88. Oxford, 1990.

"Poet's Love or Composer's Love?" In *Music and Text*, edited by S. P. Scher, 177–92. Cambridge, 1992.

"Ambiguity and Reinterpretation in Chopin." In *Chopin Studies 2*, edited by John Rink and Jim Samson, 140–60. Cambridge, 1994.

"Thinking (about) Music." *Proceedings of the American Philosophical Society*, 138, no. 4 (1994): 469–75.

"Edward T. Cone Makes a Plea for Good Citizenship." *Musical Times* 135, no. 12 (December 1994): 734–38.

"The Pianist as Critic." In *The Practice of Performance: Studies in Musical Interpretation*, edited by John Rink, 241–53. Cambridge, 1995.

"Attacking a Brahms Puzzle." *Musical Times* 136, no. 2 (February 1995): 72–77.

"Adding Up Beauty and Truth" (Article/Review of Edward Rothstein: *Emblems of Mind: The Inner Life of Music and Mathematics*). *Yale Review* 83, no. 4 (October 1995): 121–34.

"'Am Meer' Reconsidered: Strophic, Binary, Ternary." In *Schubert Studies 5*, edited by Brian Newbould, 112–26. Aldershot, 1998.

"Repetition and Correspondence in *Schwanengesang*." In *Companion to Schubert's Schwanengesang*, edited by Martin Chusid, 53–89. New Haven, 2000.

POEMS

"Hills of Judea." *Palestine Tribune* 2, no. 9 (1946): 10.

"You Two." *Perspectives of New Music* 9 no. 2; 10, no. 1 (1971): 58.

"In Memoriam R. H. S." *Perspectives of New Music* 23, no. 2 (1985): 123.

Index

Page numbers in italic type indicate musical examples.

Abbate, Carolyn, 63
Academie des Beaux-Arts, 159
Agawu, Kofi, 34
Allgemeine musikalische Zeitung, 153n2
American Musicological Society, 2
appoggiatura, 24–25
atonality, 13, 40
Augenmusik, 56

Babbitt, Milton, 1, 173
Bach, J. S., 53, 56; Christmas Oratorio,
  182; Italian Concerto, 177; Toccata in D
  major, 187; *Well-Tempered Clavier*, 20
Balakirev, Mily Alexeyevich, 171
Bartók, Béla: Improvisations, Op. 20, 45;
  Out of Doors Suite, Op. 20, 45; String
  Quartet No. 5, 45
Beach, David, 20n
Beethoven, Ludwig van, 11–12, 135, 156
—*An die ferne Geliebte*, 53
—compositional sketches, 23, 122
—*Leonore* No. 3, 54
—Lydian mode of, 38–39
—Piano Sonatas: Op. 27 No. 2 in C-sharp
  minor ("Moonlight"), 16, 18, 30; Op.
  53 in C major ("Waldstein"), 20–23,
  21–22, 33; Op. 101 in A major, 33; Op.
  106 in B-flat major, 10, 28, *28*; Op. 109
  in E major, 58–59
—Piano Trio, Op. 1 No. 1, 20
—String Quartets: Op. 59 No. 3, 22; Op.
  131 in C-sharp minor, 29; Op. 132 in A
  minor, 38–39, 41
—Symphonies; No. 3, Op. 55 (*Eroica*),
  30–31, 191, 195–96; No. 5, Op. 67,
  22–23; No. 6, Op. 68 (*Pastoral*), 168,
  182–83, 184; No. 9, Op. 125, 22, 34,
  154
—Variations: Op. 35 ("Prometheus"), 30–
  31; Op. 120 ("Diabelli"), 29, 130
Berg, Alban: *Lyric Suite*, 53; Violin
  Concerto, 53

Berlioz, Hector, 145, 170–72; *Fantastic
  Symphony*, 51, 53–54, 170, 183; *Grand
  traité d'instrumentation*, 171–72;
  Memoirs, 14–15; Requiem, 31; *Roméo
  et Juliette*, 31–32, *32*
Blackmur, R. P., 56–58, 121, 123, 132
Boas, George, 190
Brahms, Johannes, works of: implied
  melodies in, 29; Intermezzo in B-flat,
  Op. 76 No. 4, 43; Piano Trio, Op.
  8, 123–26, 133; Symphony No. 4,
  Op. 98, 31
Bruckner, Anton, Symphony No. 5, 34

Cappi & Diabelli (publishers), 153
Chézy, Helmina von, 137
Chopin, Frédéric: Ballade No. 1 in G
  minor, Op. 23, 23, *23*; Ballade No. 2,
  Op. 38, 43; Ballade No. 4 in F minor,
  Op. 52, 23n; Mazurka, Op. 41 No. 4,
  28; Prelude in F major, 42
chorale melodies, 53
Cingria, Charles Albert, 181–82, 188–89
compositional criticism, 119, 122–23, 130,
  134, 135–36, 147
Cone, Edward T.: biographical notes on,
  1–2; *The Composers Voice*, 2, 81,
  84–85, 93, 170–71; "On Derivation,"
  10; "Sound and Syntax," 9, 43; "The
  World of Opera," 85–86, 88–89
Corelli, Arcangelo, Christmas Concerto,
  182
Craft, Robert, *Explorations and
  Developments*, 184
culture, as shared experience, 14

Dallapiccola, Luigi, *Quaderno musicale di
  Annalibera*, 46–47
Debussy, Claude, works of: *Beau soir*, 164;
  Brouillards (Preludes II), 44, 167;
  Cloches à travers les feuilles (Images II),
  161, 166; *En blanc et noir* (Preludes II),

100–101, 103, 162–63; *Siegfried*, 35, 80, 82, *83*, 87–89, *88*, 94, 98–99; *Tristan und Isolde*, 25–28, *26*, 165, 166, 168; *Walküre*, *26*, 35, 82–83, *86*, 86–87, *87*, 89–94, *90*, *92*, 97–98, *100*, 100–104, *101*, *102*, *103*, *104*. *See also* leitmotivic system

Weber, Carl Maria von, 170; Piano Sonata in E minor, Op. 70, 24, *24*
Webern, Anton, Variations for Piano, Op. 27, 40, 46
Weinberg, Henry, 40
White, Eric, 180, 187, 188
Wind, Edgar, 122